First, Second, and Third John

ΠΑΙΔΕΙΑ 🔲 paideia
COMMENTARIES ON
THE NEW TESTAMENT

GENERAL EDITORS

Mikeal C. Parsons, Charles H. Talbert, and Bruce W. Longenecker

ADVISORY BOARD

First, Second, and Third John

GEORGE L. PARSENIOS

Baker Academic

a division of Baker Publishing Group
Grand Rapids, Michigan

© 2014 by George L. Parsenios

Published by Baker Academic
a division of Baker Publishing Group
PO Box 6287, Grand Rapids, MI 49516-6287
www.bakeracademic.com

Printed in the United States of America

Library of Congress Cataloging-in-Publication Data

Parsenios, George L.
    First, Second, and Third John / George L. Parsenios.
        pages cm. — (Paideia : commentaries on the New Testament)
    Includes bibliographical references and index.
    ISBN 978-0-8010-3342-1 (pbk.)
    1. Bible. Epistles of John—Commentaries. I. Title.
BS2805.53.P37 2014
227'.94077—dc23   2014027924

Unless otherwise indicated, all quotations from the Letters of John are the author's own translation.

14 15 16 17 18 19 20   7 6 5 4 3 2 1

For Fr. Zosimas of Xenophontos

Contents

Figures and Tables

Figures

Tables

Foreword

Paideia: Commentaries on the New Testament is a series that sets out to comment on the final form of the New Testament text in a way that pays due attention both to the cultural, literary, and theological settings in which the text took form and to the interests of the contemporary readers to whom the commentaries are addressed. This series is aimed squarely at students—including MA students in religious and theological studies programs, seminarians, and upper-division undergraduates—who have theological interests in the biblical text. Thus, the didactic aim of the series is to enable students to understand each book of the New Testament as a literary whole rooted in a particular ancient setting and related to its context within the New Testament.

The name "Paideia" (Greek for "education") reflects (1) the instructional aim of the series—giving contemporary students a basic grounding in academic New Testament studies by guiding their engagement with New Testament texts; (2) the fact that the New Testament texts as literary unities are shaped by the educational categories and ideas (rhetorical, narratological, etc.) of their ancient writers and readers; and (3) the pedagogical aims of the texts themselves—their central aim being not simply to impart information but to form the theological convictions and moral habits of their readers.

Each commentary deals with the text in terms of larger rhetorical units; these are not verse-by-verse commentaries. This series thus stands within the stream of recent commentaries that attend to the final form of the text. Such reader-centered literary approaches are inherently more accessible to liberal arts students without extensive linguistic and historical-critical preparation than older exegetical approaches, but within the reader-centered world the sanest practitioners have paid careful attention to the extratext of the original readers, including not only these readers' knowledge of the geography, history, and other contextual elements reflected in the text but also their ability to respond correctly to the literary and rhetorical conventions used in the text. Paideia commentaries pay deliberate attention to this extratextual repertoire in order to highlight the ways in which the text is designed to persuade and move its readers. Each rhetorical unit is explored from three angles: (1) introductory matters; (2) tracing the train of thought or narrative or rhetorical flow of the argument; and (3) theological issues raised by the text that are of interest to the contemporary Christian. Thus, the primary focus remains on the text and not its historical context or its interpretation in the secondary literature.

Our authors represent a variety of confessional points of view: Protestant, Catholic, and Orthodox. What they share, beyond being New Testament scholars of national and international repute, is a commitment to reading the biblical text as theological documents within their ancient contexts. Working within the broad parameters described here, each author brings his or her own considerable exegetical talents and deep theological commitments to the task of laying bare the interpretation of Scripture for the faith and practice of God's people everywhere.

Mikeal C. Parsons
Charles H. Talbert
Bruce W. Longenecker

Preface

My previous research and writing have focused on the Fourth Gospel, but one cannot for very long study that book without turning one's attention closely to 1–3 John. Writing this commentary has provided an invaluable opportunity to reflect on the connections that link these texts, and I would like to thank the editors of the Paideia series for asking me to produce this volume. C. Clifton Black deserves special thanks for the personal support and encouragement he offered from the very start. Charles Talbert, Mikeal Parsons, and Bruce Longenecker have offered insightful editorial help, and they showed tremendous patience when the volume took much longer to complete than originally planned. Their suggestions improved the book in every instance. From Baker Academic, James Earnest guided the work from beginning to end with expert care, while Rachel Klompmaker prepared the beautiful artwork, and the various Baker editors were always insightful, saving me from more than a few embarrassing errors. Portions of the introductory chapter reproduce elements from my essay "A Sententious Silence: First Thoughts on the Fourth Gospel and the *Ardens* Style," in *Portraits of Jesus: Essays in Honor of Harold W. Attridge*, edited by Susan Myers; and portions of the commentary on 2 John reproduce elements from my essay "'No Longer in the World' (John 17:11): The Transformation of the Tragic in the Fourth Gospel." *Harvard Theological Review* 98 (2005): 1–21. Both texts are used here by permission. Finally, this book is dedicated as a small token of friendship to Fr. Zosimas of the Holy Monastery of Xenophontos on Mt. Athos.

Abbreviations

General

AT	author's translation	i.e.	*id est*, that is
BCE	before the Common Era (= BC)	NT	New Testament
		OT	Old Testament
ca.	*circa*, approximately		
CE	the Common Era (= AD)	rev.	revised
cf.	*confer*, compare	trans.	translator, translation, translated by
ed.	edition, edited by, editor		
d.	died	x	times
fl.	flourished in (year)	v./vv.	verse/verses

Bible Texts, Editions, and Versions

JB	Jerusalem Bible	NASB	New American Standard Bible
KJV	King James (Authorized) Version	NEB	New English Bible
		NIV	New International Version (2011)
LXX	Septuagint, the Greek Bible		
NABRE	New American Bible, Revised Edition	NRSV	New Revised Standard Version
		RSV	Revised Standard Version

Ancient Manuscripts, Papyri, and Inscriptions

P.Flor.	*Papiri greco-egizii, Papiri Fiorentini*. Supplementi Filologico-Storici ai Monumenti Antichi. Milan, 1906–15.	P.Oslo	*Papyri Osloenses*. 3 vols. Oslo, 1925–36.
		P.Oxy.	*The Oxyrhynchus Papyri*. 75 vols. London, 1898–2010.

P.Ryl.	*Catalogue of the Greek and Latin Papyri in the John Rylands Library, Manchester.* Manchester, UK, 1911–52.		PSI	Pubblicazione della Società Italiana per la ricerca dei papiri Greci e Latini in Egitto. *Papiri Greci e Latini.* Florence, 1912–.

Ancient Corpora

OLD TESTAMENT

Gen.	Genesis
Exod.	Exodus
Lev.	Leviticus
Num.	Numbers
Deut.	Deuteronomy
Josh.	Joshua
Judg.	Judges
Ruth	Ruth
1–2 Sam.	1–2 Samuel
1–2 Kings	1–2 Kings
1–2 Chron.	1–2 Chronicles
Ezra	Ezra
Neh.	Nehemiah
Esther	Esther
Job	Job
Ps(s).	Psalm(s)
Prov.	Proverbs
Eccles.	Ecclesiastes
Song	Song of Songs
Isa.	Isaiah
Jer.	Jeremiah
Lam.	Lamentations
Ezek.	Ezekiel
Dan.	Daniel
Hosea	Hosea
Joel	Joel
Amos	Amos
Obad.	Obadiah
Jon.	Jonah
Mic.	Micah
Nah.	Nahum
Hab.	Habakkuk
Zeph.	Zephaniah

Hag.	Haggai
Zech.	Zechariah
Mal.	Malachi

DEUTEROCANONICAL BOOKS

Bar.	Baruch
1–2 Esd.	1–2 Esdras
Tob.	Tobit
Wis.	Wisdom of Solomon

NEW TESTAMENT

Matt.	Matthew
Mark	Mark
Luke	Luke
John	John
Acts	Acts
Rom.	Romans
1–2 Cor.	1–2 Corinthians
Gal.	Galatians
Eph.	Ephesians
Phil.	Philippians
Col.	Colossians
1–2 Thess.	1–2 Thessalonians
1–2 Tim.	1–2 Timothy
Titus	Titus
Philem.	Philemon
Heb.	Hebrews
James	James
1–2 Pet.	1–2 Peter
1–3 John	1–3 John
Jude	Jude
Rev.	Revelation

OLD TESTAMENT PSEUDEPIGRAPHA

4 Ezra	*4 Ezra*
Jos. Asen.	*Joseph and Aseneth*

Other Ancient Authors

SENECA THE ELDER

Suas.   *Suasoriae = Declamations*

SENECA THE YOUNGER

Ep.   *Epistulae morales = Moral*
Epistles

TACITUS

Hist.   *Histories*

Series, Collections, and Reference Works

ANF   *The Ante-Nicene Fathers.* Edited by A. Roberts and J. Donaldson. American ed. 10 vols. Buffalo, NY: Christian Literature Publishing, 1885–96.

BDAG   *A Greek-English Lexicon of the New Testament and Other Early Christian Literature.* By W. Bauer, F. W. Danker, W. F. Arndt, and F. W. Gingrich. Chicago: University of Chicago Press, 2000.

LCL   Loeb Classical Library

NPNF   *The Nicene and Post-Nicene Fathers.* Edited by P. Schaff and H. Wace. 2nd series. 28 vols. Repr. Peabody, MA: Hendrickson, 1994.

First, Second, and Third John

Introduction to the Letters of John

A letter is a second self. People write letters when separation prevents speaking face-to-face, and the letter bridges the divide, making the absent person present. As an example of how letters convey the personal presence of their authors, Plutarch (ca. 46–120 CE) records what happened when the Athenians captured the letter carriers of Philip of Macedon (382–336 BCE). The Athenians read all the official letters addressed to Philip from his generals, as one would expect in a time of war. They left one letter unread. It was a letter to Philip from his wife. They did not even open this letter but sent it back to Philip, with the seal unbroken, and so demonstrated what Plutarch calls "the thoughtful kindness of the Athenians" (*Demetr.* 22.2). By refusing to eavesdrop on the intimate exchange of husband and wife, the Athenians treated a private letter like a private conversation between two people in their midst. The captured letter represented the personal presence of its author. In this same spirit, Demetrius of Phalerum (350–280 BCE) says that "one writes an image of one's soul when one writes a letter" (*Eloc.* 227). In his own *Letter* 9, Basil of Caesarea (329/330–379 CE) says that "words truly are images of the soul." A letter is a second self, stamped with the character of its author.

But if the Letters of John show us the soul of their author, they do so "only through a glass darkly" (1 Cor. 13:12). Far from providing a window into the personality and character of the one who writes them, these letters cloak their author in anonymity. The author does not stand alone in being anonymous. The recipients are also unknown, apart from the Gaius mentioned in 3 John 1, and his identity is hardly clear. The Letters of John tell us virtually nothing about why they were written and who read them. By contrast, some letters in the NT reveal a great deal about the circumstances in which they were composed. First Corinthians tells us more than most. Because 1 Corinthians was written by Paul, we can compare it to the many other letters that come from Paul. Because it was written to Corinth in the middle of the first century, we can coordinate what we read in 1 Corinthians with what we know in general about the Greek cities of the Roman Empire. Copious comparative material helps us to read between the lines of what Paul wrote and fill in the gaps in our knowledge.

The Letters of John present a different circumstance (Lieu 2008). Precious little can be gleaned from these letters regarding the people and problems that produced them since 2 and 3 John are the shortest writings in the NT, and they identify their sender only by the cryptic title "the Elder." Their recipients are just as obscure: 2 John is sent to the enigmatic "Elect Lady and her children," and 3 John tells us the name of its recipient—a certain Gaius—and refers to a figure named Demetrius. In 3 John we also hear of a conflict between the Elder and a certain Diotrephes, but the very brevity of the letter keeps us from knowing who any of these men are, or why they oppose each other. As for 1 John, it is much longer than the other two letters, and it contains an elaborate polemic against beliefs that it opposes; but it mentions nothing about where or when it was written, who sent it, to whom it was sent, and who specifically is committing the wrongs it seeks to correct. The echoes of the circumstances that produced 1–3 John are far more muffled than those that reverberate around 1 Corinthians.

And yet, if 1–3 John differ from 1 Corinthians in conveying little detail about their context and circumstances, they just as surely resemble 1 Corinthians in being produced in the midst of what Margaret Mitchell calls an "*agōn* of interpretation" (Mitchell 2010, 18; see also Mitchell 2003). The Greek term *agōn* means "conflict or trial," and people in the Greek world were said to struggle in an *agōn* if they were contending in anything from a courtroom trial to a wrestling match. Mitchell applies the label "*agōn* of interpretation" to Paul's Corinthian Letters because Paul regularly makes corrective comments like "I wrote to you in my letter . . . not at all meaning . . ." (1 Cor. 5:9). He struggles with his readers over the proper interpretation of his message. He had taught them something. They had misunderstood him. He writes 1 Corinthians to correct them. In his elaborate efforts at correction and clarification, Paul explains and interprets not only his own former words but also the words of Scripture, the words of the Corinthians themselves, and even his own personal behavior.

A similar "*agōn* of interpretation" lies behind 1–3 John. The view adopted in this commentary is that these letters represent one side in a struggle over the proper meaning of the Gospel of John (Smith 2009). In these letters, the heirs of the Johannine tradition are contending over a theological tradition that they share in common. A tense tone permeates each epistle, and this tension comes boiling to the surface in verses like: "They went out from us, but they did not really belong to us. For if they had belonged to us, they would have remained with us; but their going showed that none of them belonged to us" (1 John 2:19). So 1–3 John are the surviving relics of a contentious "*agōn* of interpretation."

What specific factors might have caused this conflict? This simple question has inspired complicated answers. If 1–3 John reflect an *agōn* over the meaning of the Gospel of John, the *agōn* extends and expands when we attempt to interpret the letters themselves. Questions about the meaning, function, and historical setting of 1–3 John have initiated their own *agōn* of interpretation, and the remainder of this introduction will survey the contours of the various debates, beginning with a discussion of the relationship of the Letters to the Gospel.

The Relationship of the Letters to the Gospel

Raymond Brown states that the Letters of John were never meant to be read apart from the Gospel (1982, preface). The present commentary relies on the same presupposition and will argue that 1–3 John are interpretations of the Fourth Gospel. Other scholars, of course, explain the connections between the Gospel and the Letters in other ways, especially when it comes to deciding the order in which the documents were written. Some imagine that the Letters came first, others that the Gospel came first, and still others argue that the production of these various texts involved a more complicated process in which several texts were being written contemporarily with one another. The following discussion will not begin with a survey of scholarly opinion, though, but with a survey of the relevant primary texts, comparing the evidence from the Gospel of John with the evidence of 1–3 John. Several other

Terms Used in John and 1 John but Not Elsewhere in the New Testament

Anthrōpoktonos

John 8:44: *"You are from your father the devil, and you choose to do your father's desires. He was a murderer* [anthrōpoktonos] *from the beginning and does not stand in the truth, because there is no truth in him."*

1 John 3:15: *"All who hate a brother or sister are murderers* [anthrōpoktonoi], *and you know that murderers* [anthrōpoktonoi] *do not have eternal life abiding in them."*

Paraklētos

John 14:16: *"And I will ask the Father, and he will give you another Advocate* [paraklēton], *to be with you forever."* (See also 14:26; 15:26; 16:7.)

1 John 2:1: *"My little children, I am writing these things to you so that you may not sin. But if anyone does sin, we have an Advocate* [paraklēton] *with the Father, Jesus Christ the righteous."*

commentators have studied the common elements in these texts with great care (Brooke 1912; Brown 1982; Painter 2002). Their work provides the basis of what is presented here.

The similarities of the texts are most obvious at the level of vocabulary. Some important terms in John and 1 John occur nowhere else in the NT, like *paraklētos* (see sidebar on previous page). Listing these uniquely Johannine terms alone, however, does not show just how broad and deep are the connections. Even terms that are not unique to the Johannine tradition are used with a high degree of frequency and exclusivity in the Johannine literature, especially in John and 1 John. These two texts—John and 1 John—rely on the same limited and repeated set of terms. So extensive are the connections between the two that almost all the contents of 1 John correspond to something in John (Brooke 1912, ix). Table 1, abbreviated from John Painter's exhaustive charts (2002, 63–73), shows how certain words appear with greater frequency in the Johannine texts than they do in other texts. The comparative categories are the Synoptic Gospels, the Pauline corpus, the entire NT, and each of the Johannine texts individually.

Table 1. Characteristic Language of the Gospel and Letters of John

		Synoptic Gospels	Gospel of John	1 John	2 John	3 John	Paul	NT
agapan	(to love)	26	36	28	2	1	33	141
agapē	(love)	2	7	18	2	1	75	116
alētheia	(truth)	7	25	9	5	6	47	109
alēthēs	(true)	2	4	2	–	1	4	26
alēthinos	(true)	1	9	4	–	–	1	28
alēthōs	(truly)	8	7	1	–	–	1	18
hamartanein	(to sin)	7	3	10	–	–	17	42
hamartia	(sin)	24	17	17	–	–	64	173
ginōskein	(to know)	60	56	25	1	–	50	221
hina	(in order to)	152	147	20	5	2	249	673
martyrein	(to testify)	2	33	6	–	4	8	76
martyria	(testimony)	4	14	14	–	–	2	37
menein	(to abide)	12	40	24	3	–	17	118
oida	(I know)	72	85	15	–	1	103	321
skotia	(darkness)	3	8	6	–	–	–	17
skotos	(darkness)	11	1	1	–	–	11	30
phōs	(light)	15	23	6	–	–	13	73
pseudos	(falsehood)	0	1	2	–	–	4	10
pseustēs	(liar)	0	2	5	–	–	3	10

Certain words immediately rise to the surface. For example, the verb *agapan* (to love) and the noun *agapē* (love) occur more in John than they do in Matthew, Mark, and Luke combined, and they appear 46 times in the five chapters of 1 John—an average of just over 9 times in each chapter. The words *mar-tyrein* and *martyria* are similar. Taken together, these words occur 113 times in the entire NT, and 71 of those instances are in the Gospel and Letters of John—almost 70 percent of the total. The concept of truth is also important. If we consider together the various nouns, adjectives, and adverbs referring to the notion of "truth," the vast percentage of their occurrences would be in John and 1 John, especially the noun *alētheia*, for which almost half of the total usages (45 of 109) are in the Johannine literature. Two terms related to falsehood (*pseudos* and *pseustēs*) are not common in the NT as a whole, but 10 out of these words' 20 total usages are in the Johannine literature. Finally, the verb *menein* is used in the entire NT 118 times, but the word is found 67 times in the Gospel and Letters of John. Examples of characteristic vocabulary could be multiplied further. The examples shown here make it clear enough, though, that John and 1–3 John rely on a similar set of fairly limited terms, and these words are not nearly so common in other books of the NT. A further point is worth stressing. Although the bulk of the following discussion will focus on 1 John, the list above shows that characteristic Johannine terms like "truth," "abide," and "testimony" appear with some prominence in 2–3 John as well. Their appearance in all three letters, as well in as the Gospel, points to a distinctive Johannine vocabulary. Attuning one's ears to this specialized vocabulary is the first stage in recognizing the similarity between 1–3 John and the Gospel of John.

But it is only the first stage. Not only are particular words shared by the various texts but these same words are also combined in similar phrases and sentences. Common syntactical structures and common clusters of words are formed around this shared vocabulary (Brooke 1912, i–x). It is one thing to see, for instance, that terms related to "truth" are common in the Johannine literature, but it is even more compelling to list the various phrases that build around the word "truth," as in table 2 (modified from Painter 2002, 66–68):

Table 2. Common Phrases and Syntax in John and 1 John

1 John		John	
1:6	We do not do the truth	3:21	the one who does the truth
1:8	the truth is not in us	8:44	truth is not in him
2:21	is not of the truth	18:37	everyone who is of the truth
3:19	we are of the truth		
4:6	spirit of truth	14:16–17	Paraclete, the spirit of truth
		16:13	the spirit of truth

In all these cases, terms are clustered in very similar ways. The most compelling example is the phrase "to do the truth." The expression is a common

Semitic idiom in the OT, but it appears in the NT only in the Johannine literature, serving as a link between the Gospel and the Letters. Many other phrases are also shaped around common vocabulary, as table 3 shows.

Table 3. Further Common Phrases Shared by John and 1 John

1 John		John	
1:8	we have no sin	9:41	you would not have sin
2:11	he walks in the darkness	8:12	shall not walk in darkness (cf. 11:9, 10; 12:35)
2:28	abide in him	15:4, 7	abide in me (cf. 14:10; 6:56)
3:1	be called children of God	1:12	authority to be children of God
3:2	we are children of God		
3:4	everyone who does sin (cf. 3:8, 9)	8:34	everyone who does sin
3:14	we have passed from death into life	5:24	he has passed from death into life
4:16	we have known and believed	6:69	we have believed and known
5:4	conquers the world and this is the victory that conquers the world	16:33	I have conquered the world
5:9	if we receive the witness of men	3:33	the one receiving his witness
		5:34	but I do not receive the witness of men

Even larger literary structures than just phrases and sentences are also built around this shared vocabulary. Commentators regularly note, for example, that both John and 1 John begin with prologues that include the same key terms, like "word" (*logos*) and "beginning" (*archē*). John opens by describing the Word that was *in* the beginning, while 1 John opens by describing the word that was *from* the beginning. These twin texts will receive fuller comment in the appropriate place in the commentary, but it is important here to notice that both John and 1 John open with prologues that share the same vocabulary. John and 1 John share a common manner of concluding as well. As the Gospel winds toward its final chapter, John 20:30–31 says:

> Jesus performed many other signs in the presence of his disciples, which are not written in this book; but these things [*tauta*] are written that you may believe that Jesus is the Christ, the Son of God, and that believing you may have life in his name. (see also John 21:25)

Several key terms and phrases in this passage from John find a corollary in a similar statement near the close of 1 John (5:13):

> I wrote these things [*tauta*] to you so that you may know that you have eternal life, who believe in the name of the Son of God.

Both texts refer to "these things" that are "written," and both texts connect "belief" in the "Son of God" to "having" either "life" or "eternal life."

The connections with the Gospel are not confined to 1 John. Third John 13 has a similar resonance, even if in a slightly muted form. Like the phrase in John 20, it apologizes for not writing more when the author says,

> I had much more that I should write you, but I do not wish to write it out with pen and ink.

Thus the Fourth Gospel and 1 John not only open with prologues that resemble each other but they also draw near to their conclusions with summary statements that resemble each other. Third John seems to share in this relationship, at least as it relates to the closing formula.

More can be said at a further level of abstraction. The opening and closing sections of Johannine texts share another common quality, the reference to the notion of testimony through the verb *martyrein* (to testify) and the noun *martyria* (testimony). The Gospel of John begins by referring repeatedly to the testimony of John the Baptist, first in the prologue (1:7–8) and then in the opening line of the narrative (1:19): "This is the testimony [*martyria*] given by John. . . ." The final lines of the Gospel return to this term by underscoring the testimony of the Beloved Disciple: "This is the disciple who is testifying [*martyrōn*] to these things and has written them, and we know that his testimony [*martyria*] is true [*alēthēs*]" (21:24). Testimony (*martyria*) also serves as a framing device in 1 John. First John opens by referring to testimony (1:2) and then winds to its close by saying in 5:11, "And this is the testimony [*martyria*], that God gave eternal life to us, and this life is in his Son." Third John unfolds according to the same structure. The opening lines of 3 John refer to the brothers who testify (*martyrountōn*) about the manner in which Gaius walks (3 John 3), and the letter closes (3 John 12) by commending Demetrius and saying, "We testify [*martyroumen*], and you know [*oidas*] that our testimony [*martyria*] is true [*alēthēs*]." This last line has the added quality of reminding one of John 21, where it refers to the testimony of the Beloved Disciple, and announces, "We know [*oidamen*] that his testimony [*martyria*] is true [*alēthēs*]" (21:24). Once one accounts for the changes in the person of the verbs between 3 John 12 and John 21:24, the two statements seem evocative of each other, especially because of the common reliance on the terms "know," "testimony," and "true."

Thus 1–3 John share with the Gospel of John not only a common vocabulary and basic syntactical structures but also larger structuring devices. To borrow a musical analogy, the texts not only use the same individual notes but also combine those notes into similar harmonies. The commonalities are both broad and deep.

Even so, similarity is only half the matter. The various points of correspondence that we have just surveyed also show how different the texts are. The first and best case of such similarity-in-difference comes from a comparative reading of the prologues of John and 1 John. Both prologues rely on similar terms, such as *logos* (word) and *archē* (beginning), but the meaning of the terms is different in the different texts. The "beginning" referred to in John 1:1 is the cosmic beginning, before the creation of the world. The "beginning" that 1 John 1:1 has in mind is the beginning of Jesus's earthly ministry. Similarly, John 1:1 refers to Jesus as the "Word," but 1 John 1 applies the term "word" to the preaching of the apostles. In both cases a "word" has its origins in the "beginning," which suggests an obvious connection between the texts, but the character of the word and the time frame of the beginning are not at all the same. A common set of terms and a common style are deployed differently in each text. Broad similarities are elided by important differences.

These complications extend to theological questions and to matters of content. One common issue is that the Johannine Letters ascribe to the Father things that the Gospel ascribes to Jesus. The famous "new commandment" offers a good example. In the Fourth Gospel, the command to "love one another" comes from the mouth of Jesus on the night when he was betrayed. He twice tells his disciples, "Love one another" (John 13:34; 15:12). The same command appears in the Letters (1 John 3:11, 23; 2 John 5), only now it is the command not of Jesus but of the Father (1 John 3:23). Matters become even more complicated when one compares the Gospel and Letters on a theological level. Some interpreters argue that the theology of the Letters and the theology of the Gospel are so different as to be incompatible. C. H. Dodd is an eloquent spokesperson for those who hold this view: "Eschatology, the Atonement, the Holy Spirit: these are certainly no minor themes in Christian theology. In all three the First Epistle of John represents an outlook widely different from that of the Fourth Gospel" (1946, liv). This bold statement is too stark, but for precisely this reason it provides a helpful starting point for discussion. The distinctions are real but not utterly irresolvable. Painter (2002, 59) elegantly and efficiently shows that Dodd overemphasizes the differences in each of these three areas of thought—eschatology, atonement, and the Holy Spirit.

The oversimplification is most obvious in eschatology. Dodd assumes that the Gospel has a thoroughly realized eschatology, in which the gifts of the end times are already available here and now, while 1 John has an entirely future eschatology, in which only the return of Christ will inaugurate a new world and a new way of existing. The Gospel certainly assumes a realized eschatology, which is most obvious in a verse like John 5:24: "Very truly I tell you, anyone who hears my word and believes him who sent me has eternal life and does not come under judgment, but has crossed over from death to life." But this present experience is not total or complete. Jesus still points to a future and final fulfillment of the promise of new life, as when he says at 14:3, "And if I go and prepare a place for you, I will come again and take you to myself, so that where I am, there you may be also." John 14:3 is not alone. Other phrases also have a future orientation (5:21–29; 6:39, 40, 44, 54; 12:48; 17:24).

The hope of the Gospel is oriented toward the future, even as it affirms that the gifts of the future are available in the present. Jesus clarifies this dual eschatological hope: "A time is coming and now is when the dead will hear the voice of the Son of God and those who hear will live" (5:25). First John shares in this dual hope, emphasizing both a future and a realized eschatology. Attention to the future is certainly more pronounced in 1 John, as when 3:2 says, "Dear friends, now we are children of God, and what we will be has not yet been made known," and yet a concern for the present is hardly absent. First John 2:8 says, "Yet I am writing you a new command; its truth is seen in him and in you, because the darkness is passing and the true light is already shining" (see also 5:20). These two verses in 1 John seem to reflect the theology of the Fourth Gospel, in which "the time is coming, and yet now is."

John and 1 John are also not so far apart on the role of the Spirit. To be sure, the Spirit is nowhere in 1 John called "the Paraclete," nor is the full panoply of imagery that the writer of John applies to the Spirit present in 1 John. Other things, though, are held in common. The Spirit of Truth in John 15:26–27 inspires the disciples to offer witness to Jesus, while in 1 John 4:2 the spirit of truth shows the difference between true confession and the confession of false prophets, who are antichrists. This is not exactly the same thing, but in both cases the Spirit of Truth empowers true witness in the face of opposition. On the question of atonement, it is true that John never calls Jesus an "atonement for our sins" (*hilasmos peri tōn hamartiōn hēmōn*, 1 John 2:2), but John does open by announcing that Jesus is the "Lamb of God who takes away the sin of the world" (John 1:29). Sacrificial atonement may not be prominent in the Gospel, but it does seem to lie somewhere behind this announcement of John the Baptist. The theology of the two books is either more compatible (in the case of eschatology) or not nearly so incompatible (in atonement and the Spirit) as some assume. The theological visions of the two books do not separate them. The visions are related. To assume that they are related, however, only begets a further question: *how* are they related?

Chronology of the Letters

The present commentary assumes that the Letters represent a later period in the history of the Johannine tradition than the Gospel, but not every commentator shares this view. Three general approaches predominate. One view finds recent expression in the work of Judith Lieu (2008). While Lieu recognizes the various literary and syntactical connections that unite the various texts just surveyed, she argues the following in her commentary (17):

11

> The position taken here is that there is no compelling evidence of a direct literary relationship between 1 John and the Gospel in anything like the latter's current form; on the contrary, the consistent subtle differences of wording, inference, context, and combination even where parallels appear close suggest that both writings draw independently on earlier formulations.

Lieu prefers to avoid the question of the literary dependence of one text (or texts) on another; she chooses to refer to a collective "Johannine tradition" in a way that implies nothing about whether one document is a source or model for the others (2008, 18). In making this argument, she echoes, in a slightly modified form, the sentiments expressed earlier by scholars like Georg Strecker, who also ascribes the similarities of the various Johannine texts to "the independent language and world of the Johannine school" (1996, 9n8).

The benefit of this position is that it so sharply deviates from the current standard reading (which assumes the literary dependence that Strecker and Lieu deny), reminding us to be careful about how much we presume to know about these mysterious letters. In her effort to resist the standard reading, Lieu helpfully avoids excesses in the standard view. For instance, the eminent Raymond Brown (1982, 116–30) seems to go beyond the evidence in arguing that 1 John and John actually share the same outline, beginning with a prologue (1 John 1:1–4 and John 1:1–18), followed by two major blocks of narrative in John (1:19–12:50 and 13:1–20:29) and two blocks of argument in 1 John (1:5–3:10; 3:11–5:12), ending with a closing formula that is followed by an epilogue (1 John 5:13, 14–21 and John 20:30–31; 21:1–25). Lieu (2008, 17) rightly argues that we might be seeing the connections too closely if we imagine two texts of such very different genres imitating each other to such a great degree. But even if she is correct to remind us that the evidence is complicated, her caution might go too far in the other extreme by suggesting that the evidence is so complicated and so mysterious as to defy any effort to decide whether the texts are linked by literary dependence.

The copious lists of similarities sampled above suggest otherwise. The larger structural bonds that connect the texts are even more suggestive in showing literary dependence, and they make it extremely difficult to imagine how a "Johannine tradition" does not rely on literary dependence in some form. The opening lines and closing formulas shared by 1 John and the Gospel of John are the best place to see the problems with Lieu's approach, since it seems difficult to imagine that, in an unrelated and nonimitative fashion, the same Johannine tradition led two authors to refer in their opening lines to so many common terms. The two texts mention either what was "from the beginning" (*ap' archēs*) or "in the beginning" (*en archē*) and then proceed to use several common phrases such as "in the presence of God" (*pros ton theon* in John 1:1) and "in the presence of the Father" (*pros ton patera* in 1 John 1:2), and common terms such as "testimony," "light," "word," and "life." This kind of close association suggests more than a coincidence arising from a common tradition. If the various terms and phrases that the texts share were randomly scattered throughout the works, then their similarities might be merely coincidental. But the fact that 1 John and John both employ these common phrases and words in their opening lines suggests that one of them is imitating the other. The same is true of the summary phrases that appear in John 20:31 and 1 John 5:13, as recognized above. More than a common tradition seems to be at work when two texts not only use the same words but also use them in the same places. This is why the vast majority of scholars assume that one of the Johannine texts is the model for the others, which leads us to the next question. If one text is copying the other, which text is copying which?

The monumental commentary of Urban C. von Wahlde (2010) argues that the Gospel copies its prologue from 1 John. The initial and most primitive form of the Fourth Gospel took shape prior to the writing of 1 John, he argues, but the final form of the Gospel copies 1 John. Support for this theory relies on first accepting several presuppositions about the source and editorial history of the Johannine tradition, especially as this relates to the Gospel. That matter cannot be discussed here in full since it would distract us too far from our present concern (but see Parsenios 2012a). It is important to stress, however, that von Wahlde has strong support for his theory. A chief piece of evidence in his favor comes with the use of the term "Paraclete." In John 14:16, Jesus refers to the Spirit as "another Paraclete." No one else is ever called a Paraclete in the Gospel, which makes it difficult to see why Jesus adds the adjective "another." Yet 1 John 2:1 refers to Jesus as "a Paraclete before the Father." This could very well mean that 1 John preceded the Gospel. If Jesus is first called a Paraclete in 1 John, and if 1 John was written before the Gospel, then the Gospel could very naturally refer to the Spirit as "another Paraclete." The first Paraclete is Jesus in 1 John, and the Spirit is "another Paraclete" in the Gospel, written later.

The present commentary will argue the opposite and assume that the Gospel precedes 1–3 John. The prologue is again a decisive text. To assume that 1 John was written before the Gospel, we would have to imagine that the author of 1 John first coined the phrase "from the beginning" in the opening line of 1 John for reasons unknown, and that subsequently the Fourth Evangelist recognized a possible connection between this phrase and the phrase "In the beginning" from Gen. 1:1. The Evangelist then changed the phrase "from the beginning" into the scriptural phrase "In the beginning." Such a scenario does not seem likely. More likely is the possibility that the Evangelist first used the phrase "In the beginning" in the Gospel as a way to connect the story of God's work in Jesus to the story of God's work in Genesis by repeating the phrase from Genesis, "In the beginning." Then, later, 1 John changed this evocative phrase into the new formula "from the beginning" and reapplied the new phrase to a new problem in a new setting in the letter.

13

Rhetoric and the Opposition

If the author of these letters has obscured himself behind a veil of silence, that same veil covers the people to whom he writes and, even more, the people whom he opposes. The gaps in our knowledge provide room for scholarly debate, and interpreters have found several different ways to reconstruct the opponents against whom the author writes. Scholarly opinion varies so widely because the author does not consistently tell us who the opponents are, or even what they believe—even as he says a great deal about them. He paints a rhetorical portrait of them in order to interpret them for his readers. The opponents are "antichrists" and "false prophets" (2:18–22; 4:1, 3), and these labels tell us how the author of 1 John understands the opponents and how he wants his readers to understand them. But he does not tell us what the opponents themselves think. The rhetorical portrait in the letters is our only access to the opponents. On one level, then, the rhetoric of the letters is an obstacle to reconstructing the opponents and the problems plaguing the community. The veil of silence that covers the opponents is a veil of words.

And yet for some scholars the rhetoric of the letters does not impede histori-cal reconstruction of the opponents but facilitates historical analysis. Duane Watson has argued not only that the rhetorical style and shape of the Letters of John rely on ancient rhetorical categories but also that particular categories were chosen in order to respond to specific problems in the Johannine orbit (1989a; 1989b; 1993). For instance, Watson shows that 1 John relies on the rhetorical technique of "amplification," wherein an author repeatedly returns to and develops a particular set of ideas to "amplify" their importance (1993). But this is not merely a literary or rhetorical insight; it also has historical consequences. Watson argues that 1 John relies on "amplification" in order to win the greater adherence of its readers to the Johannine tradition in the face of the opponents who undermine that tradition. Rhetoric and historical reconstruction are tightly linked in his work.

Other interpreters connect the rhetoric of the letters to historical recon-struction in a different way, and their work will provide the impetus for the rhetorical concerns of this commentary. For these interpreters, the rhetorical presentation of the opponents not only shows us how to understand the rift in the community but also actually shows that the rift was not so great. They view the heated rhetoric of 1–3 John as mere rhetoric, and the supposedly permanent rift in the community as nothing more than a minor squabble among people still living in communion. This way of reading is articulated clearly by Pheme Perkins, who deserves to be quoted at length to make her position as clear as possible:

> Scholars who are not sensitive to the language of oral cultures often misinterpret statements about opponents in ancient writings. You would get the impression

from reading some modern interpreters of the Johannine letters that the community was being violently ripped apart by the debates to which the author refers. In an oral culture, infused with rhetoric at every level, minor debates could produce major rhetorical responses that were often not indicative of the nature of the problem. . . . The point of rhetoric was to use every means possible to see that one's own position, the true or good one, prevailed over its "bad" opposition. Even sciences and medicine were discussed in terms of conflicts between forces, of battles that had to be won. (1978, xxi–xxii)

With this in mind, the heated rhetoric of the Johannine Letters might not imply such an elaborate schism. Perkins writes:

When the author speaks of his opponents having broken fellowship with his community, we perhaps have to think of the various types of feud and breaking off of association that occur in close-knit oral societies. . . . Such disputes do not destroy the whole fabric of a community. . . . Several hours after the most dire exchange of insults and threats, the opponents may be going about their business as though they had never fought. (1979, xxii–xxiii)

According to Perkins, we should not imagine some grand schism existing behind these letters but something more like a family quarrel that, once it blows over, is forgotten and a thing of the past. Fellowship continues.

Two aspects of this approach will be influential in what follows, with qualifications. First, the suggestion by Perkins that the quarrel in these letters is best compared to a family fight is helpful. The Letters of John regularly rely on familial language when they refer to the members of the church, as in the regular practice of addressing the readers as children (1 John 3:1, 2; 5:2; 2 John 1, 4, 13; 3 John 4) or "my little children" (1 John 2:12, 28; 3:7, 18; 4:4; 5:21). This may be an important sociological move on the part of the author. In antiquity, when people converted to a minority religion like Judaism or Christianity, they often strained or completely severed their ties to their natural families. Philo of Alexandria writes about the situation of Gentiles who became Jewish proselytes. By abandoning the polytheism of their past to follow the one God of Israel, they also abandoned the various family, social, and political ties connected to Greek and Roman religion. Since such proselytes had lost their former friendly and familial relations, Philo writes, "Let them not be denied another citizenship or other ties of *family and friendship*, and let them find places of shelter standing ready for refugees to the camp of piety" (*Spec. Laws* 1.52). Jews or pagans who follow Christ experience the same loss of family and friends, and so use kinship language to describe their relations to members of their new faith (see "Theological Issues" following section 2:12–3:10). This familial character of Christian community plays a subtle role in the conflict behind these letters. For example, 1 John 2:9–10 refers to those who remain in the community as those who love their brothers, and to those who leave the community as those who hate their brothers.

But the familial character of the conflict raises the issue of how complete and total the conflict was. While some interpreters follow Perkins in downplaying the polemical edge, viewing the struggle as either not very great, or at least not very central to the argument of the letters (Lieu 1991, 5–6, 13–16, 66), others argue against this view. Raymond Brown (1982, 48–49) is prominent among them. He thinks that Perkins too quickly dismisses passages like 2 John 10–11: "If someone comes to you and does not bring this teaching, do not receive him into your house and do not say to him, 'Greetings!' For the one who says to him, 'Greetings,' has fellowship with his wicked deeds." These verses imply a serious break of fellowship that is more extreme than Perkins's approach allows. Brown's position has broad support (see Painter 2002, 88–90). One is left to ask, Is the heated rhetoric mere rhetoric, or does it reflect historical reality?

The present commentary will develop a hybrid approach to this question. Perkins and Lieu may very well be correct that the division in the community is not so great, at least not yet. While certain people have left the fellowship (otherwise 1 John 2:19 could not have said, "They went out from us"), an ongoing relationship with these people seems to exist, since 1 John 3:7 tells the readers that they "are trying to deceive you." A group of people have separated themselves from the community and seek to persuade others to follow them. And yet the readers of the letters might not yet realize just how dangerous the secessionists are. Following the argument of Perkins, the rift might not yet seem great to all members of the community. First John is written in order to make the danger plain. The forceful rhetoric of the letter may not imply that there already is a crisis. Perhaps instead it seeks to produce a crisis. Understood this way, the rhetoric is not simply "mere rhetoric" but is to be taken seriously as reflecting a grave situation for the author of 1 John. The community, as tightly knit as a family, is nevertheless susceptible to pollution by false teaching and is already experiencing some degree of division. All the community members may not yet know the danger that lies before them, and the author writes to oppose this teaching and to marginalize his opponents.

The Rhetoric of the Letters: *Sententiae* and Social Division

Since such a grave historical circumstance lies behind the forceful rhetoric of 1–3 John, more needs to be said about the rhetorical posture of the letters. A fruitful way to proceed is to focus on a rhetorical style that has not yet been explored in regard to 1–3 John: their reliance on the rhetorical *sententia*. A *sententia* (*gnōmē* in Greek) is a maxim that expresses some broadly held truth in a pithy, pointed style, such as the comment of Shakespeare's Polonius:

"Neither a borrower nor a lender be" (*Hamlet*, act 1, scene 3). Maxims like these had been discussed and divided into different types as early as Aristotle (*Rhet.* 2.21), but they had a particular prominence in the rhetoric of the early Roman Empire.

The Stoic Seneca the Younger often expresses the paradoxes of Stoic philosophy in *sententiae*. For example, he urges Lucilius not to fear the criticism of others by saying, "One must scorn scorn itself" (*contemnendus est ipse contemptus*; *Ep.* 76.4; translations of Seneca in this paragraph are taken from Holloway 1998). Elsewhere, Seneca writes of the unimportance of wealth for the Stoic sage by insisting, "The shortest way to riches is to despise riches" (*brevissima ad divitias per contemptum divitiarum via est*; *Ep.* 62.3). These *sententiae* rely on the common devices of antithesis and paradox. Equally common is paronomasia. This device exploits the various possible meanings of a word, or adds a prefix to a word, in order to create a surprising expression, as in a phrase from Seneca the Elder: "Shall, then, Cicero's scribings [*quod scripsit*] perish, and Antony's proscribings [*quod proscripsit*] remain?" (*Suas.* 7.11).

The Gospel of John expresses the paradoxes and antitheses of its theological vision by relying on a similar style of discourse. This is most obvious in a verse from John 3: "What is born of the flesh is flesh, and what is born of the Spirit is spirit" (3:5–6). Paradox is further present in the claim that "those who love their life lose it, and those who hate their life in this world will keep it for eternal life" (12:25). This line also exploits the device of paronomasia, since the paradox that death leads to life is extended by a shift from earthly life to eternal life.

The Johannine Letters share this same style, which is especially prominent in 1 John. Several *sententiae* exploit antithetical realities, as follows:

1:5:   God is light; in him there is no darkness.
2:9:   Anyone who claims to be in the light but hates a brother or sister is still in the darkness.
2:15: If anyone loves the world, love of the Father is not in him.
2:17: The world and its desires pass away, but whoever does the will of God lives forever.

Although 2 and 3 John are shorter and less rhetorically shaped than 1 John, this style nevertheless appears in 3 John: "Anyone who does what is good is from God. Anyone who does what is evil has not seen God" (v. 11).

To identify the presence of *sententiae* in the Letters of John, though, is to say simply that these letters were written in the first century in the Roman Empire, a time and a place when *sententiae* were common and popular. The bigger question is: how do these *sententiae* function? Patrick Sinclair provides an answer to his question with an elegant phrase, "*Sententiae* speak to those who understand" (1995, 33). *Sententiae* have a social function, drawing boundaries and establishing a social connection between author and audience. This was recognized as early as Aristotle, who writes:

> The maxim, as has been already said, is a general statement and people love to hear stated in general terms what they already believe in some particular connection: e.g., if a man happens to have bad neighbors or bad children, he will agree with anyone who tells him, "Nothing is more annoying than having neighbors," or, "Nothing is more foolish than to be the parent of children." (*Rhet.* 2.21, trans. Roberts and Bywater 1954)

This is how *sententiae* function in the rhetoric of the early Roman Empire. Tacitus especially uses *sententiae* to solidify the boundaries of the Roman social elite, in order to separate Romans from barbarians and from anyone who does not live like a Roman. Tacitus defines the boundaries that divide Jews and Romans, for instance, with a *sententia* rich in antithesis: "The Jews regard as profane all that we hold sacred, and yet permit all that we abhor" (*Hist.* 5.4.1). *Sententiae* continue to function in this same way in the modern world, as many have shown in the writings of Rudyard Kipling. Kipling defines the relationship between England and its Asian and African colonies with phrases like "East is East, and West is West, and never the twain shall meet" ("The Ballad of East and West"). The line that separates England from India is drawn by such maxims in order to make absolutely sure that East will always be East and West will always be West, separate and apart. Kipling's novel *Kim*, for instance, includes phrases like "Kim would lie like an Oriental." Equally pointed in its chauvinism is the line "all hours of the twenty-four are alike to Orientals." Edward Said argues that these maxims are *derived* from British perceptions of India, and in turn also *fortify* those perceptions as objective truths (2005). Social, cultural, and religious divisions find their rhetorical expression in *sententiae*.

The Johannine Letters do something similar, as when they say such things as "God is light; in him there is no darkness at all" (1 John 1:5). Light and darkness are as separate as Kipling's East and West. This rhetorical reality is also present in the Gospel of John. Just like Kipling's insistence that East is East and West is West is the comment of Jesus to Nicodemus: "That born from flesh is flesh, and that born from Spirit is spirit" (John 3:6). The immediately preceding verse (3:5) has already informed us that one born of flesh cannot enter the kingdom of heaven or, to return again to Kipling's language, never the twain shall meet. The connection to Kipling here is more than stylistic. No less than Kipling's maxims, Jesus's *sententiae* in the Nicodemus dialogue provide a rhetorical expression of stark contrast. While Kipling illustrates the contrasts between England and India, the Fourth Gospel describes the contrasts between people of the flesh and people of the Spirit, those "from above" and those "from below" (3:31).

With no less immediacy 1 John insists that its readers are also caught between two realities: to behave and believe rightly, or to behave and believe wrongly. So 3:7–8 resembles both Kipling and the Nicodemus dialogue: "The one who does what is right is righteous, just as he is righteous. The one who does what is sinful is of the devil, because the devil has been sinning from the beginning." The comment right before this verse says: "No one who continues to sin has either seen him or known him" (3:6). In other words, "never the twain shall meet." *Sententiae* shore up the boundaries that separate two realities and show that those boundaries cannot be crossed.

And yet when Kipling says of East and West that never the twain shall meet, he is saying something that is both true and false for the function of *sententiae* in the Johannine orbit. It is certainly true that flesh and darkness are utterly and irreconcilably separate from the Spirit and light. And yet the chasm between people of the flesh and people of the Spirit is not impassable. The chasm is vast, but the bridge that leads a person across this chasm is faith in Jesus Christ. The rhetorical *sententiae* of the Gospel do not define the realms of darkness and light so sharply in order to signal that people are locked in one realm or the other, with no chance to change or choose, but rather, in order to emphasize the need to choose the one over the other.

The *sententiae* of the Johannine Letters function in this way. The passage already cited above from 3 John 11 is instructive: "Anyone who does what is good is from God. Anyone who does what is evil has not seen God." But right before this sententious statement comes a warning: "Dear friend, do not imitate what is evil but what is good" (v. 11). The stark separation that the *sententiae* draw is intended to show the necessity of choosing one side or the other. The author is writing to people within his orbit, urging them to live in such a way that they remain within the realm of light. Light and darkness may be separate and apart, but people are not irredeemably consigned to one realm or the other. They can—and must—choose by their actions which realm they will inhabit. Thus 1 John 2:17 sets up the same choice: "The world and its desires pass away, but whoever does the will of God lives forever." Right before this, 2:15 says, "Do not love the world or anything in the world." The rebellious world and God are as far apart as Kipling's East and West, but this contrast is drawn not to show that believers are locked securely within one or the other category but to show the importance of choosing to stay in the light.

The rhetoric of 1–3 John, therefore, is not mere rhetoric, and the problem in the community is not a mere family squabble. It is a profound crisis. The members of the community seem not to share the author's sense of immediacy, and the extreme posture of the letter is meant to jar them into greater awareness. We should, perhaps, imagine something similar to the situation in Paul's Letter to the Galatians, where Paul is driven by such furious intensity precisely because his community is not so energized. Likewise, 1–3 John were written to combat developing errors and to inoculate the community against being infected by error.

Settings and Purposes of 1–3 John

Setting and Purpose of 1 John

For decades, the setting and purpose of 1 John were defined by reconstructing the opponents against whom the letter argues. This practice has been called into question by recent interpreters, especially by Judith Lieu (2008, 9–14). Lieu helpfully and insightfully shows how our elaborate theories about the beliefs of the opponents can often be founded on unsteady hypotheses, which too easily become the (supposedly solid) foundation for further hypotheses. Reconstructing the opponents also takes our focus away from the argument of 1 John itself.

First John is our only window into the thought of the opponents, and it gives us its own interpretation of the views it opposes. Even more important, the letter tells us very little about those views. We do not even know for certain whether all the condemned views were held by one group only or by many different groups. The letter sees these issues as part of a coherent whole, but it is not clear whether there was a coherence in the opposition. It is difficult to know where to begin in reconstructing the rhetorical situation to which the letter responds. Painter provides a helpful way forward:

> My assumption is that the Johannine Epistles are directed to the continuing Johannine community. 1 John is directed to the situation subsequent to the schism referred to in 2:18–19. It is addressed to those who have been confused and made unsure by the departure of the schismatics who were, until recently, members of the Johannine community. (2002, 85)

The schism to which Painter here refers appears in verses 2:18–19:

> Dear children, this is the last hour; and as you have heard that the antichrist is coming, even now many antichrists have come. This is how we know it is the last hour. They went out from us, but they did not really belong to us. For if they had belonged to us, they would have remained with us; but their going showed that none of them belonged to us.

The departure of some members of the community is clearly one of the precipitating factors that inspired the letter. There has been a schism, and 1 John urges the remaining believers to stay with the community and not to join the schismatic group. This concern for communal concord is not only of minor importance, and not something that comes into view only in chapter 2. The opening lines of 1 John already show the need to maintain communal concord: "We proclaim to you what we have seen and heard, so that you also may have fellowship with us. And our fellowship is with the Father and with his Son, Jesus Christ" (1 John 1:3). To leave the fellowship of the community is not to choose an equally viable option but to choose a false community. The letter is written "so that you also may have fellowship with us." In Galatians, Paul tells his readers that to choose another gospel is to choose a non-gospel (1:7). First John makes a similar point. The only path to fellowship with the Father and his Son is to abide within this one community, and within no other. Communal coherence is a major concern in 1 John.

By coordinating the contents of 1 and 2 John we gain greater insight. The evidence of 2 John suggests that this schism was not only a break in fellowship but also a disagreement over theology. Hence 2 John 7 reads, "I say this because many deceivers, who do not acknowledge Jesus Christ as coming in the flesh, have gone out into the world. Any such person is the deceiver and the antichrist." This verse evokes 1 John 2:18–19 by (1) label-ing its opponents as antichrists and (2) referring to them as "going out." Yet 2 John 7 adds a theological element to the secessionists: "They do not acknowledge Jesus Christ as coming in the flesh." Something very similar appears in 1 John 4:1–3:

> Dear friends, do not believe every spirit, but test the spirits to see whether they are from God, because many false prophets have gone out into the world. This is how you can recognize the Spirit of God: Every spirit that acknowledges that Jesus Christ has come in the flesh is from God, but every spirit that does not acknowledge Jesus is not from God. This is the spirit of the antichrist, which you have heard is coming and even now is already in the world.

Thus 2 John 7 shares several concerns with 1 John but pulls the various parts together into one problem in a way that 1 John does not. The separat-ists did not merely separate themselves; they also held a deficient Christology. Thus the rift that tears apart the community is theological, and maintaining communion with the proper community is connected to maintaining proper belief. These two issues find further coordination in other parts of 1 John, such as 4:15: "God abides in those who confess that Jesus is the Son of God, and they abide in God." First John 1:3 has already said that having fellowship with God means having fellowship with the Johannine community, and 4:15 says that abiding in God means holding the proper faith. In these and other verses (see 3:23; 5:1, 5–13), 1 John seems to connect inclusion in the proper community with adherence to the proper faith, and both are necessary for fellowship with God.

False belief is clearly a problem, but less clear is the content of the belief that is considered false. The error of the opponents is mentioned in several places in 1 John (2:22–23; 4:15; 5:1, 5), but the error is not fully explained.

21

This commentary will assume, following many commentators, that the theological issue motivating 1 John is the reverse of the problem that motivated the Gospel of John. The Gospel was written to people who refused to believe that the man Jesus is God. They saw him as a mere human (cf. John 6:42). In response, the Gospel emphasized his divinity. First John faces the opposite problem. It is written to people who are Christians and who believe that Jesus is God. But in their certainty that he is God, they have come to deny that he was a human. This is why so much emphasis is placed, in both 1 and 2 John, on Jesus having become "flesh." More certainty than this about the beliefs of the opponents is not possible.

The history of scholarship has seen many attempts to identify more specifically the opponents of 1 John as one or another of the groups known in the second century whose Christology seems to correspond to what is rejected in 1 John. For example, Ignatius of Antioch (d. ca. 98–117 CE) struggles against docetists who say that Christ only "seemed" (*dokein*) to suffer in the flesh (*Trall.* 2.1; *Smyrn.* 2). Because 1 and 2 John argue against those who say that Jesus did not come in the flesh (1 John 4:2; 2 John 7) and make several allusions to the reality and significance of Christ's Passion (1 John 1:7; 2:2; 4:10), some have argued that Ignatius and 1–2 John share the same opponents. Another well-known candidate for identifying the opposition is the figure Cerinthus (ca. 100 CE), described by Irenaeus of Lyons (ca. 180 CE; *Haer.* 1.26). Cerinthus did not believe that the earthly Jesus who existed in the flesh could be equated with the divine Christ, who was spiritual and who descended upon Jesus in the form of a dove at baptism. Cerinthus devised a scheme in which the earthly Jesus in the flesh had a particular identity that was temporarily joined to the Christ of the Spirit, but only very superficially. They were actually separate figures. Because 1 and 2 John insist that "Jesus Christ" came in the flesh, and strictly connect "Jesus" and "Christ," some say they seem to respond to Cerinthus. Gnosticism, of course, is often mentioned in this debate, because certain gnostics devalued the physical quality of Jesus's life and ministry in the manner of figures described above. But scholars continue to struggle to delimit gnostics as a social group (Layton 1995b), and there is no clear evidence in 1–3 John that the opponents adhere to the details of the gnostic redeemer story (see Layton 1995a).

In addition to second-century groups and personalities like the ones just listed, other groups have been proposed to define the teaching of the opposition behind 1–2 John (Brown 1982, 55–68), but the letters do not provide nearly enough information about the beliefs of their opponents to make a clear connection to any particular figures or groups known from other texts (Lieu 1991, 14–16). One does not need to make a specific connection to a particular group or individual, however, to learn from these second-century figures. They all show a failure to appreciate the full reality of the incarnation: they devalue the belief that Jesus appeared in the flesh. If the opponents

---

Possible Opponents behind the Letters of John

Docetists

"Be deaf, then, when someone speaks to you apart from Jesus Christ, of the family of David, of Mary, who was truly born, both ate and drank, was truly persecuted under Pontius Pilate, was truly crucified and died, . . . who was also truly raised from the dead." (Ignatius of Antioch, *Trall.* 9–10, trans. Schoedel 1985, 152)

Cerinthus

"A certain Cerinthus . . . proposes Jesus, not as having been born of a Virgin—for this seemed impossible to him—but as having been born the son of Joseph and Mary like all other men, and that he excelled over every person in justice, prudence and wisdom. After his baptism, Christ descended on him in the shape of a dove from the Authority that is above all things. Then he preached the unknown Father and worked wonders. But at the end Christ again flew off from Jesus. Jesus indeed suffered and rose again from the dead, but Christ remained impassible, since he was spiritual." (Irenaeus of Lyons, *Haer.* 26.1, trans. Unger 1992, 90)

---

of the Johannine Letters have no specific connection to known entities in the ancient world, they do reflect the same general concerns that known figures debated regarding the salvific significance—or lack thereof—that should be ascribed to the human flesh of Jesus.

Was there also a debate with the secessionists over morality? The question is hard to answer for certain. First John is clearly concerned about Christian behavior and raises the issue several times in relation to Christology. From the perspective of 1 John, belief and behavior are closely connected. In 3:23 we read, "And this is his command: to believe in the name of his Son, Jesus Christ, and to love one another as he commanded us" (see also 4:7–5:5). Likewise, the letter opens with a lengthy section on the proper way for Christians to live (1:5–2:11) and says a great deal about sin in several places (1:5–2:11; 2:28–3:10; 5:16–18), as well as the effect of Jesus's death for human sin (1:7; 2:12; 4:10). Tremendous stress is also placed on the need for Christians to love one another (2:9–11; 3:10–18). Could this emphasis relate in any way to the christological debate? It is possible. One could speculate that the opponents who rejected the sacrificial life of Jesus on earth in the flesh also rejected that they needed to live their own lives in a sacrificial manner. This would explain why 1 John 3:16–17 says:

We know love by this: that he laid down his life for us—and we ought to lay down our lives for one another. How does God's love abide in anyone who has the world's goods and sees a brother or sister in need and yet refuses help?

We can only speculate over how such comments relate to what the opponents actually taught and believed about Christology. On the one hand, it is conceivable that their very different Christology led to a very different view of morality. On the other hand, if their only deviation was in the area of Christology, the author of 1 John might connect Christology and behavior so closely in order to show that they are inherently inseparable. The opponents might have believed that their behavior could remain correct, even if they altered their Christology. The Johannine Letters connect behavior and belief in order to show that believers cannot have one without the other: true belief and true behavior are inseparable. In the end, the only thing clear is that the author of 1 John connects these issues. We cannot know what he argues against, but we can see clearly what he argues for. The loving sacrifice of Christ, when properly understood, requires his followers to live lives of loving sacrifice themselves.

Interpreters often describe this intersection of Christology and the love command under the twin titles of "Christology" and "ethics." David Rensberger rightly shows the poverty of these categories for describing 1 John:

> The epistles are not concerned with ethics. . . . The only ethical category of interest to the author is love for one another, and love rather than "ethics" seems the more appropriate heading. . . . In Jesus was revealed not only the God who is love, but [also] the good news that human beings can love one another with this same love. (1997, 35)

First John responds with such alarm to the theology and the secession of the opponents precisely because their Christology imperils the proper understanding of such love. Their anemic Christology diminishes the profundity of the incarnation, and their act of separating themselves from the broader community diminishes the love expressed through the concord of the community.

Thus 1 John is, broadly and loosely speaking, an example of paraenetic literature. The Greek word *parainesis* means "advice" or "exhortation," and a large body of paraenetic speeches and letters survive from antiquity, designed to give advice and exhortation. More specific treatment of the concept of paraenesis will be given in the commentary on 2 John, but 1 John also has a basic paraenetic quality. Essentially, paraenetic discourse has two functions: to encourage people to follow one course of action, and to dissuade them from following another (Libanius, *Epis. Styles* 5). First John certainly fits these broad criteria for paraenetic discourse: its basic concerns are to urge people to follow the true teaching enshrined within the community and to avoid the false teaching associated with those who have left the community. Second John even more closely fits the model of the paraenetic letter, and we can turn to 2 John now.

Setting and Purpose of 2 John

Second John seems to respond to the same crisis as 1 John, and to do so in the same way. Most commentators agree on this point. Commentators disagree, though, on what explains this similarity. Why did the same author write the same argument twice? Was 2 John sent to a different community? Was it sent to the same community, but following 1 John? Or, rather, was it sent before 1 John? Was it, in this way of thinking, the quick, rough draft of the argument that was sent out when the crisis first exploded, followed by 1 John when time had permitted a longer, more reflective response? Or did it actually accompany 1 John? It is hard to know for sure which of these scenarios corresponds to reality. We can only say for certain that 2 John closely resembles 1 John. In at least one important way, though, 2 John differs from 1 John: we see that 2 John actually tells its audience how to respond to the secessionist opponents. In verses 10–11, readers are told not even to welcome anyone who teaches a different theology from the one approved by the author. Literary issues also distinguish 2 John from 1 John. While the genre of 1 John is difficult to discern, 2 John is obviously a letter (see below, under "The Relationship of the Johannine Letters to Ancient Letters").

Setting and Purpose of 3 John

Third John is simultaneously the most clear and the most enigmatic of all the Johannine Letters. It is the clearest because it is the only one of the three documents that provides names for the people it mentions. It begins by praising Gaius for help that he has provided for traveling missionaries (1–8), condemns Diotrephes for refusing to provide similar help (9–10), and then urges Gaius to show further support for Demetrius (11–12). Thus it is a letter of recommendation, a type common in ancient epistolography. When journeying abroad, travelers would need the support of people dwelling in the areas they visited. A letter of introduction/recommendation from a person who was known in the foreign land would win the support of locals for the unknown traveler. But if the status of 3 John as a letter of introduction/recommendation is clear, the relationship of 3 John to the problems raised in 1–2 John is not at all clear. Diotrephes rejects the emissaries of the Elder. Does this mean that Diotrephes is one of those who has left the community, the secessionists described in 1–2 John? Some believe that we can say nothing positive about Diotrephes in this regard (Lieu 2008, 265–66), while others believe that he is indeed a secessionist (Painter 2002, 361–65). This commentary will follow the position laid out by Brown (1982, 732–39), who argues that nothing specific can connect Diotrephes to the secessionist group. After all, if the Elder teaches not to receive emissaries from opposing groups in 2 John, why would he be angry if Diotrephes did not receive any emissaries? Indeed, why would such emissaries even be sent?

Further, no clearly doctrinal problems are attached to Diotrephes. The only error on his part is to reject the agents sent from the Elder. This act of rejection is an act of inhospitality, according to the conventions governing letters of introduction, but it is not a dogmatic error, and not obviously connected to the problems appearing in 1–2 John. And yet, at a certain level of abstraction, there is an oblique way to connect 3 John to the problems of 1–2 John. Diotrephes may not have been a member of the secessionist group, but he might still have been motivated by the problems between the Elder and the secessionists when he refused to welcome the agents of the Elder. It is possible that he no longer knew whom to trust, given the presence of traveling missionaries (as in 2 John), and so refused to welcome any traveling teachers, even those sent by the Elder. This is the position taken in the commentary, but it cannot be proved beyond a reasonable doubt.

The Letters in Relationship to One Another

Though it is not entirely clear how all these letters fit into a coherent narrative of activity, it is, nevertheless, reasonably clear that they all were produced by the same source. Shared vocabulary is the most immediate tie that binds the three texts, as seen in the discussion above. The texts can be bound together even more closely. At first, 1 and 3 John seem the most remote and different, but these two texts do not exist in isolation. They stand together alongside 2 John, and each has important connections with 2 John. Regardless of the order in which the separate documents were produced, we can see 2 John as the link that holds the other letters in a single chain. Both 2 and 3 John, for instance, share the same sender, "the Elder." This makes their link secure. In the same way, 2 John and 1 John address the same basic theological problems and the same schism. When 2 John 7 refers to "many deceivers who do not acknowledge Jesus Christ as coming in the flesh," one cannot help but hear an echo of 1 John 4:2: "Every spirit that acknowledges that Jesus Christ has come in the flesh is from God." Thus 2 John is the common ground that shows the shared origin of 1 and 3 John. Each of them is so tightly connected to 2 John that they are reasonably connected to each other. Because the author of 2 John seems to have written 1 John and 3 John, we can surmise that the same author (or authors) wrote them all. But if the same author wrote all three documents, the one thing he changed was his manner of presentation. The manner of writing in 2 and 3 John is typical of ancient letters, but 1 John is much more distant in form from a standard letter. To explain the differences, we must look now at the conventions of ancient epistolography.

The Relationship of the Johannine Letters to Ancient Letters

The most definitive elements of an ancient letter come in the opening line. As John Muir (2009, 1) says succinctly, "Most ancient letters are easily recognizable. . . . They begin with 'A to B, greetings' (or a slight variation of that) and usually end with a single word of good wishes 'Farewell' or 'Best wishes.'" A letter from Cicero in 58 BCE to his colleague Atticus (*Att.* 3.7) begins with three Latin words: *Cicero Attico sal*, where *sal* is short for *salutem dicit*, "offers greetings." These three words can be translated roughly as "Cicero [sender] offers greetings [the greeting] to Atticus [recipient]." A Greek letter from a certain Apollonios in third-century Egypt demonstrates the model in Greek as follows (P.Oxy. 2783): *Apollonios Artema tō adelphō chairein*, which can be roughly translated, "Apollonios [sender] to his brother Artemas [recipient], greetings [the greeting]." As a good example of the type in the NT, 1 Thessalonians (1:1) opens as follows:

Senders: Paul, Silvanus, and Timothy,
Recipients: To the church of the Thessalonians in God the Father and the Lord
             Jesus Christ:
Greeting: Grace to you and peace.

This pattern appears not only in almost all the Letters of the Pauline corpus (Rom. 1:1–7; 1 Cor. 1:1–3; 2 Cor. 1:1–2; Gal. 1:1–5; Eph. 1:1–2; Phil. 1:1–2; Col. 1:1–2; 2 Thess. 1:1–2; 1 Tim. 1:1–2; 2 Tim. 1:1–2; Titus 1:1–4; Philem. 1–3; Hebrews alone opens without such an epistolary greeting) but also in every other letter in the NT, though with some variations.

2–3 John and Ancient Letters

Following these standard conventions, 2 and 3 John begin by naming both their senders and recipients. They both identify their sender as "the Elder," and 2 John is sent to "the Elect Lady and her children," while 3 John is addressed to a certain Gaius. They also share many other elements with the typical ancient letter. For instance, 3 John offers a wish for good health (v. 2), a thanksgiving (v. 3), a standard promise to follow up the letter with a personal visit (vv. 13–14), and the offering of greetings to and from a third party prior to a farewell (v. 15). In addition, 3 John is classified as a letter of introduction or recommendation, a category of letter that will be further discussed in the commentary on 3 John. Second John is more generally a paraenetic letter. Paraenetic letters were often used as opportunities to offer advice to distant friends, relatives, and associates.

1 John and Ancient Letters

Because 1 John begins with an introductory paragraph that is often called a prologue, and because it lacks the epistolary opening that is found in 2 and 3 John, it is rare for commentators to classify the document as a letter. The evidence does not entirely prevent calling it a letter, of course. Support for seeing 1 John as a letter comes first from the early church, which had no trouble calling it a letter (Lieu 2008, 5). Also, 1 John does contain certain other features common in letters, which should not be ignored. Hans-Josef Klauck writes (2006, 343), "The motif of joy in 1:4 . . . , the frequent reflection on the act of writing by *graphō* (2:1, 7, etc.) and *egrapsa* (2:14, etc.), and the repeated direct address of the audience can all be considered indications of an epistolary act of communication." It is certainly possible that the epistolary introduction to 1 John was removed when it was collected with the other Johannine Letters. It is sometimes argued that the opening and closing elements of a letter could be removed when collected, or they could drop out when letters were incorporated into a larger literary work (Stowers 1986, 20), like the letters collected in the histories of Thucydides and Herodotus (Trapp 2003, 23, 37, for examples). But the evidence for this is not unambiguous. It is possible that when these histories were written (fifth century BCE), the opening epistolary forms had not yet solidified completely. If this is so, then the standard epistolary features of these excerpted letters were not removed but never actually existed (Muir 2009, 1). Given these complications, the safest conclusion is to recognize that the epistolary quality of 1 John is not at all clear. This commentary will call 1 John a letter, but with the recognition that this label is more convenient than it is certain.

Authorship

Questions about the authorship of 1–3 John align along two broad areas of inquiry: (1) Do all three letters share the same author? (2) Did the author of the Gospel write the Letters? Scholarly responses to these questions are almost as numerous as there are scholars. The position of this commentary is that the three letters are the product of a single mind, given their close association on various levels. All three letters also share common features with, and allude in various ways to, the Fourth Gospel, suggesting associations with that book as well (see earlier discussion under "The Relationship of the Letters to the Gospel"). Irenaeus of Lyons (fl. 180) attributed the Gospel and 1–2 John to John the son of Zebedee already in the second century (*Haer.* 3.16.5, 8), and a comment by Origen (184–253) suggests that 2 and 3 John were considered by some to be the product of the same disciple in the third century (preserved in Eusebius, *Hist. eccl.* 6.25.9–10). An even earlier notice of the existence of the Johannine Letters comes from Papias (early second century), who knew of "the former letter of John and likewise that of Peter" (in Eusebius, *Hist. eccl.* 3.39.17). Even so, the final acceptance and inclusion of all three letters in the canonical Scripture was a long process, with many fits and starts even in the fourth century (Lieu 1986; C. Hill 2004). By the later fourth century, the famous Festal Letter of Athanasius (367), the Synod of Hippo (393), and the Council of Carthage (397) all accepted the three Letters of John, but 2–3 John never appear in the corpus of writings of John Chrysostom (d. 407) or of Theodore of Mopsuestia (d. 428).

Scholarly approaches to the problem of authorship span a broad spectrum. Raymond Brown believes that the antiquity of the tradition about Johannine authorship means that John the apostle was the source of the theology and traditions expressed in the Gospel. Yet he adds (1) that the final form of the Gospel shows refinement and development of these traditions and (2) that he cannot prove John as the source of these traditions to someone who does not take seriously either the ancient ecclesiastical traditions or the claims of the Gospel itself to be the product of an eyewitness (1966, 1.cii). The letters, Brown adds, were written by a later leader in the Johannine community (1982, 69–115). Judith Lieu adopts a polar-opposite position and emphasizes both the anonymous quality of these letters and their differences in purpose and form from one another (2008, 2–9). She recognizes that they have certain qualities in common, and so can be gathered together into a group under the label "Johannine," but emphasizes their uniqueness from one another and their anonymity. Finally, some have argued that both the Gospel and the Letters were not written by John the disciple but by John the elder (Hengel 1989; Bauckham 2007). Papias of Hierapolis (early second century) mentions a group of "elders" who transmit the traditions of the apostles (Eusebius, *Hist. eccl.* 3.39.3–4), (although it is not entirely clear how these elders relate to the apostles), and among them he lists John the elder. Scholars have tried to connect this John the elder to the elder who wrote 2–3 John, on the assumption that ecclesiastical tradition confused John the elder and John the disciple. However, these arguments always rely on accepting several contested interpretations of ancient texts, and then rely on these contested interpretations as the basis for further interpretations of other texts, until one loses confidence in the practice (see Lieu 1986, 12–14, 55–63; Rensberger 1997, 19).

It is beyond the scope of the present format to evaluate and explore all the relevant evidence and all the scholarly debates about authorship. A few tentative things can be said about this point, though. Irenaeus represents an ancient tradition that attributes at least the Gospel of John and some combination of 1–2 John to John the disciple. Other ancient testimonies complicate matters, but none of them is as unambiguous as Irenaeus (see Painter 2002, 44–50). As Brown noted above, not everyone accepts this ancient ecclesiastical tradition, and it is not possible to prove a connection to the historical John while following the canons of critical historical study. Furthermore, the documents themselves do not claim common authorship. The Gospel is attributed to the "Beloved Disciple," 2–3 John are attributed to the "elder" and 1 John is anonymous. These facts cannot be ignored. But neither do I see any reason to deny the traditional attribution to John the disciple of any of these texts, as long as this attribution is understood in a broad sense, meaning that the documents may not have come from the pen of John, the son of Zebedee, but at least from his

---

Irenaeus Attributes John, 1 John, and 2 John to John the Son of Zebedee

Adversus haereses 3.16.5

"As John the Lord's disciple affirms, saying, 'But these things are written that you might believe that Jesus is the Son of God, and believing might have eternal life in his name' (John 20:31). . . . Wherefore also in his Epistle he has borne this witness unto us: 'Little children, it is the last hour: and as you have heard that Antichrist comes, now many Antichrists have appeared, whereby we know that it is the last hour' (1 John 2:18–19)."

Adversus haereses 3.16.8

"His disciple John in the aforementioned Epistle bade us fly from them, saying, 'Many deceivers have gone out into this world, who do not confess Jesus Christ come in the flesh. This is a deceiver and an Antichrist' (2 John 7). . . . And again he says in the Epistle, 'Many false prophets are gone out into the world' (1 John 4:1)." (trans. Painter 2002, 48–49)

Irenaeus is writing circa 180 CE. The latter passage conflates 2 John 7–8 and 1 John 4, suggesting that perhaps he knew them as one epistle.

---

orbit of followers and from the teaching associated with him. There seems to me no reason to deny this. Luke Timothy Johnson makes a similar claim in regard to a different biblical book when he argues that the Epistle of James was produced by James of Jerusalem, the "brother of the Lord" mentioned by Paul (Gal. 1:19). Johnson writes, "I will not try to do the impossible and demonstrate beyond the possibility of cavil that James of Jerusalem was indeed the author of James, even though I share the view that preponderance of evidence makes that position one that can be held with a high degree of confidence" (2004, 3; for a different point of view on James, see Allison 2013).

This does not mean, however, that critical historical arguments must be put aside in evaluating the authorship of the epistles, especially when it

---

Reference to 1 John 4:2–3 in Polycarp's *Letter to the Philippians*

"Let us be eager with regard to what is good, and let us avoid those who tempt others to sin, and false brothers, and those who bear the name of the Lord hypocritically, who lead foolish people astray. For everyone who does not confess that Jesus Christ has come in the flesh is antichrist." (6.3–7.1 [ca. 115 CE], trans. Holmes 2007, 289; cf. 1 John 4:2–3; 2 John 7)

---

comes to assessing their relationship to the Gospel. I am simply more and more convinced that one can reasonably believe that the Gospel and Letters of John are products of the same mind, whether that mind is a single person or a collective body, because the books seem bound to one another at various levels of abstraction. We have already seen above that they share a common vocabulary, combine that vocabulary into common expressions, and share larger rhetorical and structural complexes (see above, "The Relationship of the Letters to the Gospel" and "The Rhetoric of the Letters: *Sententiae* and Social Division"). The commentary that follows will try in various ways to show that the Gospel and Letters share additional commonalities which bind them very closely. These shared qualities will be cataloged briefly at the close of the commentary on 1 John, in the "Theological Issues" section following 5:21.

And yet the historical question about authorship, while obligatory in the commentary format, is not the only way to explore the anonymous authorship of these letters. Judith Lieu very helpfully emphasizes that all the documents in the Johannine tradition mask the identity of their authors. The Gospel lists explicitly the names of many of Jesus's disciples, but its own author is identified not by name but only by the epithet "the disciple whom Jesus loved" (21:20, 24). The very title that reveals his identity also conceals it. The Letters are similarly reluctant to name their authors. Although ancient letters identify their sender as a matter of course, 1 John tells us nothing at all about its author. Also, 2 and 3 John operate like the Gospel. They simultaneously reveal and conceal the identity of their author by identifying him not by a name but by the epithet "the Elder" (2 John 1; 3 John 1). Anonymity seems intentional in all of these texts. Lieu refers to "the chosen anonymity of the letters" as "a deliberate technique in the Johannine literature" (2008, 9). Whether we have in mind the Beloved Disciple of the Gospel of John, the Elder of 2–3 John, or the total silence of 1 John, all four texts are alike in being produced by an author who obscures himself. This commentary will understand such anonymity as an important statement on the nature of discipleship in the Johannine tradition (see the "Theological Issues" section following 1:1–4).

Date and Place of Composition

Because this commentary assumes that the Letters follow the Gospel, the date of the Letters—at least in part—depends on the dating of the Gospel, but assigning a date to the Gospel is more complicated than it once was. The Fourth Gospel was often assigned to the late first century, on the traditional belief that the earliest manuscript of John, $\mathfrak{P}^{52}$ (P.Ryl. 3.457), is to be dated to the early second century. Brent Nongbri has shown that such a specific date is not so certain, so the date of the earliest manuscripts of the Gospel is now less clear (2005). But Charles Hill (2004, 418–19) argues that 1 John 4:2–3 and 2 John 7 are referenced in Polycarp's *Letter to the Philippians* (7.1), which is generally dated to about 115 CE (Holmes 2007, 272–79). Against a long history of suspicion that the Gospel of John was read only by gnostic interpreters until the late second century, Hill (2004, 421–43) also argues convincingly that much earlier writers, like Ignatius of Antioch, cited the Fourth Gospel in the early years of the second century. The Gospel had to be written before this then, and if the Gospel seems to have been produced sometime in the last two decades of the first century, the letters would have been written soon thereafter. The letters themselves tell us nothing about their place of origin. Tradition has often connected the Gospel and Letters of John to the city of Ephesus or its environs, and the very first reference to the Letters of John comes in the *Letter to the Philippians* of Polycarp. Because Polycarp was bishop of the city of Smyrna, a close neighbor of Ephesus, the Ephesian origin of the letters seems a plausible assumption but hardly one that can proven beyond any doubt (cf. von Wahlde 2010, 14–15).

Outline of First John

Introductory prologue (1:1–4)

The light and the darkness (1:5–2:11)

Three boasts: "If we say . . ." (1:5–2:2)

Three boasts: "Whoever says . . ." (2:3–11)

Who are the children of God? (2:12–3:10)

"I have written . . . I am writing" (2:12–14)

God and the world (2:15–17)

The Christ and the antichrists (2:18–27)

Born from above, born from below (2:28–3:10)

Love for God, love for one another (3:11–4:21)

Love one another (3:11–18)

Believe in the Son (3:19–24)

True teaching is "from God" (4:1–6)

True fellowship is "from God" (4:7–21)

Testimony and witnesses (5:1–21)

Witnesses (*martyriai*) for God's Son (5:1–12)

Martyrs (*martyres*) for God's Son (5:13–21)

Outline of Second John

Epistolary prescript (1–3)

The true faith and the true way of life (4–6)

The false faith and the false way of life (7–9)

False teachers and hospitality (10–11)

Epistolary farewell (12–13)

Outline of Third John

Epistolary opening (1–4)

Hospitality for missionaries (5–8)

The inhospitality of Diotrephes (9–10)

The recommendation of Demetrius (11–12)

Epistolary closing (13–15)

1 John 1:1–4

Introductory Prologue

Introductory Matters

The opening lines of a literary work serve as a threshold that a reader crosses in order to leave behind the broader world of human experience and enter into the more limited world of a text. Some interpreters have compared a written work's opening lines to the introitus of a piece of music, which introduces listeners to the musical composition that follows (Betz 1995, 92). Others have looked to architecture and compared the opening lines of a book, like the prologue of the Gospel of John, to the opening staircase of an ancient temple, which ushers one from the mundane world of the public street to the sacred space of the divine presence (Phillips 2006, 1–2; but see Fish 1980). The opening lines of 1 John function like such a threshold, but not in the usual way. These opening lines invite us into the world of the text by stopping us short and forcing us to pause. Complicated syntax and a peculiar use of key terms keep the reader from smoothly moving forward. If these verses orient us to the text that follows, they do so only by disorienting us. The misdirection is not haphazard, though. It has a theological purpose, grounded in the incarnation. Through the incarnation, according to 1 John, the invisible, immaterial God has become a person whom we can touch and see (1:1–4), while still continuing to be the God whom no one has ever beheld (4:12). A world in which God has become flesh, and yet continues to be the immaterial God, is a new and mysterious world, a world of paradoxes. God is infinitely distant and apart, and yet at the same time intimately present and near. He has been revealed, and yet remains concealed. Ephrem the Syrian neatly expresses this reality when he writes about the incarnation as follows:

> Who will not give thanks to the Hidden One, most hidden of all,
> Who came to open revelation, most open of all,
> For he put on a body, and other bodies felt Him,
> Though minds never grasped Him? (*Hymns on Faith* 19.7, trans. Brock
>   1992, 28)

When Ephrem says, "He put on a body, and other bodies felt Him," one hears a poetic restatement of 1 John 1:1: "That which we have seen and our hands have touched." Ephrem's phrase "minds never grasped Him" corresponds to a later verse, 1 John 4:12: "No one has ever seen God." The revelation of God in the incarnation does not mean that humans now understand all there is to understand about God, or even that we understand what has been revealed with mathematical certainty. It means, rather, that we are invited into a mystery that everyday patterns of speech cannot express. Ephrem presents his own theology in a poetic format for precisely this reason, so that (like all Greek and Syrian patristic writers) he can emphasize the paradoxes that lie at the heart of the incarnation. On this point, Sebastian Brock writes, "For this purpose poetry proves a far more suitable vehicle than prose, seeing that poetry is much better capable of sustaining the essential dynamism and fluidity that is characteristic of this sort of approach to theology" (1992, 24). The opening lines of 1 John operate in the same fashion: they orient us toward a paradoxical view of the world by necessarily disorienting us. Three points of confusion are especially prominent: (1) authorial anonymity; (2) style and syntax; (3) and the relationship between 1 John and the Gospel of John.

Authorial Anonymity

We call 1 John a letter, following a precedent extending back to ancient Christian commentators. In many ways the text behaves like a letter, but it does not begin like a letter. Ancient letters ordinarily open by naming their senders and recipients, and then by offering a greeting. The First Letter of John is different. It tells us neither who sent it nor to whom it was sent, and so we know very little about the circumstances that produced the document. To many interpreters, the lack of such an opening means that the document should not be understood as a letter at all (see "Introduction to the Letters of John").

Style and Syntax

The second source of confusion and of scholarly discussion is the unusual prose style of 1:1–4. Here, too, we find opacity. Opacity does not mean sloppiness, though, and George Strecker (1996, 8) and Martin Culy

(2004, 1–2) rightly argue that this style not only seems intentional but also shows an obvious plan. The circuitous syntax is easy to follow once one recognizes that the author has employed a "topic construction" (Culy 2004, 2). In a topic sentence, the item to be stressed is placed at the start of the thought in order to give it prominence. In the case of 1 John 1:1, the phrases that are given focus are the several relative clauses placed in apposition to one another. Their relationship to the rest of the sentence is not at first clear. The text simply begins by saying, "that which we have heard, that which we have beheld with our eyes, that which we have seen and touched with our hands, concerning the word of life—" (1:1). These clauses are the direct objects of the verb *apangellomen*, "we announce," but *apangellomen* does not appear until two verses later, in 1:3. Between these opening relative clauses and their accompanying verb stands a lengthy parenthetic comment in 1:2, which further delays the coordination of all the pieces of the discourse. The effect of these various delays and misdirections is to give the reader pause and to create a heightened tension that draws the reader into the discourse.

The topic construction focuses on what "we have seen and heard," which clearly refers to the incarnate Jesus, but the name of Jesus is not given until 1:3. The most important name is thus delayed. The same effect exists in the Gospel of John, where the name of Jesus is not mentioned until 1:17, and Jesus himself does not appear in the narrative until 1:29. He does not speak until 1:38 (Culy 2004, 2). When all these effects are understood in concert in 1 John, the reader is simultaneously drawn forward into the text and repelled by the unusual syntax. Or, to repeat the language from above, the reader is oriented to the text by being disoriented.

The Relationship between 1 John and the Gospel of John

A similar quality characterizes the relationship between the opening lines of 1 John and the opening lines of the Gospel of John. The first four verses of 1 John seem in many ways to echo the prologue to the Gospel by employing the same key terms, such as "word" (*logos*; John 1:1, 14; 1 John 1:1); "life" (*zōē*; John 1:4; 1 John 1:1, 2); "testify/witness" (*martyria/martyrein*; John 1:7, 8, 15; 1 John 1:2); "beheld" (*heōraken*; John 1:18; *heōrakamen*; 1 John 1:1, 2, 3); "saw" (*etheasametha*; John 1:14; 1 John 1:1); Father (John 1:14, 18; 1 John 1:3); Son (John 1:14, 18; 1 John 1:3).

Connections between John and 1 John extend beyond the mere repetition of key terms. Phrases and styles of speech are also shared in common. For example, the Gospel famously opens by announcing, "In the beginning was the Word," while 1 John opens with the phrase "that which was from the beginning" (1:1). The relationship between the two phrases is more obvious in Greek, where in both cases the term "beginning" (*archē*) is the object of a preposition and is joined to the verb of "being" (*ēn*, "was") as follows:

John 1:1	*en archē ēn*	<u>In</u> the beginning *was*
1 John 1:1	*ēn ap' archēs*	*was* <u>from</u> the beginning

Similarly striking is the parallel use of the preposition *pros*. John 1:1 famously says that the "Word was *with* God," which translates the unusual phrase *pros ton theon*. First John repeats this unusual phrase yet varies the preposition's object, saying that the Word of life was "with the Father," *pros ton patera* (1:2). The use of *pros* with the accusative case as a preposition meaning "with" is uncommon. The fact that this uncommon usage appears in the opening lines of both texts suggests a relationship between the two works. Thus in various ways they are strikingly similar.

And yet their similarity is a similarity-in-difference. The same words and phrases are used, but they are not used in the same way. While the Fourth Gospel opens (1:1) by speaking of the word (*Logos*) that was *in* the beginning (*archē*), and 1 John discusses the word that was *from* the beginning (*archē*, 1:1), the respective meanings of "beginning" are different. In the Gospel, Jesus is the Word who existed in the beginning, where the term "beginning" refers to the time before creation. The point is clear: the Word existed before the world was created. By contrast, the "beginning" in 1 John cannot refer to a time before the existence of the physical world, since it so clearly refers to something physical that can be touched and seen and heard (1:1). Thus the same terms are used in both prologues, but they are used in very different ways, reflecting different realities and rhetorical concerns.

To sum up briefly, the opening lines of 1 John disorient the reader in various ways. First, the document does not open like a typical letter, so we do not know who sent it or to whom it was sent. Second, whatever information 1 John does provide in its opening lines is presented in a swirling array of phrases that have an obvious meaning in the end, but only after one is led along a circuitous path. Finally, the opening verses of 1 John evoke the language and style of John but in a way that makes the relationship between the two texts difficult to determine. The shared language is familiar, but only in an oblique and opaque manner. These apparent forms of madness are not without method, though. Such acts of misdirection and confusion seem designed to prepare us for the argument that follows, which is centered on the mysterious character of the incarnation.

---

1 John 1:1–4 in the Rhetorical Flow

▶ **Introductory prologue (1:1–4)**

Tracing the Train of Thought

1:1. First John opens by referring to **that which was from the beginning** (*ex archēs*). This phrase has generated considerable discussion among commentators, not only because of its similarity to the opening phrase of the Fourth Gospel but also because it is not immediately clear when "the beginning" was. Several possibilities present themselves. The term "beginning" is common in the Johannine literature, occurring eight times in the Gospel (1:1, 2; 2:11; 6:64; 8:25, 44; 15:27; 16:4), and ten times in 1 and 2 John (1 John 1:1; 2:7, 13, 14, 24 [2x]; 3:8, 11; 2 John 5, 6). Because the word does not always appear in the same context, it seems to carry different shades of meaning in different settings. Such an elastic use of language is not at all unusual for the Johannine literature. For example, the term *pneuma* in John 3:8 refers to both the wind and the Holy Spirit—a shift in reference that takes place within a single sentence. Different shades of meaning over the range of entire texts are thus very plausible, and other meanings of the term "beginning" may be operative in other verses in 1 and 2 John. But the sense in 1 John 1 seems to be that expressed in various NT texts that use either the noun *archē* (beginning) or the verb *archein* (to begin) in reference either to Jesus's baptism (Mark 1:1; Luke 3:23; Acts 1:22) or to the beginning of Jesus's ministry (John 6:64; 15:27; 16:4). This is clearly how the word is understood in 1 John 2:7; 3:11; and 2 John 5, 6. "From the beginning" in 1:1, then, means "from the first association" with Jesus (Brown 1982, 157). To say that the teaching extends "from the beginning" means that it is grounded in the life and ministry and teaching of Jesus.

A further matter that deserves attention is the possible legal quality of the phrase "from the beginning." The expression "from the beginning" is a technical phrase in legal proceedings, appearing not only in Greek and Latin courtroom rhetoric but also in scenes from dramas that imitate a legal setting. The phrase is not only legal, of course; it also has a more general usage and is found in the opening lines of narratives of all sorts. To introduce a narrative with the phrase "from the beginning" is a way to alert the reader

> **Jesus as the *Archē* in the Book of Revelation**
>
> *"I am the Alpha and the Omega, the first and the last, the beginning* (archē) *and the end."* (22:13)

that an elaborate and full narrative will follow (Carey 1992, 93). In Plato's *Symposium* (174.1), for example, when Apollodoros begins to recount the speeches that took place at a dinner party so long ago, he says, "But it might be better for me to try to tell you the whole story right from the start [*ex archēs*]." Alongside this general use of the phrase exists a specific usage that applies to the legal *narratio*, the part of the speech in which a person presents his version of the events in question during a courtroom trial. As Alan Sommerstein says, "The phrase is regularly used by prosecutors in introducing their narrative of the facts of the case" (1989, 192). Lysias, for example, opens his speech *Against Eratosthenes* by saying, "Nevertheless, I will try to inform you of the matter from the beginning [*ex archēs*] as briefly as I can" (12.3). Demosthenes does the same in his speech *Against Conon* (54.2): "I shall state to you from the beginning [*ex archēs*] each incident as it occurred in the fewest words I can" (cf. also Lysias 32.3; Isocrates, *Nic.* 7.3). Playwrights followed these rhetorical models in staging trial scenes and legal scenarios of various kinds. In the famous trial that takes place in Aeschylus's *Eumenides*, for example, the goddess Athena dubs the chorus leader "the prosecutor [*ho diōkōn*]" and invites the leader to recount the details of the issue in dispute "from the beginning [*ex archēs*]" (line 583). Plautus's *Andria* shows the same device in Roman comedy, when the character Simo initiates a legal narration by saying, "You will hear the whole story from the beginning [*a principio*]" (cf. Scafuro 1997, 361). Thus in legal texts as well as in texts that imitate legal scenarios the phrase "from the beginning" is a technical forensic expression.

A legal reading of this phrase in 1 John not only relies on such external evidence, though, but also on the legal context of the phrase in both 1 John and the Gospel of John, where the expression "from the beginning" is joined with the language of testimony, *martyria*, an inherently legal term (Lincoln 2000; Meeks 1967, 65). In John 15:27, Jesus says to the disciples, "You also are to testify [*martyreite*] because you have been with me from the beginning [*ap' archēs*]." The term "testify" (*martyroumen*) is used here in 1 John 1:2, adding the same legal color to the expression. The testimony of the author is grounded in what he saw and heard "from the beginning." In the Gospel of John, the disciples can provide trustworthy testimony because they know the facts of the case, thoroughly and from the very start. In the same way, the argument of 1 John will be a prosecution of the opponents' false beliefs based on the same solid testimony.

A further point can be made about the notion of testimony and its value in the Johannine literature. The Gospel famously opens by referring in its prologue several times to the testimony of John the Baptist (1:7–8, 15), and as soon as the prologue ends, the first line of the narrative of the Gospel is "This is the testimony [*martyria*] given by John" (1:19). The Fourth Gospel returns to testimony as it draws to a close and refers to the testimony (*martyria*) of the Beloved Disciple (21:24). Very similar is the function of testimony in 1 John, which not only opens by referring here in 1:1 to testimony, but returns to this notion again in 5:10–11. Third John does the same by discussing the testimony of the faithful in its opening lines (v. 3) and then by referring to the testimony that people provide for Demetrius as its argument concludes (v. 12). The notion of testimony, then, has a prominent position at both the start and the conclusion of the Fourth Gospel, 1 John, and 3 John. This common device can very likely be understood as a development from the legal character of the Gospel of John, in which Jesus collects testimony on his behalf from various quarters. Those who continue to live by the pattern he laid out (the author of 1 John and his fellow believers) also continue to offer testimony.

The various relative clauses that follow in 1 John 1:1—**that which we have heard, that which we have beheld with our eyes, that which we have seen and touched with our hands**—share two qualities in common. They all refer to sensory perception (hear, see, touch), and they all have first-person plural ("we") verbs. The "we" subject of the verbs continues in 1:2–4 and is so common in 1 John that Raymond Brown refers to "the striking 'we' motif" of this letter (1982, 158). In these opening lines, there is a strong separation between "we" who send the letter and "you" who receive it. The separation between the two groups will soften as the letter proceeds, since the "you" who are addressed also seem to have access to the knowledge of what was given in the beginning (2:7). Likewise, the author will later refer to himself as "I" when he describes the task of writing (2:1, 7, 8, 12–14, 21, 26; 5:13, 16). In these early lines, though, there is an important rhetorical reason for referring to the author as "we" and the recipients as "you."

In Greek and Roman authors, the careful use of such personal pronouns helped to reinforce community boundaries (Parsenios 2012b). The Roman historian Tacitus often separates Romans from non-Romans in his writing by referring to the Romans as "us." For example, he writes, "The Jews regard as profane all that we [*nos*] hold sacred, and yet permit all that we [*nobis*] abhor" (*Hist.* 5.4.1). By referring to "we" in this way, Tacitus "clearly and unmistakably co-opts his reader into an 'us-against-them' relationship based on Roman partisanship and solidarity" (Sinclair 1995, 19). Tacitus regularly draws the reader into his view of reality with the careful and selective use of first-person plural verbs and pronouns. This use of *nos* and *noster* in Tacitus should be understood not as something akin to the so-called royal we but as the *pluralis sociativus*, the "associative plural" that establishes a bond with the reader (Sinclair 1995, 19). The same phenomenon appears in other texts as well, such as in Longinus's *On the Sublime*. Longinus's concern is to distinguish Romans from Greeks. He writes of Greek authors as "we" and refers to his Roman patron Terentianus and other Romans as "you" (12.4–5). A telling comment of Timothy Whitmarsh defines this device well: "This schematic polarity between 'we' and 'you' then is not so much an articulation of a self-evident fact as an artful structuring device, designed to create a dilemma for the reader: which side are you on? Are you with 'us' or 'them'?" (2001, 69; see also 68).

The Johannine literature uses the same device in the same way. When Jesus speaks to Nicodemus in the Fourth Gospel, Jesus initially and naturally refers to himself as "I" and to Nicodemus as the singular "you" in Greek (cf. 3:3, 10). As the conversation proceeds, Jesus modifies his persona. He suddenly speaks of himself as "we" and refers to Nicodemus as "you" in the plural, as follows (3:11–12):

> I tell you, we speak [*laloumen*] of what we know [*oidamen*] and testify [*martyrou-men*] to what we have seen [*heōrakamen*]; yet you do not receive [*lambanete*]

our testimony. If I have told you [*hymin*] about earthly things and you do not believe [*pisteuete*], how can you believe [*pisteusete*] if I tell you [*hymin*] about heavenly things?

Interpreters have long identified three groups in John, and the use of pronouns is related to these groups. Jesus refers to himself and those who believe in him as "we." Other people are not in this group and reject Jesus. But there is a third group, a middle group standing between the "we" who stand around Jesus and "those" who oppose Jesus. This group is the "you" of Nicodemus. In John 12:42 we again hear of this middle group: "Nevertheless many, even of the authorities, believed in him. But because of the Pharisees they did not confess it, for fear that they would be put out of the synagogue." Between the "we" that represents the explicit followers of Jesus and the people who explicitly oppose Jesus stands the "you" of those who believe, but who believe in a way that needs to be corrected and encouraged. To quote Whitmarsh, they need to choose: "are you with 'us' or them?" (2001, 69).

The point of separating people into groups is not to suggest that they are locked into predetermined states that they cannot escape, but precisely the opposite. As Leander Keck so rightly argues, John does not emphasize the distinction between people of the Spirit and people of the flesh in order to define two polar realities to which people are irrevocably bound. Rather, John emphasizes the difference between the two in order to underscore the immediate necessity for people to cross from one pole to the other, from flesh to Spirit (Keck 1996, 277). In John 8, a stark distinction is made between those who follow Jesus and those who do not (8:25–27). But John does not leave the matter there, with two groups locked in their respective realms. Jesus adds, "I told you that you would die in your sins, for you will die in your sins unless you believe that I AM" (8:24). The operative phrase here is the last one: "unless you believe that I AM." Those who reject Jesus can choose a different destiny. They can be born from above—if they believe. The necessity of making a choice is made urgent.

"We" Greeks Opposed to "You" Romans in Longinus's *On the Sublime*

"*Wherefore it is, I suppose, that the orator shows . . . all the glow of a fiery spirit. . . . And it is in these same respects, my dear friend Terentianus, that it seems to me (supposing always that we Greeks are allowed to have an opinion upon the point) that Cicero differs from Demosthenes in elevated passages. . . . Our orator* [i.e., Demosthenes] . . . *can as it were consume by fire and carry away all before him, and may be compared to a thunderbolt or flash of lightning. . . . This, however, you* [i.e., Romans] *will be better able to decide.*" (12.3–5, trans. Rhys-Roberts, LCL)

Precisely this rhetoric operates in 1 John. A group designated as "we" is writing to a group designated as "you." But there is a third group—the opponents of the author and his allies. We hear of them when we read, "*They* went out from us, but they were never of us; for if *they* had been of us, *they* would have remained with us" (2:19). The addressees, designated as "you" and lying somewhere between "we" and "they," seem to be in danger of falling away just as "they" did. That is the reason for the letter, to urge the readers to maintain what was heard from the beginning. The recipients of the letter are still within the fold, but they are in danger of leaving it. In this sense, the use of plural pronouns to describe separate groups is of a piece with the regular use of rhetorical *sententiae* (maxims, or aphorisms), which is common in the Johannine literature (see "The Rhetoric of the Letters: *Sententiae* and Social Division" in the introduction).

A long tradition of interpretation has attempted to sort out more precisely the identities of these various groups in 1 John. The opponents of the author are often understood to represent some form of docetism or gnosticism (see "Setting and Purpose of 1 John" in the introduction) because they seem to accept that the human Jesus was truly God but not truly human. In this way of thinking, his divinity is certain but not his humanity. He entered the world in a way that seemed human but was not actually and fully human. At least some of the opponents seem to ascribe to such a belief.

Just as much, if not more, attention has been paid to the identities of the author and his allies. Much of the debate revolves around whether the author is an actual eyewitness of Christ's ministry. The repeated emphasis placed on actually seeing, touching, and hearing (1:1–4) the realities that are the subject of the letter leads many to insist that the author is an actual eyewitness of the events he describes. Others reject this view. Brown (1982, 160) suggests that this is a false debate, based on a long tradition in the Bible and in early Christian authors of collapsing the distance that separates the later people of God from their earlier history. For example, the prophet Amos (2:10) says to his readers, who lived long after the exodus, "I brought you up out of the land of Egypt and led you forty years in the wilderness." Gregory of Nazianzus (*Orat.* 39.14) similarly says to his fourth-century CE audience, "We ran with the star, and we adored with the Magi," even though they live three hundred years after the birth of Christ. The same telescoping of time is a feature of the hymnography of the Greek Orthodox Church. A central hymn from the Matins for Good Friday (the fifteenth Antiphon) announces, "*Today* he is suspended on a tree who suspended the earth amidst the waters." What happened thousands of years ago is said to be "today," just as Amos says that the Israelites of his day were led out of Egypt and just as Gregory of Nazianzus says that his fourth-century audience witnessed the birth of Christ. Finally, Irenaeus says to his audience in the late second century, "We could have learned in no other way than by seeing our Teacher, and hearing his voice with our own ears" (*Haer.*

5.1.1). Here the "we" is the body of believers who "heard" Jesus, even though they lived long after his earthly ministry. The "we" in whom Irenaeus counts himself is a generation of Christians who lived long after the ministry of Christ. And yet in some sense they share the experience of those who beheld the incarnation. A similar usage of "we" may operate in the Johannine Letters. To accept such an argument is not to demand a minimalist view of authorship, nor does it rule out the possibility that here we have eyewitness testimony. It is simply to change the emphasis of the question from the identity of the one who sees,

> ### The Eternal Today
>
> *"Today, Hades groans and cries out,*
> *'My authority has been destroyed.*
> *I took one who died, as though he were mortal,*
> *But I am powerless to contain him.*
> *Along with him I lose all those over whom I had ruled.*
> *I had held the dead from all ages, but behold, He raises them all!'*
> *Glory to Your Cross and Your Resurrection, O Lord!"*
>
> (Greek Orthodox Hymn from Saturday Vespers in Holy Week, Sticheron, sung at "Lord, I Have Cried," trans. Dedes)

and to place it rather on what is seen, and on the universal and timeless character of what was seen—God in the flesh.

The various forms of sensory perception in 1:1 underscore the reality of the incarnation when this verse announces, "We have heard . . . we have seen with our eyes . . . we have looked at and touched with our hands" (1:1). These statements about sensory perception show their significance when they are connected to what is said later in 1:2: "the life that was with the Father was revealed to us." This is a clear statement about the incarnation and can be seen as a restatement of the famous phrase in the prologue to John, "The Word became flesh" (1:14). The emphasis is different, though. John begins with the divine life of the Word, while 1 John begins with the earthly life of the incarnate Jesus. The Gospel opens by referring to the time when the Word was "with the Father" (1:1) because it was written to prove and to demonstrate that the man Jesus was actually God. First John begins at the other side of the calculus, with the humanity of Jesus, emphasizing that he could be seen, touched, and heard (1 John 1:1). While the Fourth Gospel emphasizes that Jesus was really God, 1 John stresses that God was really the human Jesus (Smith 2009, 375). In 1 John, the opponents of the author already believe that Jesus is divine. In fact, so high is their belief in his divinity that they neglect his humanity. To combat this mistake, the letter opens by underscoring the human side of the incarnation, its palpability. Emphasis will be placed on the reality of Jesus appearing in the flesh throughout 1 and 2 John (cf. 1 John 4:2; 2 John 7). Those who reject the reality of the incarnation are like those throughout human history who have refused to see and hear the work of God. Psalm 115 insists that the idols of the nations are mute and dumb and blind, and those who worship them will be equally unperceiving. This may well explain why 1 John draws to a close by insisting, "Guard yourselves from idols" (5:21). To follow any other god than the one preached here is to follow a false god, with the spiritual insensitivity of those who worship idols.

First John 1:1 draws to a close by referring to that which our hands have touched **concerning the word of life.** When 1 John refers to the "word of life," does the term "word" (*logos*) in this phrase carry the same christological weight that it does in the Johannine prologue, referring personally to Jesus? Many commentators believe that it does, but just as many believe the term means something akin to "message." Support for translating the word as "message" comes from the rest of 1 John. Every other instance of the term *logos* in 1 John is impersonal (1:10; 2:5, 7, 14; 3:18). The term functions in this same impersonal sense throughout the Gospel of John, apart from the prologue. After Jesus is personally called "the Word" in the prologue, such a personal sense of the term is never used again in John. The term *logos* in the narrative body of John always means "message" or "commandment," and carries no personal quality. A good example appears in John 5:24: "Very truly, I tell you, anyone who hears my word [*logos*] and believes him who sent me has eternal life, and does not come under judgment, but has passed from death to life." This is the sense of the term generally in 1 John, where we read of those who "keep his word" (2:5) and of "the old commandment, which is his word" (2:7; see also 1:10). The "word" in 1 John seems to be the message about Jesus. When 1 John 1:1 refers to the "word of life," the phrase seems to mean "the message about life" regarding new life in Jesus, as distinct from the false message peddled by the opponents. The phrase "word of life" seems not to apply to a person but to an impersonal word, a message, or a teaching.

If this seems the most likely reading, the other reading is not wholly implausible. First John 1:1 may very well refer to Jesus as the "Word of life" in its opening lines in a personal sense, and then thereafter employ the term *logos* to refer to the message about Jesus in an impersonal sense. This would imitate the procedure of the Fourth Gospel, which applies the term "Logos" personally to Jesus in its prologue (1:1, 14), but thereafter it uses the term to

> ### Sensory Perception in Psalm 115:4–8
>
> *"Their idols are silver and gold, the work of human hands.*
> *They have mouths, but they do not speak; eyes, but do not see.*
> *They have ears, but do not hear; noses, but do not smell.*
> *They have hands, but do not feel; feet, but do not walk.*
> *They make no sound in their throats.*
> *Those who make them are like them, so are all who trust in them."*

mean "message" or "commandment" (see 5:24 cited above). While the weight of probability lies with those who see the term *logos* as impersonal in 1 John, the very presence of the ambiguity may signal that there is no need to definitively choose one side or the other.

1:2. The same problem becomes even more complicated in the next line, with the parenthetic comment in 1:2: **And the Life was revealed and we have beheld it and we testify and we announce to you the eternal Life that was with the Father and was revealed to us.** At first these phrases are puzzling and difficult to unpack. The easiest way to read them is to begin with the second phrase, where we hear about "the eternal Life that was with [*pros*] the Father and was revealed to us." The phrase "with the Father" uses the pronoun *pros* in the same way that the prologue to John says, "The Word was with [*pros*] God" (1:1). Does this cryptic phrase refer personally to Jesus? The opening lines of the prologue to the Gospel of John call Jesus the Word, and then say that in him was Life (1:1–4). If this similarity with the Gospel has any value for reading 1 John, the personal "Word" of John seems to be equivalent to the "Life" in 1 John 1:2. In both cases, the Word/Life that was "with" the Father was revealed to humanity. Referring to Jesus as "the Life" in 1 John is very natural because, even in the Fourth Gospel, the Word has life (1:4), and Jesus calls himself "the Resurrection and the Life" (11:25). When the letter says that "the Life" was revealed and was available to be seen and touched and heard, this is equivalent to the Gospel's saying that the Word became flesh (1:14).

1:3. The point of the entire letter is clarified here near the close of the prologue, with the mention of fellowship (*koinōnia*) in 1:3: **in order that you might have fellowship with us, and our fellowship is with the Father and with his Son, Jesus Christ.** The rhetoric of these opening lines forces a decision on the readers, to make them answer the question, "Are you with us or not?" The immediacy behind that question is now clear, since having fellowship (or not) with "us" implies having fellowship (or not) with God. The term *koinōnia* does not appear in the Gospel, and the noun form of the term appears in 1 John only in this cluster of verses in 1 John 1:3–7, where it is used four times. Having such fellowship with other believers, however, is not at all alien to John's Gospel, where the image is that of "being one" with fellow Christians (17:11, 21, 22, 23). The idea of having fellowship with God is also an extension of the notion of "abiding" in the Fourth Gospel, especially in the famous image of the vine in John 15. The language of abiding in God is very common in 1 John (cf. 2:5–6 and comments thereon). But this promise of fellowship with God is mentioned after a circuitous series of clauses that underscore the importance of the incarnation and the divine status of the human Jesus. Jesus was with the Father, and then was revealed in the flesh. The point is clear: fellowship with God is possible through the incarnation, and only through the incarnation. If the opponents have a false view of the incarnation, they are imperiling their fellowship with God. The readers of 1 John are thus being advised regarding the immediacy of their decisions about their faith.

1:4. The opening section of the letter comes to a close in 1:4 by explaining another reason for writing: **in order that our joy [*chara*] might be complete/ fulfilled [*peplēromenē*].** In 1:3 we are given one reason for the writing: "in order that you might also have fellowship with us." Now another reason is given. The language of "joy" (*chara*) vaguely conjures the standard expression of greeting that usually opens a letter in the wider culture, *chairein* (greetings), but this epistolary association is made only vaguely. A more immediate reason for the mention of joy comes from within the Johannine tradition itself, where the fulfillment of joy is a common theme (Brown 1982, 173–74). John the Baptist announces, for instance, "He who has the bride is the bridegroom. The friend of the bridegroom, who stands and hears him, rejoices greatly at the bridegroom's voice. For this reason my joy has been fulfilled" (John 3:29; see also 7:8). The term *chara* appears nine times in the Gospel of John, and eight of the nine instances (all except in 3:29) occur in the Farewell Discourses (John 13–17). In these chapters, joy is a gift that will come to the disciples after Jesus has risen from the dead, and the Gospel shows the fulfillment of this promise after the resurrection, as we read, "At the sight of the Lord, the disciples rejoiced" (20:20).

But the joy of the community is based in having fellowship not only with the Lord but also with one another. One of the important statements about joy in the Farewell Discourses comes in John 17, where Jesus prays to the Father as follows: "Holy Father, protect them in your name that you have given me, so that they may be one, as we are one. . . . But now I am coming to you, and I speak these things in the world so that they may have my joy made complete in themselves" (17:11–13). Joy for the believers comes not only from fellowship with the risen Lord but also from the fellowship they share with fellow believers. Thus the two purposes given for the letter in these opening lines coincide. The letter is written to ensure that the recipients have fellowship with the Father and the Son, and also that they might have fellowship with the author and the community he represents. In this way, the joy of the community will be fulfilled.

Theological Issues

The opening lines of 1 John emphasize that Jesus is immediately present in the incarnation yet distant and remote in his divine identity. The author of the letter has a similar character as the God he describes. He is at the same time both present and remote. His presence is almost palpable, even as it remains hidden and impossible to identify. The author speaks of himself repeatedly as "I" and as part of a collective "we," and yet he remains anonymous. This anonymity is the topic of the present theological comment, since it provides insight into the notion of discipleship in the Johannine literature. The present discussion applies not only to 1 John, where the author is not mentioned at all, but also to 2 and 3 John, where the author is identified only by the epithet "the Elder." The author is hidden in all three letters. Judith Lieu has insightfully argued that this anonymity is an intentional technique in all the documents in the Johannine corpus, beginning with the Gospel (2008, 9). The anonymity of the author in each Johannine document guides us to reflect further on the nature of discipleship that these books convey. We can begin to see this by looking at the first anonymous author, the Beloved Disciple who produced the Gospel.

The Gospel of John is attributed to the enigmatic "disciple whom Jesus loved" (21:20, 24) but we never learn this disciple's name. We know him only obliquely. Harold Attridge (2012) argues that this is by design and is connected to the role of the Beloved Disciple as witness par excellence (21:24). The reader who struggles to learn the identity of the Beloved Disciple will return again and again to the text in order to clarify the nature of the Beloved Disciple's witness. But the concept of witness is a "vortex" (Attridge 2012, 29), drawing the reader ever more deeply into the text and to other witnesses, because so many other figures—John the Baptist, the Scriptures, the Father—are all witnesses to Jesus (John 5:31–46). Eventually the reader is left with no other witness but "the Word enfleshed, nailed to a cross. If one can understand that witness, then everything else will make sense. No other witness will count for ought" (Attridge 2012, 29). The anonymity of the Beloved Disciple is designed to do nothing else than to point to Jesus, and to cause people to see through him to Jesus. His very anonymity witnesses to Jesus. To see the Beloved Disciple is to look through him to Christ.

The author of 1–3 John seems to function in the same way. To see him is to look through him to Christ and, more specifically, to the Christ of the Gospel of John. Raymond Brown shows how this is true by noting the similarity in style that 1 John shares with the Fourth Gospel. He defines this similarity in an elegantly pointed statement: "The Johannine Jesus *speaks* as the author of the Johannine Epistles writes" (1982, 24, emphasis original). When 1 John opens, for instance, by emphasizing what "we" have seen and testified to, an obvious echo is heard from Jesus's conversation with Nicodemus in John 3:11, where Jesus refers to what "we" have seen and testified to. The author of 1 John couples his anonymity with an imitation of Jesus. When the author speaks, one hears the voice of Jesus.

A compelling comment of Origen elevates this discussion to a higher order of contemplation. When Origen interprets the Johannine scene at the foot of the cross, he focuses on Jesus's conversation and actions with the Beloved Disciple and Mary. John 19:26–27 reads, "When Jesus saw his mother and the disciple whom he loved standing beside her, he said to his mother, 'Woman, here is your son.' Then he said to the disciple, 'Here is your mother.' And from that hour the disciple took her into his own home." Origen sees more than a symbolic act here. The Beloved Disciple, he says, does not become "like" Jesus, nor does he simply take on a role that Jesus once performed when he becomes the son of Mary. He does not become "like" Jesus. He becomes Jesus. Origen says,

> We may therefore make bold to say that the Gospels are the firstfruits of all the Scriptures, but that of the Gospels that [Gospel] of John is the firstfruits. No one can apprehend the meaning of it unless he has rested on Jesus's breast and received from Jesus Mary to be his mother also. He must become another John, and must have shown to him, as to John, by Jesus himself Jesus as he is. For if Mary . . . had no other son but Jesus, and yet Jesus says to his mother, "Woman, behold thy son," and not "Behold, you have this son also," then he virtually said to her, "Lo, this [i.e., John] is Jesus, whom you have borne." Is it not the case that everyone who is perfect lives himself no longer, but Christ lives in him? (*Comm. Jo.* 1.6; *ANF* 10:300, modified)

Thus when the Beloved Disciple is handed over to Mary, and Mary to the Beloved Disciple, John conforms his life to the life of Jesus. The Beloved Disciple has taken on the role of Christ. Anonymity and imitation combine so that when one seems to see the disciple, one actually sees Christ. For Origen, to be a disciple of Christ is to become "another Christ." When Jesus says to Mary, "Here is your son," he means that John has conformed his life to the life of Jesus to such an extent that he can say in the words of Paul, "It is no longer I who live, but Christ who lives in me" (Gal. 2:20). The shape of John's life is conformed to Christ. He is a christomorph.

Jeffrey Hamburger has discovered a small group of images in medieval Western art that depict John the Evangelist—understood as the author of both the Gospel and Letters—as a christomorph in a variety of ways (for the following survey of images, see Hamburger 2002, 43–64). The images range in date from the ninth to the fifteenth centuries. Amounting to only a couple dozen pieces in total, these illustrations convey the same idea in a variety of ways, depicting John as someone whose life is uniquely conformed to the life of Christ.

The Language of Jesus and 1 John Compared

The author of 1 John writes like the Jesus of the Gospel speaks. In the Fourth Gospel, Jesus says, "Very truly, I tell you, we speak of what we know and testify [*martyroumen*] to what we have seen [*ho heōrakamen*]" (John 3:11). The author of 1 John writes, "We have both seen [*heōrakamen*] and testify [*martyroumen*] and declare to you. . . . What we have seen [*ho heōrakamen*] and heard we declare" (1 John 1:2–3).

Figure 1. Christ enthroned in majesty. Weingarten Gospels, Tours, ca. 830.

Figure 2. John the Evangelist, enthroned in majesty, facing the viewer in the manner of Christ in the same manuscript. Weingarten Gospels, Tours, ca. 830.

One such image appears in a fifteenth-century Psalter from Freiburg. At first glance, the image is a typical depiction of Christ at the moment of creation, with the central figure raising his right arm in a gesture that is very common for the depiction of the Christ-Logos as he points to the world when it is created. But the image is not at all typical. The central figure is not Christ but the Beloved Disciple, who is identified with absolute certainty in the inscription above his head. And he does not point to the creation of the world told in Genesis, the beginning of biblical history, but rather to various scenes from Christian history. The upper roundel, for example, refers to the birth of Christ and is circumscribed by a text that reads "And the Word became flesh" (John 1:14).

Other examples are just as emphatic in casting John as a christomorph, especially in relation to the other evangelists. In the Weingarten Gospels, dating to the early decades of the ninth century, Jesus is seated upon an orb at the frontispiece to the Gospel collection. John is seated in a similar posture soon thereafter, while the other evangelists are given other poses, not at all like those of Christ. A group of miniature portraits that were added in about the year 1000 to a Carolingian Gospel book originally from the diocese of Mainz in Trier do something similar. These miniatures depict the synoptic evangelists as authors seated at their desks, writing their Gospels, while John is depicted facing the reader, just as Christ does, underscoring the special identification of John and Jesus. The other evangelists are portrayed in profile and writing,

Figure 3. John the Evangelist, seated in glory, facing the viewer in the manner of Christ in the same manuscript. Miniature added at Trier, ca. 1000, to a Gospel book from St. Maximian, Mainz, ca. 900–950.

Figure 4. Luke the Evangelist, writing at his desk. Miniature added at Trier, ca. 1000, to a Gospel book from St. Maximian, Mainz, ca. 900–950.

while John faces the viewer directly, raising his hand in a gesture of address comparable to Christ's gesture of blessing. Like Christ, who both embodies and also displays the Gospel on his knee, John holds a book on his own left knee.

An even more explicit portrayal of the christomorphic John appears in the Limburg Gospels from the beginning of the eleventh century. Each of the evangelists is depicted in a way that emphasizes their divine inspiration. Matthew looks upward while he writes and witnesses Christ in majesty. Mark is also shown writing his Gospel, and Luke faces the viewer head on, framed by curtains from the temple. But John is depicted from within an almond-shaped mandorla, as only Christ is depicted.

All these images, as well as the comments of Origen, derive from the special insight that the Beloved Disciple shows in the Gospel of John. He has a special proximity to Jesus. But the Beloved Disciple and the Elder are not alone in enjoying this special insight and union with God. Conformity to Christ—becoming a christomorph—is a defining quality of discipleship in the Johannine literature for all disciples.

One of the most compelling comments in 1 John regarding discipleship is the statement from 1 John 2:6: "The one who says that he abides in him ought himself to walk just as that one walked." The earthly life of the Christian is supposed to be a mirror image of the earthly life of Christ. Every Christian is supposed to be a christomorph. Other texts in 1 John make the same point, as when 2:3 says, "And in this way we know that we have known him: if we keep his commandments." Such imitation is equally pronounced in 1 John 4:19: "We love, because he first loved us." Discipleship means conformity to the life of Christ.

Other images in 1 John make the same point. Thus 1:3 speaks of "fellowship with the Father [God]," and one of the most common terms in the Johannine Letters for describing this fellowship is the verb *menein*, "to abide/dwell." The abiding/dwelling that is implied by this word is a mutual indwelling of God and believers. By walking as Christ walked, believers abide in God (2:6), but the opposite is also true: "If we love one another, God abides in us" (4:12). There is more here than symbolic language, as 3:24 makes clear: "The one who keeps his commandments abides in him, and he [God] in him [the believer]. In this we know that he abides in us—he has given to us from his Spirit." Thus imitation is not just moral copying but a spiritual connection between God and the believer. The believer abides in God, and God in the believer. The profundity of this connection is finally and fully expressed in 1 John 3:2: "We will be like him, for we shall see him as he is." What is in view here is not merely moral imitation but spiritual indwelling.

The depth and profundity of such a christomorphic life can be explicated more fully by looking at a particular scene in the Gospel of John, that of the blind man from John 9. The man in John 9 who was born blind provides the best example of the combination of anonymity and discipleship that the Beloved Disciple shows. Jesus promises his disciples in John 15–16 that they will be hated as their Lord was hated. In detailed and compelling ways, the activity and experiences of the blind man in John 9 are a mirror image of the activity and experiences of Jesus in John 7–8. Both Jesus and the blind man, for instance, are driven away after being interrogated. Throughout chapters 7 and 8, Jesus is interrogated by the leaders of Israel. Legal language about judgment and witness dominates the debates. In the end, the leaders of Israel condemn Jesus for blasphemy, expel him, and wish to stone him (8:59). The same thing operates in the case of the blind man. He is interrogated by the Pharisees until he is expelled from the synagogue for being a sinner (9:34). Jesus and the man born blind are also both questioned over their identity: the crowds cannot determine whether Jesus is a prophet or the Christ (7:40–41; cf. 7:25–27); and regarding the blind man, "The neighbors and those who had seen him before as a beggar began to ask, 'Is this not the man who used to sit and beg?'" (9:8).

In both cases, there is also a *schisma*. In the debates over identity, both Jesus and the man born blind create a division (*schisma*) among their interlocutors, some holding one position and others another (7:41–43; 9:16). But the most compelling feature of the shared fate of Jesus and the blind man has not to do with what people say about them but with what they say about themselves. In one statement, the man born blind identifies himself with a simple phrase that might be easily overlooked and its significance missed. But in light of the other associations between Jesus and the blind man, this phrase carries considerable significance. John 9:8–9 reads: "The neighbors and those who had seen him before as a beggar began to ask, 'Is this not the man who used to sit and beg?' Some were saying, 'It is he.' Others were saying, 'No, but it is someone like him.' He kept saying, 'I am [*egō eimi*].'" Just a few verses before this one, at the end of chapter 8, Jesus was almost stoned for saying to his interlocutors (8:58), "Very truly, I tell you, before Abraham was, I am [*egō eimi*]." When Jesus uses this phrase, he applies to himself the divine name that God used to reveal himself to Moses, of which we hear in Isa. 52:6 LXX: "My people shall know my name; in that day (they shall know) that 'I AM' [*egō eimi*] is the one who speaks" (cf. LXX of Exod. 3:14 and Isa. 43:25). As Brown writes:

> No clearer implication of divinity is found in the Gospel tradition, and "the Jews" recognize this implication. Leviticus [24:]16 had commanded: "He who blasphemes *the name* of the Lord shall be put to death; all the congregation shall stone him." We are not sure what the legal definition of blasphemy was in Jesus' time; but in John's account the use of the divine name represented by *egō eimi* seems to be sufficient. (1966, 367)

The last verse in John 8 ends with Jesus's use of the divine name, which leads immediately into the episode of the blind man in John 9, when the blind man also says, "I am [*egō eimi*]" (9:9). In light of the many ties that bind the blind man in John 9 to the activity of Jesus in John 7–8, this phrase sounds striking on the lips of the blind man, and more than striking—perhaps also as blasphemous to some modern ears as the original statement of Jesus sounded to those who tried to stone him. But I think we should take it seriously, in a particular way. It is clearly not a christological statement with the same force as the comment of Jesus, but neither should we dismiss it as irrelevant, coming only a few verses after the same comment was on the lips of Jesus. In his *Ambiguum* 21, Maximus the Confessor reflects on the nature of discipleship in a way that is very appropriate for understanding the Johannine notion of abiding in God, and how it applies to the issue of discipleship in the case of the blind man. Maximus writes:

> Those who choose the pure and undefiled life of the Gospel, through their strict exercise of the commandments, take possession of the likeness of the good things of the age to come, and are made ready by the Word through the hope that they will be spiritually vivified by their union with the archetype of these true things, and so become living images of Christ, or rather become one with

Him through grace (rather than being a mere simulacrum), or even, perhaps, become the Lord Himself, if such an idea is not too onerous for some to bear. (21.15, trans. Constas 2014)

This comment of Maximus expresses well the teaching on discipleship in 1–3 John. Fellowship with God and abiding in God are a direct result of the incarnation, in which God entered humanity and opened the possibility of union with him. Where there had been separation from God, there now is union with God. The anonymity of the author of both the Gospel and the Letters of John makes a great deal of sense in light of this notion of discipleship, because the process of following Christ means nothing less than becoming, in the words of Maximus, "living images of Christ" and "the Lord Himself." The individual disciple, and in this case the individual author, no longer reflects his own individuality but rather the person of Christ. Anonymity points not into oblivion but to the Lord himself.

1 John 1:5–2:11

The Light and the Darkness

Introductory Matters

The argument that makes up the body of the letter opens at 1:5, and the first line of thought extends to 2:11. At least two structural markers define 1:5–2:11 as a discrete section. First, the references to light and darkness in 1:5–7 and in 2:8–11 serve as bookends to mark off everything between them as a discernible unit. Second, this section contains a catalog of six claims about behavior and belief, which the author introduces only in order to reject them (Rensberger 1997, 49–50). The first three of these claims (1:6, 8, 10) share the same opening line, "if we say." The latter three share a different opening line, "whoever says" (2:4, 6, 9). In each case, the opening claim is corrected and replaced by more accurate teaching. The false teaching is quoted only in order to correct it. Paul often relies on the same device, quoting the slogans that were used in his communities in order to adjust them and to develop his own argument. In 1 Cor. 6:12, for instance, Paul first quotes the slogan "All things are lawful for me," only so that he can add the phrase "but not all things are beneficial." In 1 Cor. 8:1, Paul quotes a slogan that says, "All of us possess knowledge," in order that he can correct it by adding, "Knowledge puffs up but love builds up." A similar style of argument seems to be at work here in 1 John. False teaching is expressed in the form of slogans in order to facilitate correction.

Some interpreters are puzzled by the focus in this section on behavior instead of belief. Raymond Brown wonders why ethics, and not theology, is the first thing discussed in 1 John: "It is surprising that the first overt attack

Anthropology and Theology in Athanasius

"You may wonder why we are discussing the origin of human beings when we set out to talk about the Word's becoming human. The former subject is relevant to the latter for this reason: it was our sorry case that caused the Word to come down, our transgression that called out his Love for us, so that he made haste to help us and to appear among us. It is we who were the cause of his taking human form." (Inc. 1.4)

on dangerous ideas is in the moral sphere. One might have expected the author to begin with the christological errors that are so much on his mind throughout 1 John" (1982, 230–31). The larger flow of the letter, though, justifies this manner of beginning. Throughout 1 John, the emphasis on thinking rightly is never far removed from the need to live rightly. Belief in the incarnation does not exist in the abstract but must show forth in a life lived a certain way. Anthropology and theology are tightly connected.

Tracing the Train of Thought

Three Boasts: "If We Say . . ." (1:5–2:2)

1:5. The body of the letter begins in 1:5, and the phrase that transitions from the introductory prologue to the argument proper is the same phrase used in the Fourth Gospel to transition from its prologue to its narrative proper. Here 1 John 1:5 begins with the phrase **And this is the message** (*kai estin hautē hē angelia*), while John 1:19 begins with the phrase "And this is the testimony" (*kai hautē estin hē martyria*). The Gospel of John, once again, looms large as a model for 1 John.

And yet as soon as this striking parallel between 1 John and John appears we are immediately cautioned to remember that the similarity between the two documents is often a similarity-in-difference. The phrase **God is light and in him there is no darkness at all** is at first reminiscent of the claims in the Gospel of John that Jesus is the light—except that the Gospel never says that God is light. While imagery related to light is applied to Jesus on several occasions and in several different ways (8:12; 9:5; 12:35, 46), nowhere in the Fourth Gospel is the Father ever said to be light. This is the first example of a circumstance that will recur many times, whereby the Johannine Letters ascribe to God things that the Fourth Gospel ascribes to Jesus. In the Gospel, for instance, Christians abide in Jesus (15:4–10),

1 John 1:5–2:11 in the Rhetorical Flow

Introductory prologue (1:1–4)

▶ The light and the darkness (1:5–2:11)

   Three boasts: "If we say . . ." (1:5–2:2)

   Three boasts: "Whoever says . . ." (2:3–11)

but in 1 John they abide in God (2:5–6; etc.). Likewise, the Fourth Gospel places the command to love one another in the mouth of Jesus (13:34; etc.), but 2 John 4–6 ascribes the love command to God (for further discussion, see "The Relationship of the Letters to the Gospel" in the introduction).

And yet if the statement that "God is light" does not appear in the Gospel of John it has ample precedent in the biblical witness and in the ancient world in general (Johnson 2003, 125–27). Light is associated with God from the point of creation, since light was the first thing God created (Gen. 1:3–6). When God was present among Israel in Egypt, he was a light to his people (Exod. 10:23). Psalm 27:1 announces, "The Lord is my light," and Wis. 7:26 says that wisdom is a "reflection of eternal light." Numerous other passages make the same point in different ways (Pss. 43:3; 56:13; 78:14; Isa. 2:5; 9:2; 60:1–3). The NT continues this language and imagery (2 Cor. 4:5–6; 1 Tim. 6:16; 1 Pet.

2:9), especially in the elegant statement in James 1:17: "Every generous act of giving, with every perfect gift, is from above, coming down from the Father of lights, with whom there is no variation or shadow due to change."

The Gospel of John is especially rich in light imagery, applying the symbol of light to Jesus already in the opening lines of the prologue: "In him was life, and the life was the light of all people. The light shines in the darkness and the darkness did not overcome it" (1:4–5). Soon thereafter comes the notice that "the true light that enlightens everyone was coming into the world" (1:9). Numerous other passages apply the imagery of light to Jesus (3:19; 5:35; 8:12), which makes it all the more striking that when Judas leaves the table to betray Jesus, we are immediately told by the Evangelist, "It was night" (13:30). The darkness is incompatible with the light. Such an opposition between light and darkness is dominant for 1 John. Thus "God is light and in him there is no darkness at all."

In the OT, the relationship between light and darkness is actually more complicated than this NT imagery suggests. Light and darkness do not always stand in stark

Wikimedia Commons/Man Vyi

Figure 5. Depiction of Jesus as the Light of the World. Saint Lawrence Parish Church, New Jersey.

opposition. Isaiah 45:7, for example, puts the following phrase in the mouth of God, "I form light and create darkness, I make weal and create woe; I the LORD do all these things," while in Exod. 20:21 God appears to Moses from within "thick darkness." The sharper contrast between light and darkness is a product of intertestamental Judaism. *First Enoch* concludes with a division between those who please God "in shining light" (108.13) and those who are "born in darkness" (108.15). The Dead Sea Scrolls also prominently use this imagery (1QS 1.9–10; 3.19–4.14). Other NT texts associate Christians with the light and nonbelievers with the darkness (Acts 26:18; Col. 1:13; 1 Pet. 2:9).

1:6–7. The first erroneous teaching is expressed in 1:6: **If we say that we have fellowship with him and yet we walk in darkness, we lie and do not do the truth.** The term "fellowship" (*koinōnia*) deserves attention first. Raymond Brown argues that the term is introduced into the discussion by 1 John (1982, 186, 232). Brown's argument begins from the assumption that fellowship is brought into the discussion as a way to counteract the opponents' misunderstanding of what it meant "to abide in" (*menein en*) and "to be in" (*einai en*) God. John Painter argues for the opposite position, believing that this is one of the opponents' teachings that 1 John seeks to correct. Regardless of who introduced the term into the discussion, it is important to affirm that *koinōnia* is not a typical Johannine word. It appears nowhere in the Gospel of John and only four times in 1 John (1:3, 6–7). How does it function? The many uses of the term in Paul shed some light on the matter. Of the fifteen uses of the term in the NT outside of 1 John, thirteen are in Paul, and seven of these are in the Corinthian correspondence. Painter turns to the Corinthian correspondence to understand the function of *koinōnia* in John, connecting the problems with idolatry in Corinth with the statement about idolatry that concludes 1 John (5:21). Painter (2002, 327–30) writes, "The context of Paul's use of this language in 1 Corinthians may be a warning to take the final exhortation of 1 John at face value and as a serious warning: 'Little children, guard yourselves from idols' (1 John 5:21)." This may be correct. And yet another set of problems regarding "fellowship" appears in Paul's Letters to the Corinthians, which can take the term in a different direction, and in a direction more closely connected to the immediate context of its usage in 1 John. In 2 Corinthians especially, the term often refers to the fellowship shared by Christians with one another. Thus 2 Cor. 8:4 refers to the "sharing [*koinōnia*] in this ministry to the saints," while 9:13 refers to "the generosity of your sharing [*koinōnia*]

Walking in Light, Walking in Darkness at Qumran

"In the hand of the Prince of Light [is] *the dominion of all the Sons of Righteousness; in the ways of light they walk. But in the hand of the Angel of Darkness* [is] *the dominion of the Sons of Deceit; and in the ways of darkness they walk."* (1QS 3.20–21, trans. Charlesworth 1996, 71)

with them and with all." The related term *koinōnos*, "fellow" or "partner," has a similar function in 2 Cor. 1:7 and 8:23. The term not only refers to fellowship among believers; it also refers to union with God (cf. 1 Cor. 1:9; 10:16; 2 Cor. 13:13). If it can involve both union with God and union with fellow believers, then its function in 1 John is clearer. Those who left the communion defended by 1 John seem to believe that they can have fellowship with God but not fellowship with the author of 1 John and his community. First John argues otherwise. Having fellowship with God cannot be separated from the need to maintain unity with fellow believers.

Verses 6–7 ground this fellowship in the way that one "walks." In the Bible the metaphor of walking is a common way to refer to one's way of life (Pss. 1:1; 15:2; Rom. 6:4; 8:4; 14:15; cf. Rensberger 1988, 51–52). Another common biblical phrase occurs in 1 John 1:6b but sounds more peculiar to modern ears: **we do not do the truth.** The phrase "to do the truth" is common in the OT (LXX: 2 Chron. 31:20; Neh. 9:33) and is especially common in later Jewish writings (Tob. 4:6; 1QS 1.5; 5.3; 8.2). In the Johannine tradition, though, the phrase has a special significance because the notion of truth has a particular prominence (John 1:14, 17; 4:23–24; 8:31–32; 14:6; 16:13; 17:17–19; 18:37; 1 John 2:8; 3:18–19; 4:6; 5:20; 2 John 1–4; 3 John 3–4). The "truth" refers to the eternal truth that was revealed only in Jesus. Other gifts had come from God before, but "grace and truth came through Jesus Christ" (John 1:17). To "do the truth" as it is understood here is to make one's ethical life correspond to one's belief. Within the broader flow of this section, the statement must also have something to do with those opponents who were once part of the same community and fellowship as the author, of whom the author says in 2:19, "They went out from us, but they were never of us. For if they had been of us, they would have remained with us." There was an inherent falsehood about the faith of such believers, and this falsehood must be avoided.

First John 1:7 offers the positive alternative to the false teaching of 1:6, but 1:7 puzzles the reader when it says that **he is *in* the light.** The phrase seems odd after reading in 1:5 that "God *is* the light." We can assume that "he" in verse 7 is God, because God is the antecedent in 1:5 to the several pronouns in 1:5d, 6a, 7b, and 10b–c. But how does one reconcile the statement that God *is* the light with the statement that God is *in* the light? There is ample Johannine precedent for such a shift in imagery. As Jesus prepares to depart the world, for example, he tells his disciples in John 14:4, "You know the way where I am going" (AT). But then suddenly, instead of speaking of the way on which he travels, Jesus insists, "I AM the way" (14:6). So too Jesus tells his disciples that he is the Good Shepherd, and that the Shepherd enters the sheepfold through the gate (10:2). Then immediately, although he is still speaking about shepherds and sheep and a gate, Jesus no longer says that he enters *through* the gate, but instead insists, "I AM the gate" (10:7). To say that God is the light and then that God is in the light relies on a similar shift in imagery. First John does the same thing in other places, as in 4:7–8, where we are told "Love is *from* God" (4:7) and then also "God is love" (4:8). In the present case regarding light, the shift in focus is probably determined by how believers are told to walk "in the light" (1:7a), and the imagery applied to God is assimilated to this phrase. Believers should be in the light as God is in the light. In this sense we are called to imitate God (Brown 1982, 201).

The logic of 1:7 is also difficult to trace, especially when one reads the verse in light of Pauline theology (Brown 1982, 202). There is, of course, nothing unusual about saying that **the blood of Jesus his Son cleanses us from all sin**. The same idea is expressed in similar language in Romans in two places. At 3:25 Paul refers to Jesus as the one "whom God put forward as a sacrifice of atonement by his blood, effective through faith. He did this to show his righteousness, because in his divine forbearance he had passed over the sins previously committed." Later, at 5:9, Paul adds, "Much more, . . . now that we have been justified by his blood, will we be saved through him from the wrath of God" (see also Rom. 8:3). In spite of the similar cluster of ideas, though, 1 John 1:7 seems at first blush to contradict Paul. In the thought of Paul, the blood of Jesus has the power to save because any human works are ineffectual. Does 1 John say the opposite? In 1 John the blood of Jesus cleanses us from sins only **if we walk in the light**. The saving value of the blood of Jesus seems to depend on human activity. And yet the contradiction with Paul here is only apparent and not real. Romans and 1 John have in mind very different rhetorical situations, and this explains their different formulations. Romans is concerned with how one becomes the people of God, whether by works of the law or by faith in Christ. Does one leave behind the old life of sin by following the law of Moses, or by means of the sacrificial death of Christ? The question is how one becomes a believer. First John is written to people who already are believers, urging them to continue to adhere to the faith of their initial conversion. It is not concerned with how we become justified before God (to use Pauline language) but with how we *maintain* this status after having accepted it. Paul is no less concerned about this when he asks, "Should we continue in sin in order that grace may abound? By no means! How can we who died to sin go on living in it?" (Rom. 6:1–2). Far from disagreeing, 1 John and Romans are very near to each other, once we compare 1 John to the right part of Romans.

The Letters of John explain the salvation that Jesus offers in a variety of ways, using a variety of terms, including the following (Brown 1982, 203):

forgive (*aphienai*)	1 John 1:9; 2:12
take away (*hairein*)	1 John 3:5
destroy (*lyein*)	1 John 3:8
atonement (*hilasmos*)	1 John 2:2; 4:10
cleanse (*katharizein*)	1 John 1:7, 9

This cleansing is accomplished through the blood of Jesus, which immediately calls to mind the sacrificial cult of ancient Israel. Leviticus 17:11 explains the procedure: "For the life of the flesh is in the blood, and I have given it to you for making atonement for your lives on the altar; for, as life, it is the blood that makes atonement." Hebrews 9:22 explains further, "Indeed, under the law almost everything is purified (*katharizetai*) with blood, and without the shedding of blood there is no forgiveness of sins." First John 2:2 will develop further this notion of sacrifice, but nothing further is said at this point. Here we learn only that to walk in the light is to be pure and to be cleansed from every sin. That much is straightforward and clear.

1:8. The next verse makes the line of argument less clear: **If we say that we do not have sin, we deceive ourselves and the truth is not in us.** Up to this point the trajectory of thought has connected walking in the light, doing the truth, and being cleansed from sin. Now 1:8 claims that light and truth are inherently connected, not to avoiding sin, but to acknowledging sins. One walks in the light and avoids the darkness precisely by acknowledging that one sins. The idea seems to be that the confession and the admission of sins are the antidote to the self-deceptiveness that leads to confusion and to darkness. The incorrect boast here is to say that one has no sins. The proper act is to confess sins.

The singular term "sin" is used in 1:8, but below in 1:9 the plural noun is used: "sins." The use of the plural shows that what is in view is not some abstract concept of sinfulness, but concrete actions that require actions in return. The commission of sins in real acts is corrected by the confession of sins in a real act. The idea of confessing sins to others, even publicly, is also attested elsewhere in the NT (Mark 1:5; Acts 19:18; James 5:16).

Certain puzzles persist in 1:8. In the first case, why is it permissible to say that one walks in the light, but not that one has no sin? How are those functionally different? Walking in the light seems to imply purity, but the only way to walk in the light is to confess that one has sin. Once the blood of Jesus cleanses believers from sin, in what sense does sin remain? This question is perhaps the easiest to answer in light of what will be said later in 2:1: "My little children, I am writing these things to you so that you may not sin. But if anyone does sin, we have a Paraclete with the Father, Jesus Christ the righteous." The pastoral efforts of the author explain the confusion. He holds up an ideal of walking in the light and being sinless, even as he comforts those who fall short of the ideal (Rensberger 1997, 54).

If that were the only problem, the matter could be left there. The problematic statements regarding sin are made even more complicated in light of what is said several chapters later, in 1 John 3:4–9. The passage deserves to be quoted in full in order to make the difficulty plain:

Everyone who does sin also does lawlessness; and sin is lawlessness. And you know that he was made manifest in order that he might remove sins. And there is no sin in him. Everyone who abides in him does not sin. Everyone who sins has neither seen him nor known him. Children, let no one deceive you. The one who does righteousness is righteous, just as he is righteous. The one who does sin is from the devil, because from the beginning the devil is a sinner. The Son of God was revealed for this reason—to undo the works of the devil. Everyone who is born of God do not do sin, for his seed abides in him, and he is not able to sin, because he has been born of God.

The statements about sin in 1:7–10 insist that the only way to walk in the light and the only way to have fellowship with God is to recognize that one has sin. Acknowledging sin is the only means for fellowship with God in 1 John 1. But in the passage just quoted from 3:4–9, the only ones who abide in God and who are born of God are those who do *not* sin. These statements are irreconcilable, and the contradiction seems to be intentional (see below, under "Theological Issues" following commentary on 1:5–2:11).

First John 1:8 speaks of "having sin." The idiom of having sin, or not, is found in the Gospel of John, where the phrase "to have sin" occurs four times, referring to those who reject Jesus. To have sin is to oppose Jesus. At 15:22, 24, Jesus says, "If I had not come and spoken to them, they would not have sin; but now they have no excuse for their sin. . . . If I had not done among them the works that no one else did, they would not have sin." Similarly, at John 19:11 Jesus tells Pilate, "The one who handed me over to you has a greater sin." But the most important passage comes from John 9, after Jesus heals the man born blind. Jesus tells the Pharisees, "If you were blind, you would not have sin; but now that you claim you can say, 'We see,' your sin remains" (9:41). In each of these cases, people who reject Jesus imagine that they do so as an expression of their sinless purity. They believe that they are in intimate union with God and could not ever imagine that their work against Jesus means that they "have sin." This very sense of purity is their undoing. The same applies even to those who claim to have no sin in 1 John 1:8. Following the true God in league with the true community (see 1:1–4) does not imply that one is without sin. To imagine that one cannot still separate oneself from God by sins is an error, and the confession and acknowledgment of sins is an important corrective for this error. The opponents of Jesus in John 9 showed their sin by imagining that they were without sin and dwelled in the light. According to 1 John 1:8, to occupy the realm of light and truth is not to avoid sin but to accept it and confess it. This is what maintains one in fellowship with God.

1:9. If we confess our sins, he is faithful and just, so that he will forgive us our sins and cleanse us from every injustice. At first one might imagine that God's justice would distance sinners from the divine presence. That is not the sense here (see Brown 1982, 209). The claim that God is faithful recalls Deut. 7:9, "Know . . . that the LORD your God is God . . . the faithful God who maintains covenant loyalty with those who love him and keep his commandments."

In a way that is similar to 1 John 1:9, Paul applies this image in relation to Christ (1 Cor. 1:9): "God is faithful, by whom you were called into fellowship [*koinōnia*] with his Son, Jesus Christ." To say that God is faithful means that he is faithful to the relationship he has established with those who believe in him. In 1 John, Jesus is also called just (2:1, 29; 3:7), and because he is just, he has no tolerance for sin (3:5–6). And yet because God is just means that he does not reject the sinner. So 1:9 ends by explaining what it means for God to be just: he forgives our sins and cleanses us from all injustice (Painter 2002, 156). In the same way that humans walk in the light, not by denying their sin but by acknowledging their sin, so also God shows that he is just, not by rejecting the sinner but by forgiving and cleansing the sinner. The point is neatly expressed in Isa. 45:21, where God is said to be "a righteous God and savior."

1:10. If we say that we have not sinned, we make him a liar, and his word is not in us. This verse articulates the third false claim that needs to be refuted. This third claim is much like the second one. Although 1:10 seems merely to repeat the false teaching expressed in 1:8, here it takes a different form. While 1:8 said in the present tense, "If we say that we do not have sin," now 1:10 expresses the same matter in the perfect tense by saying, "If we say that we have not sinned . . ." Some believe that the change from present to perfect tense carries interpretive meaning (cf. Painter 2002, 157), but the net effect of the two statements is the same: humans do not live without sin. And yet if 1:10 is a repetition it is not a mere repetition. While the claim about humans not sinning seems to be the same, the effect of that claim is not at all the same. In 1:8 those who claimed that they have no sin were guilty of deceiving only themselves. Their error hurt or affected no one but themselves. In 1:10 their error affects God: their error makes God a liar. God regularly and consistently speaks about human sin in the OT (Schnackenburg 1992, 84; Brown 1982, 211). At Gen. 8:21 we read, "I will never again curse the ground because of humankind, for the inclination of the human heart is evil from youth." Psalm 14:3 sees sin as equally pervasive: "They have all gone astray, they are all alike perverse; there is no one who does good, no not one." Thus those who reject the clear teaching of God in Scripture deny the need to be saved from sin, a need to which Scripture testifies. For this reason, "his word is not in" those who deny that they have sinned.

2:1. My little children, I write these things to you in order that you not sin, and yet if someone sins, we have an advocate with the Father, Jesus Christ the just. The argument now enters a new phase, though in a very real way remains the same. A new tone is introduced by addressing the readers as "my little children" (*teknia*), and this will be a common address from this point forward (2:12, 28; 3:7, 18; 4:4; 5:21). A similar word for children, *paidia*, will also be used (2:14, 18; 3:7). Believers are no longer addressed as a shapeless collective "you," but are now addressed in a term used by the Johannine Jesus when he addresses his disciples at 13:33. Further, the Elder refers to himself now for the first time in the singular form "I," after referring to himself as part of a collective "we" prior to this (cf. 1:4).

And yet despite these shifts in tone the concerns and content of the argument continue to be the same, especially regarding the sins of believers and the work of Jesus. There is every hope that believers will not sin, but God has provided Jesus in order to deal with the reality of sin.

Three labels are given to Jesus in 2:1–2 that explain his work in relation to the sins of human beings: *paraklēton, dikaion, hilasmos*. The second term, *dikaion*, means "just" or "righteous" and is the one most easy to explain in this context. To call Jesus "just" here is to call him merciful and to emphasize his desire to save—not destroy—those who sin. At 1:9 God was called just, and then it was immediately said that God will forgive sins and cleanse sinners from all injustice. To call God just does not imply that he eradicates sinners, but that he forgives them. The same point is now made here of Jesus. If anyone commits sin, Jesus is standing in the presence of the Father in order to accomplish this very same work of mercy and forgiveness of sins.

It is in this character that Jesus operates as *paraklētos*. The meaning of the term here in 1 John is fairly straightforward, carrying the sense of an advocate before a judge. When Philo describes the meeting of Joseph with the brothers who left him for dead, Joseph tells them not to worry, and not even to call for some intercessor or advocate to appeal to the judge. Joseph says (Philo, *Joseph* 40, trans. Yonge 1993): "Be not cast down; I give you complete forgiveness for all the things that you have done to me. Do not think that you want anyone else as a mediator [*paraklēton*]." In another place, Philo provides even closer parallels to the use of *paraklētos* here in 1 John (Lieu 2008, 62–63). In this text, Philo (*Rewards* 165–67, trans. Yonge 1993) imagines the return to true belief of those who abandoned Judaism but are now repenting. When they return to the land of Israel, they will have three *paraklētoi*:

The clemency and the kindness of the one to whom they appeal
The holiness of the founders of the nation
The reformation of those who are being led to the solemn treaties

Although none of these entities is a personal intercessor like Jesus the *Paraklētos*, this text is indeed important comparative material because of its describing advocates on behalf of sinners under the label *paraklētos*.

The noun *paraklētos* appears in the NT only here and in the Gospel of John. In the Gospel, the term is applied only to the Holy Spirit (14:15–17, 25–26; 15:26–27; 16:5–11, 12–15), and it is impossible to reconcile the activity of Jesus as Advocate in 1 John with any of the activities of the Spirit-Paraclete in the Fourth Gospel. In 1 John, Jesus performs only one function as Paraclete, while the Paraclete of the Gospel performs many different duties: teaching the disciples things that they could not understand during Jesus's earthly ministry

(14:26), testifying on behalf of Jesus (15:26), and proclaiming only what was heard from Jesus (16:13–14). The Paraclete will also fill the void left by the departure of Jesus by, in some sense, making the absent Jesus present. The Paraclete thus imitates and continues the work of Jesus, even after Jesus has returned to the Father. In the words of Raymond Brown, "Since the Paraclete can come only when Jesus departs, the Paraclete is the presence of Jesus when Jesus is absent" (1970, 1141). In this sense, the Spirit has a consolatory function (Parsenios 2005a, 77–109), and the Spirit continues on earth the ministry of Jesus, even after Jesus has returned to the Father.

None of these functions seems relevant for the title Paraclete as applied to Jesus here at 2:1, but one further function of the Paraclete-Spirit in John seems closer to the function of Jesus as Paraclete in 1 John—the function of the Paraclete-Spirit as prosecutor. John 16:8 says, "When the Paraclete comes, he will convict the world about sin and righteousness and judgment" (AT). The ministry of Jesus in John is dominated by legal concerns, and the Paraclete will continue Jesus's legal battle against the world after Jesus returns to the Father (Parsenios 2010, 35, 63). But even this function only partly explains what we find in 1 John. In the Gospel, the Paraclete prosecutes and exposes the sin of the world. In 1 John, Jesus seems to be a defending advocate for the believers. Both are legal functions, but are very different functions. One is as a prosecutor, the other as a defender. But if it is difficult to reconcile the work of the Spirit as Paraclete and the work of Jesus as Paraclete, the meaning of the term "Paraclete" in 1 John is fairly straightforward. Jesus is an intercessor with the Father on behalf of believers. The same is said of Jesus in Romans and Hebrews (Rensberger 1997, 56):

Who is to condemn? It is Christ Jesus, who died, yes, who was raised, who is at the right hand of God, who indeed intercedes for us. (Rom. 8:34)

Consequently he is able for all time to save those who approach God through him, since he always lives to make intercession for them. (Heb. 7:25)

2:2. In addition to being labeled *dikaios* and *paraklētos*, Jesus is next said to be the *hilasmos peri tōn hamartiōn hēmōn*. Possible translations of *hilasmos* extend along a very broad spectrum. Some understand the term to have strong sacrificial associations, and so render it as the NRSV has, "atoning sacrifice." Others deny any sacrificial sense to the word, and so render the phrase in English with "he is forgiveness for our sins," where the word "forgiveness" translates *hilasmos* (Lieu 2008, 60–64). This commentary will allow a certain ambiguity by rendering the phrase in English as **an atonement for our sins**. This suggests sacrificial imagery, but leaves room for some interpretation of the word as well.

The noun *hilasmos* occurs ten times in the LXX, where it often means simply "forgiveness." Psalm 130:4 (129:4 LXX) reads, for instance, "For with you is forgiveness [*hilasmos*]." The term can also, of course, convey the meaning of sacrifice when it is used in Lev. 25:9, where the Day of Atonement is called *hēmera tou hilasmou*. Within the NT, the noun occurs only here and later in this same letter, at 4:10. The several cognate forms of *hilasmos* are common in the LXX and appear as well in the NT: *hilaskesthai* occurs eleven times in the LXX and twice in the NT (Luke 18:13; Heb. 2:17); *exilaskesthai* has over one hundred appearances in the LXX but none in the NT; *hilastērion* is found twenty-seven times in the LXX and twice in the NT (Rom 3:25; Heb. 9:5); *hileōs* is used thirty-five times in the LXX and twice in the NT (Matt 16:22; Heb. 8:12). Accounting for these words does not necessarily solve the dilemma, though, because their meanings are arrayed along the same spectrum as *hilasmos*. They sometimes carry sacrificial imagery, but need not necessarily do so (Brown 1982, 217–21).

> ### Hilaskesthai in the New Testament
>
> #### Hilaskesthai with a Sacrificial Meaning
>
> "Therefore he had to become like his brothers and sisters in every respect, so that he *might be a merciful and faithful high priest in the service of God, to make a sacrifice of atonement* [hilaskesthai] *for the sins of the people.*" (Heb. 2:17)
>
> #### Hilaskesthai without a Sacrificial Meaning
>
> "God, be merciful [hilasthēti] *to me, a sinner!*" (Luke 18:13)

There are several reasons to think, however, that *hilasmos* refers to the sacrificial death of Jesus on the cross. It seems to make little sense in 2:2 to call Jesus "forgiveness." The assumption that the term here means simply forgiveness and carries no sacrificial meaning is based on the belief that the immediate context makes no reference to the death of Jesus (Lieu 2008, 64). This is not exactly accurate. A few verses earlier we read, "The blood of Jesus cleanses us from every sin" (1:7), a phrase that we must bear in mind when, only a few verses later, we read that Jesus is a *hilasmos* concerning our sins. The blood of Jesus is thus sacrificed like the sacrifice on the Day of Atonement (Lev. 16:16; 25:9).

If this conclusion resolves one set of problems, it only opens another. If the death of Jesus is a sacrifice for sins, what kind of sacrifice is it? The noun *hilasmos* and its cognates listed above all lie behind the English term "hilarity," and so refer to making something pleasant or agreeable, but scholars are divided over precisely how the death of Jesus makes humans agreeable to God. The two chief possibilities are the categories of "propitiation" and "expiation." Propitiation focuses on God, and especially on the wrath of God. A propitiatory understanding of sacrifice means that humans are made agreeable to God because the blood of Jesus assuages God's wrath. Expiation refers not to God but to humans. In an expiatory understanding of sacrifice humans are made agreeable to God because human sin is wiped away or cleansed by the sacrificial death of Jesus. Which of the two is operative here is not immediately clear. The Gospel is of little help in solving the dilemma. John 1:29 announces, "Here is the Lamb of God, who takes away the sin of the world," which seems to refer to how Jesus will be slaughtered on the cross at the same time as the lambs prepared for Passover (19:31), but the Passover sacrifice is not a sacrifice for sins like the Day of Atonement.

There are very strong philological arguments for reading *hilasmos* as propitiation (D. Hill 1967), but the vast majority of current interpreters understand 1 John 2:2 to reflect an expiatory notion of sacrifice (comments on 2:2 in Brown 1982; Rensberger 1997; Painter 2002; Culy 2004; von Wahlde 2010). Brown connects the mention of Jesus's blood in 1:7 with the mention here of *hilasmos*, and then argues that the background of these verses lies in the sacrifice on the Day of Atonement, *hē hēmera tou hilasmou* (Lev. 25:9 LXX). The high priest sacrificed a bull and a goat "concerning all their sins" (*peri pasōn tōn hamartiōn autōn*; Lev. 16:16 LXX), just as the death of Jesus took place "concerning our sins" (*peri tōn hamartiōn hēmōn*; 1 John 2:2). Further, the high priest would pour the blood of the sacrifice over the ark of the covenant, an act described with a verb from the root *hilaskesthai*, which is taken here to mean "cleanse or purify." If this reading is correct, the sacrifice implied by *hilasmos* in 2:2 is an expiatory sacrifice.

The sacrifice of Christ is not only for believers, says 2:2, but also **for the entire world**. The statement presents a puzzle in light of the complicated place of the "world" (*kosmos*) in 1 John (Painter 2002, 103, 147, 159–60). The term *kosmos* appears just a few verses later, at 2:15, in a statement that shows the dilemma: "Do not love the world or the things in the world. The love of the Father is not in those who love the world." Where 2:2 claims that the loving death of Christ is *for* the world, 2:15 says that the love of the Father stands *against* the world. The world is the object of God's love and also opposed to God's love. This tension persists in the various uses of *kosmos* throughout 1 John. God sent his Son into the world (4:9), and the Son is the Savior of the world (4:14); but believers should not love the world or the things in the world (2:15–16), because the world does not know God or believers (3:1). Indeed the world hates believers (3:13). The secessionists who left the community went out into the world (4:1; 2 John 7) and have thus shown that they are actually "of the world" (4:5). The world opposes God and is the place of the antichrist (2:18, 22; 4:3) because it lies under the sway of the evil one (5:19).

The same tension characterizes the place of the world (*kosmos*) in the Gospel of John. On the one hand, certain passages in the Fourth Gospel suggest a positive stance toward the world. God loves the world (3:16) and sends his Son to save the world (3:17; 4:42; 12:47), and Jesus enters the world to bring both light (12:46) and life (6:35, 51). On the other hand, the world does not know him (14:17), and the ministry of Jesus brings judgment on the world (9:39; 12:31) and on those who dwell in darkness (12:35–36). But this is only so because the world hates Jesus and his followers (7:7; 15:19; 16:33). The world was created by God and is the object of God's love, but it also stands in opposition to God because it falls under the sway of evil. Jesus thus enters the world to conquer both the world (16:33) and the prince of this world (12:31). The struggle with the world continues after Jesus returns to the Father. This struggle is visible in the depiction of the world in 1 John.

Three Boasts: "Whoever Says . . ." (2:3–11)

2:3. The argument now begins a new train of thought. The discussion of sin ends in 2:2, and the discussion about the knowledge of God and the keeping of commandments marks a shift to a new area of reflection. The section from 2:3 to 2:11 is divided into three subsections (vv. 3–5, 6–8, 9–11), with each subsection including the phrase "whoever says."

The first subsection begins in 2:3: **And in this way we know that we have known him: if we keep his commandments.** The Greek phrase *en toutō* is translated "in this way" but literally means "in this." It is a common phrase in 1 John, where it occurs twelve times (2:3, 5; 3:10, 16, 19, 24; 4:2, 9, 10, 13, 17; 5:2), as well as in the Fourth Gospel, where it appears five times (4:37; 9:30; 13:35; 15:8; 16:30; Brown 1982, 248–49). The rhetorical function of the phrase is very clear, but its grammatical function is often contested. Rhetorically, the phrase elevates a particular item to the fore and forces us to pay close attention to it. From a grammatical standpoint, however, the reader sometimes struggles to see where to place the focus. Does the phrase refer to something that comes before "in this way" or to something that follows it? The next appearance of the phrase displays the problem perfectly. Verses 5–6 read:

> 2:5: Whoever obeys his word, truly in this person the love of God has reached perfection. *In this way* we may be sure that we are in him.
> 2:6: The one who says that he abides in him ought himself to walk just as that one walked.

The "in this way" clause in 2:5 above might reasonably explain the preceding or the following clause. We might know, in other words, that we are "in him" (a) if we keep his word, as we are told in 2:5, or (b) if we walk as he walked, in 2:6. The "in this way" clause could point in either direction, and we need to be aware of this problem as we proceed. The present verse (2:3) is a rare case because it excites no such controversy. The phrase is immediately clear. Believers show that they have known him by keeping his commandments.

Other common phrases and terms that will recur throughout 1 John find their first expression in this verse as well. Here in 2:3 is the first of twenty-five times in 1 John, for instance, that the verb "to know" (*ginōskein*) is used. The verb appears twice in this verse, with a slightly different nuance in each case. The first use of the word could be translated in a variety of ways, such as "to know," "to be certain," "to be sure," or other similar words, and this translation could serve in several places (2:5, 18, 29; 3:19, 24; 4:2, 12–13, 16; 5:2). The second use of the word is more technical for these letters. Knowledge is the intimacy that believers now share in fellowship with God, the relationship they have with God in light of the work of Christ. They know, in the first sense of "know," that Christ has taken away sin (3:5), that they have passed from death to life (3:14; 5:13, 15, 18, 19). This is a fact. It has happened. And yet this new life must be lived in a certain way, the second sense of "know." And so, after the certainty of knowledge is expressed, a condition is given. We know that we have known him *if* we keep his commandments.

The term "commandments" appears here for the first time as well. Commandment (*entolē*) is an important word in this correspondence and occurs seventeen more times in 1–2 John together. Sometimes the plural is used, as here, and sometimes the singular form of the noun appears. The alternation between singular and plural follows the precedent set by the Gospel, which refers to the commandment to love one another as *entolē* in the singular (13:34; 15:12) and *entolai* in the plural (14:15, 21; 15:10). This is typical Johannine variation and does not imply a different referent. The nature of the commandments of God is not made clear here, but it will be gradually clarified in the remainder of the letter. The idea of "keeping" (*tērein*) the commandment(s) is common in 1 John (2:3, 4; 3:22, 24; 5:3).

2:4–5. Here 2:4 affirms the message of the previous verse by expressing its opposite. After 2:3 has explained the behavior that accords with knowing God, 2:4 speaks of not knowing God and introduces the person who does not keep God's commandments, in order to show the poverty of the person's claim to know. **The one who says, "I have known him," and does not keep his commandments is a liar, and the truth is not in this one.** Then in different terminology 2:5 restates the message of 2:3: **but whoever obeys his word, truly in this person the love of God has reached perfection. In this way we may be sure that we are in him.** After 2:3 spoke of "keeping his commandments," 2:5 refers to the same life of obedience with the phrase "obeying his word."

Here 2:5 refers to "the love of God" (as in NRSV). The translation of this phrase is contested by both commentators and the standard versions (Rensberger 1997, 62). The Greek phrase translated "love of God" is *agapē tou Theou*. Is God here, though, the object of the love? Or is God the one whose love is shown? The RSV renders the phrase as "love for God"; the NIV agrees but adds a marginal note allowing "God's love." Either one is grammatically possible, and either one has biblical precedent. It is possible, first, to speak of human love for God in the OT (Exod. 20:6; Jer. 2:2). In the Gospel of John, Jesus three times asks Peter, "Do you love me?" (21:15–17). Given the fact that the Letters of John regularly apply to the Father sayings and language that the Gospel applies to the Son, one could possibly read 2:5 as yet another manifestation of that common device. If the disciples can love Jesus in the Gospel, then they can love the Father in 1 John.

But the Gospel of John also provides the basis for reading the phrase as referring to God's love for humanity. The word translated "perfected" is a form of the Greek verb *telein*. The term is significant, because when Jesus nears his Passion, we are told in 13:31 that Jesus loved his disciples "to the end" (*telos*). The term could be temporal, indicating that he loved them all the way to the end of his earthly life; or it could express the degree of his love and suggest that he loved them to the furthest extent possible. Either way, it refers to his loving death on the cross. In John, the last word of Jesus before he dies is translated "it is finished" (*tetelestai*; 19:30), another form of the verb *telein*. Given the association again in 1 John 2:5 of love and a form of *telein*, it is reasonable to assume that here the author has in mind God's love toward humanity. And yet one hesitates to choose one option over the other, because of what is said at 1 John 4:19: "We love because he first loved us." Human love has its foundation in God's love. The ambiguity in 2:5 may very well be intentional.

2:6. This verse introduces yet another important term for 1 John, the verb *menō*, "to abide/dwell." **The one who says that he abides in him ought himself to walk just as that one walked.** To whom does the phrase "abides in him" refer? Is it the Father or the Son? The Letters of John are often ambiguous on this point, and masculine pronouns could naturally refer to either the Father or the Son. The act of abiding has a less than clear referent in other places in 1 John, where it could refer to either the Father or Jesus (2:28; 3:6, 24; 4:13), though the language of abiding is more often applied to the Father than to Jesus. This entire section (1:5–2:11) has its focus on knowing the Father, and so abiding in this verse seems to refer to abiding in the Father.

2:7–11. Verses 7–8 are a kaleidoscope of confusion: **Beloved, I do not write to you a new commandment, but an old commandment that you had from the beginning; the old commandment is the word that you heard. Again, I write to you a new commandment, which is true in him, and in you, because the darkness is passing away and the true light is already shining.** These verses disorient us, and then disorient us again, catching off guard the reader who knows the Gospel of John. The "new commandment" famously refers in the Gospel to the commandment that Jesus gives to his disciples to love one another (John 13:34–35; 15:12). This is an important commandment, and so it surprises the reader now to hear that no new commandment is being given. The argument becomes even more confusing after this, because 2:8 contradicts 2:7 and says, "I write to you a new commandment." One wonders, which is it: new or old?

Two other factors muddy the water further. First, the previous lines alternately spoke of "keeping the commandments" (2:4) and "obeying the word" (2:5). Now these two categories are collapsed: the commandment *is* the word. Second, the veteran reader of the Gospel would be expecting to hear the content of a commandment, but no commandment is ever given. There is only reference to the commandment, not the actual delivery of the commandment.

The alternation between "old" and "new" shows the profundity of the thought of 1 John. The commandment is "old" because it was passed down "from the beginning." The phrase "from the beginning" first appeared in 1 John 1:1, where it referred to the beginning of Jesus's ministry. To say that the commandment is "from the beginning" means that it has been transmitted from the ministry of Jesus to the present. In this sense, it is "old." But the commandment is also new in the sense that it applies to the new life offered in Christ and, even more important, it was called "new" in the ministry of Christ. The commandment is both old and new; because it represents the new life in Christ, it can be called the "new commandment," but because it is also an element of the faith that has been passed down "from the beginning" and must be preserved, it is also the "old commandment." In the final measure, then, "old" and "new" mean the same thing: this commandment comes from the ministry of Jesus.

Even if one comes to grips with the commandment that is both old and new, the argument is still disorienting. Such disorienting phrasing is not foreign to the Johannine tradition. Jeffrey Staley has identified several places in the Gospel of John where Jesus similarly turns his words in on themselves, or where he says one thing but does the opposite (Staley 1988, 96–118). Staley calls this "victimization of the reader." The reader of the Fourth Gospel is made to feel the same disorientation when reading about Jesus that the interlocutors of Jesus feel when they speak to him. Several scenes in John seem to operate in this way. In the wedding at Cana, Jesus seems to refuse his mother's request to help (2:4), but then proceeds to work a miracle (2:7–8). At the beginning of John 7, Jesus tells his brothers that he will not go up to the feast (7:3–6), but then proceeds to go (7:10). Finally, at John 14:31, Jesus announces, "Arise, let us go forth," but then he proceeds to speak for three more chapters. He actually departs the Last Supper at 18:1. These verses have a similar effect on the reader. The alternation here is between the old and new commandment, therefore, it is yet another place where the author of the Letters writes in the manner that the Jesus of the Gospel speaks.

A further function of 2:7–8 is that the verses hearken back to 1:5 and so round off this opening section of 1 John. Where 1:5 referred to the message (*angelia*) that was heard "from him" and proclaimed "to you," 2:7 mentions a commandment that was heard "from the beginning" and written "to you." The association with 1:5 becomes even more obvious in 2:9–11. The section begins by distinguishing light and darkness on the basis of recognizing one's sins (1:5–9), and now ends in 2:9–11 by distinguishing light and darkness on the basis of whether one hates or loves a fellow believer.

Believers can have fellowship with the Father only by having fellowship with one another (1:3). To break off fellowship with the Father leads to a life of darkness, because the only light is God, and there is no darkness in God (1:5). To have fellowship with the community is thus to have fellowship with light and with the Father. To shun the community is to have fellowship with darkness. This explains the argument in 2:9–11. Hating a fellow believer is the same as hating God and abiding in the darkness.

Theological Issues

Among the many features of 1 John that confuse interpreters, one of the most baffling is its teaching on sin. The statements regarding sin in 1:5–2:11 are difficult to reconcile with the statements on sin in chapters 3 and 5. In chapter 1, the only way to walk in the light is to recognize one's sins, where we read, "If we say that we have no sin, we deceive ourselves and the truth is not in us" (1:10). Chapter 3 says the opposite: "Everyone who abides in him does not sin. Everyone who sins has neither seen him nor known him" (3:6). How might one respond to such obviously incompatible statements?

The first step in approaching the tension of these opposing statements is to recognize that such polarities and oppositions are pervasive in the Gospel of John as well. A seemingly insignificant moment late in Jesus's ministry helps to explain the matter. Only a few verses after he has announced that the hour of his death has arrived (John 12:31–33), Jesus says to his disciples:

> The light is with you for a little longer. Walk while you have the light, so that the darkness may not overtake you. If you walk in the darkness, you do not know where you are going. While you have the light, believe in the light, so that you may become children of light. (12:35–36)

Here Jesus emphasizes light and revelation and illumination. If the disciples want to see where they are going, and so become children of the light, they must walk in the light. But as soon as Jesus finishes speaking, the Evangelist says, "After Jesus had said this, he departed and hid from them" (12:36). He *hid* from them. Even as he teaches about light and revelation and illumination, Jesus conceals and obscures. He hides himself. This tension between revelatory light and divine darkness defines the dominant theological perspective of the Gospel of John, in which every moment of revelation is equally a moment of concealment. Something is shown, but something is also hidden.

John creates this balance between revelation and concealment by presenting the teachings of Jesus in a dialectical fashion. The word *dialectical* has many possible meanings in theology and philosophy, so one must define the word carefully while using it. Here I follow those who use the word to mean that John often puts "in dialogue" two opposing statements that seem to contradict each other, and yet he never resolves the opposition and contradiction inherent in them. Every major theological statement in the Gospel of John operates in this dialectical fashion. For instance, Jesus says, "The Father and I are one" (John 10:30), which implies that Jesus holds a divine and lofty position equal to the Father, and yet Jesus also says, "The Father is greater than I" (14:28). We are left to wonder, Is Jesus equal to the Father or not? The same dialectic appears in Jesus's miracles. Are they an important basis for faith, or not? In John, the miracles of Jesus are called "signs," and these signs are written so that we might believe that Jesus is the Son of God and the Messiah (20:31). In some cases, people see the signs and they believe, as at the wedding in Cana, where we read, "Jesus did this, the first of his signs, in Cana of Galilee, and revealed his glory; and his disciples believed in him" (2:11). But other episodes end differently. Some believe in Jesus because of his signs at the end of chapter 2, but they are not welcomed by the Lord. They are rejected. We are left to wonder, then, Are signs a proper basis for faith or not? A certain tension defines the relation between signs and faith, and in this sense signs are not unique. The same tension appears in every major theological topic in the Gospel of John (see Barrett 1982; Anderson 2007).

Why does John present his theology in this format? All these examples of dialectical tension are symptoms of a much greater paradox: the immortal God has become a mortal man. John expresses his theology dialectically in order to come to grips with the mystery inherent in the incarnation. The Son of God has become a human. When the immortal God becomes mortal, when eternity enters time, when the Creator enters creation, then these once opposing and incompatible realities are joined in a single person. Two utterly incompatible entities are now united—and yet remain polar opposites. At the very heart of the incarnation lies this basic paradox, in which two completely incompatible statements are equally true and equally need to be affirmed. The dialectical mode is intended to express this new reality. When the Word becomes flesh, it is not as though we can see the Word within the flesh. The Word that is revealed in the flesh is also by the same flesh concealed. Revelation and concealment are intimately joined.

In the wake of the incarnation, humans are not left untouched by this dialectical reality. A similar paradox now defines those who are born from above. They are invited to abide in God and to share in divine realities, and yet they still exist in mortal flesh on earth. In the divine descent of the incarnation, God moves from an utterly apophatic state (i.e., nothing positive can be said of God since he is utterly remote and distant) to a more kataphatic state (i.e., certain things can now be said about God because he has revealed himself). But as humans respond to this divine revelation, they move in the opposite direction, from existing in a totally kataphatic reality that is available to the senses, and onward to something more apophatic and mysterious, as the power of God grows within a person (Brock 1992, 79). Sebastian Brock explains this reality in the theology of Ephrem the Syrian in a passage that deserves to be quoted in full:

There is thus a twofold movement from the silence of ingratitude to vocal praises, and then on to a different sort of silence, the silence of silent praise. This movement of praise from sound to silence is seen by Ephrem as a counterpart to the movement of God from the Silence of His ineffable Being to the divine Utterance, the Word. Whereas the divine descent can be described as being increasingly kataphatic, the human ascent needs correspondingly to be increasingly apophatic. (1992, 79)

In the same way that God is caught between revelation and concealment, between apophatic and kataphatic realities in his descent to humans, so too humans are caught in the same set of paradoxes in their ascent to God. In the same way that the incarnate Lord represents a paradoxical reality, combining as he does the immaterial God and material flesh, so too do those who have fellowship with him (to use Johannine language) become characterized by this same paradoxical reality. They are still very much flesh, with all of the sinful realities that go along with being in the flesh. And yet they are also in fellowship with God, with all that that entails for being perfect and pure and holy.

John applies this sort of dialectic to Jesus, as we saw above, but also applies it to human believers when it comes to the question of human free will. In many cases in John, it appears that humans have the free will and power to believe, as when Jesus says, "You will die in your sins, unless you believe that I AM" (8:24). But in other places Jesus insists that only those who are called by the Father can believe in him, as when he says, "No one can come to me unless drawn by the Father who sent me" (6:44). So we are faced with a situation in which the burden to believe or not to believe is both within our power and yet entirely in the power of God. As we saw with Christology and the value of the signs, the polar opposite statements are equally affirmed. First John reflects the same dialectic on the part of humans, where we are told that sin is a necessary aspect of human life and so much a part of human life that one cannot deny sin (1:8, 10), and yet later we are told that Christians are not permitted to sin (3:9). Both of these statements are true, and neither can exist without the other as long as humans continue to strive for a heavenly life while they remain on earth. Human beings are caught up in the dialectic of the Lord they follow.

But this is not something merely inchoate in the Johannine literature, which later theologians like Ephrem develop more fully. Rather, this is the core of the Johannine vision of reality and of discipleship. Many figures in John stand not so much at the polar opposites of light and darkness but rather somewhere between light and darkness. All human figures in the Gospel of John exist on a spectrum between loyalty to God and loyalty to the world, and few of them are fully and completely on one side or the other. Those who are faithful are rarely completely faithful, and those who are faithless are not consigned utterly to perdition. The famous words of Alexandr Solzhenitsyn are helpful here. He writes in regard to human sin and goodness:

Gradually it was disclosed to me that the line separating good and evil passes not through states, nor between classes, nor between political parties either, but right through every human heart, and through all human hearts. This line shifts. Inside us, it oscillates with the years. Even within hearts overwhelmed by evil, one small bridgehead of good is retained; and even in the best of all hearts, there remains a small corner of evil. . . . If only there were evil people somewhere insidiously committing evil deeds, and it were necessary only to separate them from the rest of us and destroy them. But the line dividing good and evil cuts through the heart of every human being. (1992, 615)

The disciples and the opponents of Jesus in the Fourth Gospel, and in 1 John, are better understood with this quotation in mind. Nicodemus provides an important example of this shifting line between heaven and earth on the part of a disciple. He first appears in John 3 and is called a "leader of the Jews" (3:1), but he treats Jesus with greater respect than the other leaders of Israel. The Jewish leaders usually pursue and attack Jesus, but Nicodemus approaches him in a spirit of respect and goodwill. He says, "Rabbi, we know that you are a teacher who has come from God; for no one can do these signs that you do apart from the presence of God" (John 3:2). Later, when the leaders of Israel condemn Jesus, Nicodemus defends him. He asks that Jesus be judged fairly, and says, "Our law does not judge people without first giving

Figure 6. Nicodemus and Jesus by Alexandre Bida, 1874.

them a hearing to find out what they are doing, does it?" (7:51). After Jesus is executed, Nicodemus joins Joseph of Arimathea at the tomb of Christ, laden with spices to anoint the Lord for burial (19:39).

All these occasions suggest a faithful disciple, and if this were all we knew about Nicodemus, we would see him in an entirely positive light. But this is not all we know. Other features of his portrayal in the Gospel of John suggest that his status as a follower of Christ is not so stable. When he first approaches Jesus, for instance, he comes to him "at night" (*nyktos*; 3:2). The only other person to operate at night is Judas, who leaves the table of fellowship to betray Jesus just as we are told, "It was night [*nyx*]" (13:30). This small fact frames Nicodemus in a dark light. Likewise, Nicodemus defends Jesus, but only on the basis of the Jewish law. He does not defend Jesus with the full confession that the man born blind will muster in John 9, after which the man is expelled from the synagogue on account of his faith. Nicodemus defends Jesus, but only while safely holding his position among the leaders of the Jews. He does not attack Jesus, but neither does he surrender everything to follow Jesus. He is like those who do not profess their faith openly for fear of being kicked out of the synagogue (9:22). Finally, when Nicodemus accompanies Joseph of Arimathea to the tomb to anoint Jesus for burial, he takes a hundred pounds of spices to complete the job, which is an enormous amount of material for embalming the dead. It indicates that Nicodemus expects Jesus to be entombed for good, with absolutely no hope for the resurrection. Is this perfect faith?

There is thus a tension in the person of Nicodemus. He shows signs of great faith and signs of lesser faith. His conversation with Jesus starts well because he honors Jesus with the title "Rabbi," and he recognizes that Jesus comes from God. But when Jesus begins to explain the new life that he offers, Nicodemus becomes so puzzled and confused that he can only stand with mouth agape and ask, "How can these things be?" (3:9). We never hear from Nicodemus again in this conversation. He simply disappears. What we see in Nicodemus is that the life of faith is complicated and enigmatic. Or rather, faith in Christ is simple, and we are to aspire to simplicity and clarity, but our entanglements with the world catch us in a web of complexity. The line that separates God and his opponents still runs through each human heart.

The same reality persists in 1 John. To use the language of 1 John, "The darkness is passing away, and the true light is already shining" (2:8). Even so, until the return of Christ, the darkness continues, and the true light does not stand alone in the sky. The light is overcoming the darkness. But the darkness is still thick, for a time. The task of Christians is to choose light over darkness, and yet always recognize that seeking the light does not equate one absolutely with the light. The life of discipleship is a life walked on a razor's edge, where every decision is a choice between light and darkness. Bultmann makes the point well when he writes in regard to 1 John 1:9, "The Christian has never acquired the light as permanent possession through his faith. He must authenticate his faith in . . . 'walking'; he is always underway and never stands before God as a finished product, but is rather dependent on forgiveness" (1973, 21).

1 John 2:12–3:10

Who Are the Children of God?

Introductory Matters

The section ranging from 2:12–3:10 finally provides explicit details about the problems that have been lying just beneath the surface of the argument since the letter began. The preceding sections spoke in general about light and darkness, and about loving or not loving fellow believers, but little specific content was provided about the actual issues at stake. The problems are now described in greater detail. We hear of people leaving the community (2:19) and of people who not only adhere to a faulty Christology (2:22) but who also want to spread this false teaching to others (2:26). The response of 1 John to these divisions will be the focus of what follows.

In the process of discussing the trauma that is described here regarding the community's separation, though, one further matter should be kept in mind. If the community is experiencing anguish as it is torn apart, it first experienced painful trauma as it was knit together. When people join the Johannine community, they sever ties with their past. A respected line of historical interpretation of the Johannine community sees certain sayings and episodes in the Fourth Gospel as providing insight into the problems that the Johannine community faced in its devotion to Jesus (Martyn 2003). John 15:18–16:2 tells us, for instance, that believers were expelled from synagogues when they entered the Johannine circle of belief, and their anxiety may have been even more personal. When the blind man in John 9 is questioned by the leaders of Israel, his parents abandon him in his hour of need, hoping to avoid the fate of expulsion that awaits him (9:22–23). Early Christians adopt the language of family for their new community and refer to one another in 1 John as brothers (2:9–11), fathers (2:13–14), children (2:1, 18, 28), and beloved (2:7). These familial bonds replace the bonds that have been severed. The Johannine community serves as a new family for those rejected by their former family and friends. As we will see at the close of this section (under "Theological Issues"), the Johannine literature shares this characteristic with other Christian texts, as well as with Jewish writings. Converting to a new faith means joining a new family. Such a vision of the group that lies behind 1 John clarifies the nature of the problems facing the group. A grave theological debate has rent into pieces a body of believers who once saw themselves

> ### 1 John 2:12–3:10 in the Rhetorical Flow
>
> **Introductory prologue (1:1–4)**
>
> **The light and the darkness (1:5–2:11)**
>
> ▶ **Who are the children of God? (2:12–3:10)**
>
> > "I have written . . . I am writing" (2:12–14)
> >
> > God and the world (2:15–17)
> >
> > The Christ and the antichrists (2:18–27)
> >
> > Born from above, born from below (2:28–3:10)

as a single family of God's children. This theological struggle is also a very personal struggle.

Defining 2:12–3:10 as a discrete section is a somewhat artificial move. Especially hard to classify are the two brief units in 2:12–14 and 2:15–17. Elements of these verses connect them to what has preceded them as well as to what comes next. These verses will be discussed as discrete units for the sake of convenience since they are too brief to be treated on their own. The rest of the section will be divided into two broader bodies of text, 2:18–27 and 2:28–3:10, each marked off by the direct addresses "children" in 2:18 and "little children" in 2:28.

Tracing the Train of Thought

"I Have Written . . . I Am Writing" (2:12–14)

2:12–14. The section 2:12–14 continues many themes from the previous section, especially the emphasis on knowing God and the forgiveness of sins that was raised in various ways in 1:5–2:11. This section also poses several problems for the interpreter. Translating it will help to make the questions plain. The entire passage reads as follows:

2:12   I am writing [*graphō*] to you, little children [*teknia*], because your sins have been forgiven through his name.

2:13   I am writing [*graphō*] to you, fathers, because you have known the one who was from the beginning.

> **I am writing [*graphō*] to you, youths [*neaniskoi*], because you have conquered the evil one.**
>
> 2:14   **I wrote [*egrapsa*] to you, children [*paidia*], because you have known the Father.**
>
> **I wrote [*egrapsa*] to you, fathers, because you have known the one who was from the beginning.**
>
> **I wrote [*egrapsa*] to you, youths [*neaniskoi*], because you are mighty and the word of God abides in you and you have conquered the evil one.**

At the outset a few things can be affirmed about this passage, and then other questions will require further attention. First, the conjunction here repeatedly translated as "because" is the Greek word *hoti*, which can mean either "that" or "because." It would be grammatically acceptable to replace every instance of the word "because" in the above translation with the word "that." But even if this would make fine grammatical sense, it would make little sense in the argument of 1 John. To translate the word as "that" would suggest that 1 John is announcing these things for the first time to its readers. This is not reasonable. This letter was written to people who were already believers. They already know these things. First John was written to them "because" they know these things. "Because" is the only sensible translation.

This fact is connected to the paraenetic quality of 1 John (see "Setting and Purpose of 1 John" in the introduction). Paraenesis (exhortation) is often not new instruction, which people have never heard before, but a reminder of things they already know (Malherbe 1986, 124–25). In the present case, the reminder about what is known "from the beginning" is a recollection of beliefs and teaching that have their origin in the ministry of Jesus. These are not new tenets. They are not teachings thought up and expressed in 1 John for the first time. But they are important. They are foundational and must not be forgotten, particularly in the present struggle. Seneca the Younger says of paraenesis, "The mind often tries not to notice even that which lies before our eyes; we must therefore force upon it the knowledge of things that are perfectly well known" (*Ep.* 94.25, trans. in Malherbe 1986, 127). It is in this spirit that 2:12–14 reminds people of what they already know. Further support for this assumption is found in the perfect tense of the six verbs that end each clause: "have been forgiven," "have known," "have conquered," and so forth. These verses remind the readers of things they already have known and have acquired.

First John 2:12 says that sins have been forgiven because of "his" name. One can never be too certain of the identity of masculine pronouns in the Johannine Letters, because they could refer to either Jesus or the Father. Jesus seems to be the antecedent in this case, though, because Jesus seems also to have been the antecedent of the last use of a masculine pronoun in 2:8 (Brown 1982, 302). To say that sins are forgiven "because" of Jesus's name does not mean they are forgiven "through" his name, but "on account of" his name. Furthermore, the name of Jesus stands for the entire identity of Jesus. In Exod. 3:13–14, for

---

Paraenesis as Reminder of Things Already Known

"People say: 'What good does it do to point out the obvious?' A great deal of good; for we sometimes know facts without paying attention to them. Advice is not teaching; it merely engages the attention and rouses us, and concentrates the memory, and keeps it from losing grip. We miss much that is set before our very eyes. Advice is, in fact, a sort of exhortation. . . . You know that friendship should be scrupulously honored, and yet you do not hold it in honor. . . . Hence you must be continually brought to remember these facts; for they should not be in storage, but ready for use." (Seneca, *Ep.* 94.25–26, trans. in Malherbe 1986, 127)

---

example, Moses wants to know God's name, because this will reveal the depth of God's being, his whole life (Brown 1982, 302; Rensberger 1997, 72). In the present conflict with the opponents, the identity of Jesus and the value of his work on earth are precisely the source of confusion. This verse emphasizes that the special status that Christians enjoy is due to the person and being of Jesus, and of no one else, by his name and by no other. Jesus is also in view in both verses 13 and 14, as "the one who was from the beginning."

The singular significance of Jesus is even more explicit in the latter part of verse 13 and at the close of verse 15. The term *nenikēkate* (you have conquered) is the term that Jesus uses in John 16:33 when he says, "In this world you will have trouble, but take heart, I have conquered [*nenikēka*] the world." The victory over the world and evil that Christians enjoy is a victory won by Jesus. To the degree that they adhere to the teaching of Jesus "from the beginning," and to the degree that they walk as he walked (1 John 2:6), believers actualize this victory within their own lives.

The devil is here (2:13–14) called *ho ponēros*, which he is called throughout the letter (3:12; 5:18–19) as well as in the Gospel of Matthew (5:37; 6:13; 13:19, 38). Because the world is under the sway of the evil one (John 12:31; 14:30; 16:11; 1 John 5:19), conquering the evil one is akin to conquering the world (1 John 4:4; 5:4–5).

The separation of the remaining members of the community from those who have seceded is further clear in the phrase "the word [*logos*] of God abides in you" (2:14). The word (*logos*) of God, in the Gospel of John, does not abide in Jesus's opponents (5:38), but the word (*rhēma*) of God does abide in his disciples (15:7). The same is true here. The word of God abides in those who adhere to the fellowship with the community and believe as the community believes, but not in those who depart from it and from its teaching.

Several puzzles remain. The points of confusion can be summarized under the headings of similarity and difference. The verb "to write" is used in every clause, for instance, but the first three clauses use the present tense (*graphō*), while the latter three use the aorist tense (*egrapsa*). Next, why are roughly the same promises made in the first group of clauses, then repeated in the second group but with slight alterations? Finally, a variety of different groups are addressed, but they are addressed in the same way and with the same promises. The various groups addressed are youths (*neaniskoi*), children (*paidia*), little children (*teknia*), and fathers (*pateres*).

The shift in verb tense is perhaps the easiest to address. Interpreters have suggested that the present tense (I am writing) might refer to the writing of 1 John, while the past tense (I wrote) might refer to either 2 John or to some other text. Such theories are hard to prove. Further, such a change in tense is not uncommon in the Johannine literature, in which such alterations in verb tense often bring little change in meaning. This is yet another example of Johannine variation.

As for the great variety of groups that are addressed, the most reasonable suggestion is that the terms *paidia* and *teknia* refer to the whole community. The terms are used throughout the letter in this capacity (*paidia* in 2:14, 18; 3:7; *teknia* in 2:1, 12, 28; 3:7, 18; 4:4; 5:21). But the other groups subdivide the community into older and younger members—youths and fathers. The same is done in the OT (Exod. 10:9; Josh. 6:21; Isa. 20:4), where dividing people into groups on the basis of age is not at all unusual. It is possible that something similar is at work here, but a more definitive explanation is not easy to find (Brown 1982, 319).

God and the World (2:15–17)

2:15–17. A brief digression comes in verses 15–17. Verse 15 opens with a prohibition: **Do not love the world, nor the things in the world. If anyone loves the world, the love of the Father is not in him.** This verse is very much at home in the dualistic worldview of the Johannine literature, in which the "world" (*kosmos*) is a place opposed to God. The next verse is a bit more confusing, where 2:16 says, **For everything in the world—the desire of the flesh and the desire of the eyes and the pride in earthly life—is not of the Father but of the world.** The Johannine concern for the world is not usually so specific in cataloging the temptations that the world holds. The temptation of the flesh is easy to understand improperly, because flesh might immediately seem to mean "the body" or "the passions." But flesh (*sarx*) is not inherently evil. It simply signifies mundane existence. The eyes are similarly neutral. But when they are motivated by desire (*epithymia*), they are directed away from God. They focus entirely on life here and now, as opposed to being born from above and born from God (John 1:13; 1 John 4:7). More difficult to translate is the phrase rendered "pride in earthly life," which in Greek is *alazoneia biou*. The first noun, *alazoneia*, has a wide range of meaning that covers the concepts of boastfulness, pride, and arrogance. *Bios* is simply "life," but is not to be confused with the typical Johannine term for life, *zōē*. *Bios* seems to be in contrast with the life (*zōē*) that comes from God in 1 John 1:1–2, and so it may refer to a perspective on life that focuses entirely on the present world and not the eternal life that God promises. How the nouns *alazoneia* and *bios* relate to each other is not entirely clear, but their connection must have something to do with a specific arrogance, imagining that the fruits and fame of this world are enough to satisfy human needs. Again, however, the world itself is not the problem. The problem comes from a distorted perspective of worldly things and a vision bounded entirely by life in this age, neglecting the life that comes only from God (Rensberger 1997, 73–75).

Regardless of these translation difficulties, the rhetorical thrust of the passage is clear in 2:17: **And the world is passing away, as is its desire, but the one who does the will of God abides forever.** The idea that the world is passing away (*paragetai*) reminds the reader of 2:8, where it was said that the darkness is passing away (*paragetai*). In 2:8 the intention was to show that the gifts of the future are already available because "the true light is already shining." Here the point is the same, but the focus is different, turning our attention not to what is available already now but to what is awaiting in eternity: permanent abiding with God.

The Christ and the Antichrists (2:18–27)

2:18. Verse 18 opens with an excited announcement: **Children, it is the last hour!** The phrase "the last hour" (*eschatē hōra*) is otherwise unattested in the NT. The Johannine tradition knows the similar sounding phrase "the last day" (*eschatē hēmera*; John 6:39, 40, 44, 54; 11:24), but that phrase refers to the final resurrection. The "last hour" in 2:18 (2x) seems to refer to the anguish just before the end, as described by 2 Tim. 3:1–2, 5: "You must understand this, that in the last days distressing times will come. People will be lovers of themselves, lovers of money, boastful, proud, abusive, . . . having a form of godliness, but denying its power. Have nothing to do with such people!" (cf. 2 Pet. 3:3; Jude 18). First John 2:18 seems to envision a similar arrival of misleading and false Christians at the time before the end. The verse announces the arrival famously by saying, **And just as you heard that antichrist is coming . . .** The alarming announcement of the arrival of antichrist suggests that this was an expected figure, even though the term "antichrist" is unattested in the Bible, except in 1–2 John (1 John 2:18, 22; 4:3; 2 John 7). The name could mean one of two things in Greek (Culy 2004, 47–48). The prefix "anti" can connote either the idea of standing in opposition to something, or the idea of standing in place of something. An "antichrist" could thus be either a figure who fights against and opposes Christ, or a false Christ who masquerades in the guise of the true Christ. Both meanings seem to bear some relation to the activity of the opponents in 1–2 John.

First John 2:18 refers to antichrist as an expected figure ("And just as you heard . . ."), and a variety of violent figures were prophesied to come at the end times in both Jewish and Christian eschatological visions (Brooke 1912; Brown 1982, 333–37; Rensberger 1997, 76–83). The expectation of such a figure took many forms, including the monster Leviathan, or Rahab, who had warred against the God of Israel in the past (Isa. 51:9; Pss. 74:13–14; 89:10) and would also be a foe at the end of time. For example, Isa. 27:1 says of the future war between God and Leviathan, "On that day the Lord with his cruel and great and strong sword will punish Leviathan the fleeing serpent, Leviathan the twisting serpent, and he will kill the dragon that is in the sea." Earthly rulers who had warred against Israel were also expected to be locked in combat with God and his true followers in a final battle. The book of Daniel refers to the abominating desolation that took place when Antiochus IV Epiphanes (175–164 BCE) installed a statue of Zeus in the Jerusalem temple (8:13; 11:31; 12:11), and the future erection of such a sacrilege became a sign that the end was near in Daniel (Dan. 9) and in early Christian texts (Matt. 24:15). Also 2 Baruch 40.1 speaks of a final showdown with earthly rulers: "The last ruler who is left alive at that time will be bound, whereas the entire host will be destroyed. And they will carry him on Mount Zion, and my Anointed One will convict him of all his wicked deeds and will assemble and set before him all the works of his hosts" (trans. in Charlesworth 1983). Finally, 2 Esdras (4 Ezra) 11–12 begins by describing a vision of the eagle of the Roman legions: "I had a dream: I saw rising from the sea an eagle that had twelve feathered wings and three heads" (11:1), which the Messiah judges and condemns in the final days. Another opponent of God's plans who would lead the people astray in the future was "the false prophet." Deuteronomy (13:1–6; 18:20) prophesies the appearance of such a figure: "If prophets or those who divine by dreams appear among you and promise you omens or portents, and the omens or the portents declared by them take place, and they say, 'Let us follow other gods' (whom you have not known) 'and let us serve them,' you must not heed the words of those prophets or those who divine by dreams" (13:1–3).

These various Jewish figures continue to be used to describe the final battle between God and his opponents among early Christians. The dragon of Rev. 12 recalls the great beast Leviathan, and the dragon is supported by various figures that recall Jewish eschatological prophecy: the sea monster in Rev. 13; the false prophet in Rev. 16:13, 19:20, and 20:10; and the earthly kings, whom Jesus defeats after his return, in Rev. 19:11–21.

Mark 13 and 2 Thess. 2 suggest that early Christians expected a false Christ to come, an impostor at the end of time who would attempt to confuse believers, yet no similar expectation is preserved in the Fourth Gospel. But the figures from 2 Thess. 2 and Mark 13 resemble the description and work of the antichrist in 1 John, at least loosely, and suggest that the figure in view in 1–2 John is a false Christ who seeks to deceive and lead astray the faithful.

Second Thessalonians, for example, refers to this figure as the lawless one (2:9), who operates through lies (2:9) and the power of deception (*planēs*; 2:11), while Jesus exhorts his disciples in Mark 13:5 to let no one "deceive" (*planēsē*) them, and then he refers to the many who "will come in my name and say, 'I am he,'" and they will "deceive" (*planēsousi*) believers by their lie (13:6). Mark 13:21 adds, "And if anyone says to you at that time, 'Look! Here is the Messiah!' or 'Look! There he is!'—do not believe it." Such figures are "false Christs" (*pseudochristoi*; Mark 13:22) and "false prophets" (*pseudoprophētai*; Mark 13:22), who will "deceive" (*apoplanan*; Mark 13:22) people. The work of the antichrist in the Letters of John bears some resemblance to these figures from 2 Thessalonians and Mark 13, especially because the opponents in 1 John are said to be "false prophets" (*pseudoprophētai*; 4:1) who deceive (*planan*; 2:26; 3:7; *planē*; 4:6; *planos, planoi*; 2 John 7). If the figure in 1 John is related to the figure prophesied in Mark 13 and 2 Thess. 2, then the antichrist is not an opponent of Christ but an impostor of Christ, a false Christ.

The emphasis on deception in all these texts echoes the expectation of a false prophet from Deuteronomy (see above; Rensberger 1997, 78). The false prophet will lead the people of Israel astray with signs and wonders and must be removed. In turn, 1 John 4:1–3 warns about "false prophets" who have come into the world and again equates these false prophets with antichrist (see comments at 4:3; 2 John 7).

In addition, 1 John 2:18 quickly moves from a false Christ as an individual to a group of many false teachers peddling a false teaching about Christ. As soon as we hear about the singular figure called antichrist, we read that **many antichrists have appeared, which is how we know it is the last hour.** All the opponents in 1–2 John are labeled as antichrists. First John does not seem specifically troubled by a single, monstrous figure dragging Christians into deception at the end of time, but by many deceivers working in league with one another. What we seem to have here, then, is a body of false teachers and false prophets

The Wetmore Print Collection, Connecticut College

Figure 7. The Seven-Headed Beast and the Beast with Lamb's Horns by Albrecht Dürer.

leading the people astray. Their prominence and prophetic ministry are important to stress. These antichrists seem not to have been merely other Christians. They were teachers who were leading the people astray (Rensberger 1997, 78).

The shift from the singular "antichrist" to the many "antichrists" requires further comment. John of Damascus (*Orth. Faith* 4.26.1, trans. *NPNF*) offers a view that is common as a way to resolve the tension between the singular and plural. He recognizes that an individual figure is to come who is called antichrist: "in a peculiar and special sense he who comes at the consummation of the age is called antichrist." But also, in a clear allusion to 1 John 4:2–3, he also says, "Everyone, therefore, who confesses not that the Son of God came in the flesh and is perfect God and became perfect man . . . is antichrist." The individual false teachers are thus many different figures who participate in the one larger work of the single antichrist. First John expresses a similar sentiment about the relation between the one deceiver and the many deceivers. The false teachers are not motivated by the "spirit of truth" (1 John 4:6) to teach the true Christ who has come in the flesh. These many antichrists, by contrast, are motivated by the spirit of the antichrist (1 John 4:3) to teach a false Christ. As David Rensberger emphasizes, it is their deceptiveness that drives the association with a deceptive false messiah (1997, 78). They do not seem, as in Mark 13 and 2 Thessalonians, to be falsely claiming themselves to be Christ, but are rather "antichrists" in the sense that they teach a false Christ. They put a false image in the place of Christ and are themselves false brethren. As Raymond Brown writes, the traditional expectation of the impostor and the opponent of Christ is applied to those who have deviated from the Johannine traditions about Jesus and have removed themselves from the Johannine community (1982, 337).

2:19. Verse 19 shows the significance of the departure of these figures from the community by subtly adjusting the meaning of the preposition *ek/ex*. The verse says: **They went out from us, but they were never of us. For if they had been of us, they would have remained with us. But [they went out] in order that it might be made known that they are not of us.** These false prophets left the community and "went out from us" (*ex hēmon exēlthan*), where the sense of the preposition *ex* is to show separation. But this same preposition (*ek, ex*) is used for the famous Johannine phrase "to be of," as in John 10:26, where Jesus says to his opponents, "But you do not believe, because you are not of [*ek*] my sheep" (see also 18:17, 25). Those who are not "of" the community of Jesus's followers are his opponents. The same use operates here in the phrase "they were never of [*ex*] us." Thus, to go out (*ex*) from the community is to show that one is not of (*ex*) the community. Even more strongly, to leave the community is to put oneself in the place of those who persecuted the Lord, those who are not "of my sheep."

2:20–21. And you have an anointing from the Holy One and you all know. I did not write to you because you do not know the truth, but because you

know it and [you know] that every falsehood is not of the truth. In the midst of warning his readers against those who peddle a false "Christ," which means the Anointed One (*christos* in Greek means "anointed"), 1 John reminds its readers that they themselves have "an anointing [*chrisma*] from the Holy One." In this instance the "Holy One" could be either God (Hab. 3:3) or Jesus (John 6:69). Also, 2 Cor. 1:21–22 speaks of Christians being anointed (*chrisas*) by God with the Holy Spirit. Brown (1982, 369) believes that in a Johannine context the anointing here is likewise an anointing with the Spirit, associated with baptism. First John 2:21 seems to secure such a reading, since it says that this anointing empowers believers to know the truth and, in the Fourth Gospel, the Paraclete-Spirit guides believers into all truth (John 16:13). Their anointing (*chrisma*) enables them to distinguish between the false and the true Messiah (*christos*).

Several other matters deserve comment. First, the verb "you know" (*oidate*) is repeated here several times. In 1 Thessalonians, Paul regularly reminds the believers of what they already know (*oidate* in 1:5; 2:1, 2, 5, 11; 3:3–4) in order to exhort them to stand up to the struggles they face and the anguish they feel (Malherbe 2000, 84). This is another example of the paraenetic device of reminding people of things they have already learned in order to encourage them to convert their knowledge into manifest action.

The verb "you know" (*oidate*) deserves comment for another reason as well. It appeared for the first time in 1 John 2:11 and is repeated several times throughout the letter, but especially here in chapter 2 (vv. 11, 20, 21, 29). First John, before using *oida* in 2:11, defined the act of knowing with the verb *ginōskō*, which also is repeated several times throughout the letter, especially in chapter 2 (vv. 3, 4, 5, 13, 14, 18, 29). Some interpreters try to distinguish between the two senses of "knowing" in these verbs, but the distinctions do not hold up to scrutiny. Indeed, variation in vocabulary is a hallmark of the Johannine tradition, especially in the Gospel, where the same variation between these two verbs prevails. Such variation drives many of the most important concepts and terms in the Fourth Gospel. When Jesus questions Peter at 21:15–17, for instance, he uses not only two words for love (*agapan, philein*) but also two terms for caring for a flock (*boskein, poimainein*), two words for the flock (sheep, *probata*; lambs, *arnia*), as well as two interchangeable verbs for the expression "to know" (*ginōskein, eidenai*). The same variation appears in the alternation from *esthiein* (*phagein*) to *trōgein* in John 6:50–58. Especially interesting are the various terms for "seeing" (*blepein, theasthai, theōrein, idein, horan*) throughout the Gospel, as well as the alternation between *niptein* and *louein* in John 13:5–10. The sending of Jesus from the Father is referred to with both *apostellein* and *pempein*, and even the important "hour" of Jesus can be referred to as both *hōra* (2:4; 7:30; 8:20; 12:23, 27; 13:1; 17:1) and *kairos* (7:6, 8). Such a use of language is difficult to explain, but it at least reflects the rhetorical device of *variatio* (using a new word instead of repeating the same word twice), which was common in antiquity.

Verses 22–25 are incredibly complicated. These several verses speak in some detail about the nature of the false teaching of the antichrists, but readers still struggle to discern the precise nature of the error. The basic contours are clear enough; the details are murky.

2:22. Verse 22 picks up the term "falsehood" (*pseudos*) at the end of verse 21 and now personalizes it into the term "liar" (*pseustēs*), directing the character of falsehood onto the deceitful teachers: **Who is the liar, except the one who denies that Jesus is the Christ? This is the antichrist, the one who denies the Father and the Son.** If this were all we had from the teaching of the secessionists, we could understand them fairly clearly. Like the opponents of Jesus in the Fourth Gospel, the secessionists would have denied that Jesus was the Messiah (John 5 and 7–8). Some interpreters have tried to argue that such a problem afflicts the community in 1 John, on the assumption that the opposition in this letter is similar to the opposition against Jesus in the Gospel (Robinson 1962, 131; Smalley 1984, 113–14). But this seems fairly unlikely, given that the opponents in 1 John were originally members of the Johannine community, and the Gospel of John definitively states that Jesus is the Messiah and Son of God (20:31). If the opponents had accepted Jesus enough to join the community in the first place, it seems unlikely that they would need to be convinced that Jesus was the Messiah all over again.

What, then, did they believe? Some might have denied that the incarnate, earthly Jesus was really the heavenly Christ, as Cerinthus and his followers did in the second century (see "Setting and Purpose of 1 John" in the introduction). They accepted the divinity of the Savior but refused to believe that the divine heavenly Christ had actually been present in the earthly Jesus. This is the opposite of the problem in the Gospel, in which the opponents of Jesus saw him as nothing more than a man, the carpenter's son. The theology of the Gospel urged that the man Jesus was the Word made flesh. Here in 1 John the opposite problem prevails. The opponents believe that the Word has come to earth, but not that he was bound to flesh. Thus if the opponents in the Gospel saw Jesus as too exclusively human, the opponents here see him as too exclusively divine. Support for the idea that this is the false teaching, or at least close to it, comes from 1 John 4:2, which insists that Jesus Christ came in the flesh, emphasizing that the identity of the Christ and his appearance in the flesh cannot be separated. As convenient as this explanation of the opponents' Christology seems, it is not without problems. The present construal seems like a very unusual way to express such a teaching (Rensberger 1997, 80). Once we know about Cerinthus, we imagine that the evidence of 1 John *might* respond to the kinds of things that he taught, and there is nothing in the text of 1 John that would suggest otherwise. In the end we are left to speculate. The description of the false teaching is somewhat unclear.

2:23. The true teaching is more plain. Whatever the false teachers were propagating, 1 John 2:23 takes the opportunity to affirm the close connection between the Father and the Son: **The one who denies the Son does not possess the Father either; the one who confesses the Son also has the Father.** The disposition that one shows toward the Son shows also one's disposition toward the Father. The Father and the Son cannot be separated (1 John 4:15; 5:1; 2 John 9). This theological posture has its roots in the Gospel, as when Jesus says that all judgment has been given to the Son, "so that all might honor the Son just as they honor the Father. Anyone who does not honor the Son does not honor the Father who sent him" (John 5:23; cf. 12:44–45; 14:6–9; 15:23).

2:24. Verse 24 sets up a contrast between the readers and the false teachers just mentioned by placing the pronoun "you" at the very front of the sentence and saying, **You, what you heard from the beginning, let that in you abide. If what you heard from the beginning abides in you, then you also abide in the Son and in the Father.** This translation does not represent the smoothest possible English translation, but it does convey as closely as possible the word order of the Greek. The two important concerns are placed at the start of the clause, associating "you" and what was "from the beginning." The readers (you) are immediately contrasted to the false teachers, and the basis of the contrast is immediately clarified: they should allow the teaching that was heard "from the beginning" to abide in them. The sense of a teaching abiding is clarified by the curious term *proagein* in 2 John 9, meaning to advance or progress forward. Those who "progress" in 2 John 9 are contrasted with those who "abide in the teaching of Christ." Here the same idea is implicit. The false teachers move forward by moving beyond the teaching that was "from the beginning" and wrongly understanding the relationship between the Father and the Son. To abide in the correct teaching is, thus, to abide properly in both the Father and the Son, as their relationship has been understood "from the beginning."

2:25. Verse 25 is a bolt out of the blue. It seems to have little thematic connection to what precedes or follows it, adding a new dimension to the argument: **And this is the promise which he promised to us—life eternal.** As usual in these letters, we cannot be entirely sure who the third-person subject of the verb is, and thus who made the promise. John 6:40 shows that we need not make a decision, however, since it is the will of the Father that all who believe in the Son have eternal life, even as Jesus is the one who is speaking. Either the Father or the Son could have made the promise, but the close association of Father and Son in Johannine theology makes choosing irrelevant. The term "promise" (*epangelia*) is not a usual Johannine term; it appears in no other place in either the Letters or the Gospel. It is common, however, in Paul (Rom. 4:13–16; 2 Cor. 1:20; Gal. 3:14–22; Rensberger 1997, 81–82).

2:26–27. **I wrote these things to you concerning those who deceive you. As for you, the anointing that you received from him abides in you, and you have no need for anyone to teach you, but rather, just as his anointing teaches**

you about all things, being both true and not false, so also, just as he taught you, abide in him. These verses recapitulate and develop several matters that were introduced in verses 20–25. Certain issues call for closer inspection. We said above that the anointing (*chrisma*) mentioned in 2:20 was probably the anointing with the Holy Spirit. That association is made more likely here, since now we learn that the anointing has the power to teach—precisely one of the tasks ascribed to the Paraclete-Spirit in John 14:26, where the Spirit "will teach you all things and remind you of everything that I said to you." Because they are taught by the Spirit, they have no need for anyone to teach them. Why, then, is the letter written? As noted above in the discussion of 2:12–14, the repetition and affirmation of things already known is a typical feature of paraenetic discourse, not because people need further instruction, but because they need to be encouraged, under difficult circumstances, to follow what they already know is the correct course of action. Even though they are taught by the Spirit and already know what is right, they need to be reminded of it amid the spread of false teaching lest they be led astray or, in the language of 2:26, be "deceived." The nouns and verb associated with deceit are also used at 1 John 1:8; 2:26; 3:7; 4:6; 2 John 7 (see comments on 2 John 7). Here verse 27 ends by saying, "abide in him," where the pronoun "him" very likely means Jesus, who is the one through whose request the Spirit is sent into the world (John 14:16, 26). As usual, however, such pronouns could always refer to either the Father or the Son.

A new line of argument begins at 2:28 and extends to 3:10. The address "little children" (*teknia*) seems to imply a change in thought, since the previous section (2:18) began by similarly addressing the readers as "children" (*paidia*). The term *teknia* is used several others times in 1 John (2:1, 12, 28; 3:7, 18; 4:4; 5:21). Less common is *paidia*, often translated as "children" (2:14, 18). In addition to these two related terms in 1 John, all three of the Johannine Letters use the term *tekna* (children) to address the readers or to refer to Christians (1 John 3:1, 2; 5:2; 2 John 1, 4, 13; 3 John 4). Second John also refers to Christians as children (*tekna*; vv. 1, 13) who belong to their mother the Elect Lady (i.e., their home church, v. 1) and her sister (i.e., the church of the writing Elder, v. 13). Some have tried to find differences of meaning that separate these terms, suggesting, for instance, that the diminutive *teknia*, "little children," is used for people in the immediate congregation of the Elder, while the word *teknon*, "child," applies to those less familiar to the author. This is possible, but Brown (1982, 707) seems correct when he claims, "I judge it more likely that we encounter here a meaningless variant of Johannine style" (for more on variation in language and style in the Johannine tradition, see above in the discussion of 2:21). Several themes that tie this segment of the argument to other parts of 1 John will become apparent as we proceed, and one of the chief themes that defines this section is the need to imitate Jesus, to show that one is a child of God by conforming to the example set by the Son of God.

Born from Above, Born from Below (2:28–3:10)

2:28. **So now, little children, abide in him, so that when he is revealed, we might have boldness and not be shamed away from his presence at his coming.** The new line of thought marked off by the transitional phrase "so now" indicates that what is said in these verses is the natural development from what has just been said. This section further develops certain aspects of the previous section in a variety of ways, but especially by focusing on what it means to be children of God, on the nature of sin and righteousness, and on what it means for God to reveal himself.

The expectation of revelation is palpable and prominent already in the opening line, with the phrase that is here translated "so that when he is revealed." The word translated "when" is actually the word *ean*, for which a more literal rendering would be something like "if" or "if ever." But the literal reading is not the only one possible, and the term often functions as it does here, with a temporal sense to mean something closer to the Greek word *hotan*, "when, whenever."

The term translated "revealed" is the common Johannine term *phaneroō*. The verb appears four more times in the section extending to 3:10. Revelation is clearly a major theme of this part of the argument. In 1 John 1:2 "life was revealed" in the incarnation in the past, and now the community is oriented to the fuller and final "revelation" in the future with the same verb. Just as Christ "revealed" himself when he took on flesh in the incarnation, so will he "reveal" himself when he returns in glory. The term "reveal" is regularly used in the Gospel of John for the revelation of Jesus (Brown 1982, 166), such as his showing himself to his disciples following the resurrection (21:1, 14) or in the revelation to Israel at the opening of his ministry (1:31). The term is never used of the Father in the Johannine literature, so this revelation must be that of Christ.

For all the Johannine uses of the term "revealed," the Gospel never uses this term to refer to an eschatological revelation in the future. Other NT writers do use it in this way (Col. 3:4; 1 Pet. 5:4), so these lines may reflect the influence of thought patterns not entirely Johannine. And this is not the only un-Johannine term in this verse. The word here translated "his coming," *parousia*, occurs twenty-four times in the NT (e.g., Matt. 24:3, 27, 37, 39; 1 Thess. 3:13; 5:23) but is absent in the Johannine literature except here. Because language that is not typically Johannine is clustered at this point, commentators often imagine that, in some sense, there is an intrusion of non-Johannine thought in this section, and especially in this verse. There is another way in which commentators separate this section from the thought of the Gospel. Many imagine that while the Gospel of John has a very realized notion of eschatology, in which the gifts of the future are available in the present life, the Letters of John, by contrast, are largely oriented toward the future. The Letters need to rely on non-Johannine language because they express non-Johannine thought. This view is overemphasized (see introduction, "The Relationship of the Letters to the Gospel"). The Letters more closely resemble the Gospel than is sometimes reflected in scholarship, with an eschatological vision that is both realized and oriented toward the future. For the expression of a more realized eschatology, see below at 3:2–3, which balances a hope for the future with a recognition that divine blessings are available here and now.

2:29. If you know that he is righteous, you know that everyone who does righteousness has been born of him. Here for the first time appears a syntactical structure that will recur repeatedly in this section (3:3, 4, 6, 9, 10), in which the Greek word *pas* (all, every) is coupled with a participle to make a broad generalization that divides the world into two opposing groups. The purpose of this construction is to place before the members of the community two stark options, and then invite them to make a choice. Such a syntactical structure is not unrelated to the style of rhetorical *sententiae* discussed in the introduction to this commentary (see "The Rhetoric of the Letters: *Sententiae* and Social Division"). The clause "everyone who does righteousness has been born of him" marks the first example of this form. The phrase "to do righteousness" is not yet entirely clear, but 3:10 shows that to do righteousness does not mean merely to live a moral life, but something much stronger. It means to love as God loves.

3:1. Behold the kind of love the Father has given to us, such that we are called children of God. And we are. The world does not know us for this reason: it did not know him. The sentiment expressed here has its origin in the Farewell Discourses in the Gospel of John, where Jesus tells his disciples:

> If the world hates you, be aware that it hated me before it hated you. If you belonged to the world, the world would love you as its own. Because you do not belong to the world, but I have chosen you out of the world—therefore the world hates you. Remember the word that I said to you: "Servants are not greater than their masters." If they persecuted me, they will persecute you. (15:18–20)

The difference in the meaning of the enmity between believers and the world in the Gospel and in 1 John is defined by the difference in circumstances. In the Gospel, to be part of the world means to oppose Jesus. Here the world that persecutes the community is personalized in the opponents.

3:2–3. Beloved, we are now children of God, and it has not yet been revealed what we will be. It was noted above (in comments on 2:28) that many interpreters view 1–3 John in general, and this section in particular, as having an eschatology oriented toward the future and not toward the present. This verse suggests otherwise when it opens by announcing, "We are *now* children of God." Hope is also oriented toward the future, of course, because the full realization of this status is not complete: "it has not yet been revealed what we will be." One wonders how this expression relates to the next use of the verb "reveal" and especially what the subject of the verb is, when we read, **We know that when he is revealed . . .** This commentary assumes that the verb has Christ as its unstated subject. No subject is explicit, so in this case the subject of "reveal" might be impersonal, as it was in the last clause ("*It* has not yet been revealed"), or it could have Christ as its subject, as it did in 2:28. To see Christ as the subject is preferable because doing so connects the pronouns to a clear antecedent (Culy 2004, 69). The term here translated "when" is again *ean*, for which the literal translation is "if," but that here and in 2:28 should be translated "when" (see comments on 2:28). At the full revelation of Christ, **we will be like him, for we shall see him as he is. And everyone who has this hope in him purifies himself, just as he is pure.** Matthew 5:8 says that the "pure in heart shall see God," and 1 Cor. 13:12 speaks of a future vision of God at the end of time. To partake of this vision requires, of course, purification. Psalms 11:7 and 17:15 say that the just will see the face of God, thus explaining why those who will see God must make themselves holy.

3:4. Everyone who does sin also does lawlessness, and sin is lawlessness. Sin (*hamartia*) and lawlessness (*anomia*) are often treated as synonyms and paired to refer to those who do not do the will of God. Psalm 51:3 LXX, for instance, says, "I know my lawlessness [*anomia*], and my sin [*hamartia*] is ever before me." Romans 4:7 does the same: "Happy are they whose iniquities [*anomia*] are forgiven, and whose sins [*hamartia*] are covered" (see Brown 1982, 399).

3:5. And you know that he was made manifest in order that he might remove sins. And there is no sin in him. That Christ removes sins is clear in 1:9 and 2:1–2. For the sinlessness of Christ, see John 7:18.

3:6–9. The next several verses are difficult to reconcile—impossible to reconcile, actually—with the teaching on sin in 1 John 1:8–10, where we are told that those who walk in the light are those who acknowledge their sin. Now those who are on the side of God are those who *do not* sin. Verses 6–9 read: **Everyone who abides in him does not sin. Everyone who sins has neither seen him nor known him. Children, let no one deceive you. The one who does righteousness is righteous, just as he is righteous. The one who does sin is from the devil, because from the beginning the devil is a sinner. The Son of God was revealed for this reason—to undo the works of the devil. Everyone who is born of God does not do sin, for his seed abides in him, and he is not able to sin because he has been born of God.** The incompatibility of these statements with the statements on sin in 1:8–10 was addressed in the discussion of theological issues following 1 John 1:5–2:11, but two other issues merit further comment here. The statement in 3:8 that the devil is a sinner from the beginning recalls the Gospel, where the devil is called a murderer "from the beginning" (John 8:44). Does this, perhaps, relate to the murder of Abel by Cain, discussed below at 3:11–12? That is possible, since the very term used in the Gospel for murderer (*anthrōpoktonos*) will be used again in 1 John 3:15. In this sense, the "beginning" is likely not the same beginning as that in

1 John 1:1, which refers to the beginning of Jesus's ministry, but rather the primordial beginning in the early chapters of Genesis.

3:10. In this way are made manifest the children of God and the children of the devil: everyone who does not do righteousness is not from God, and he does not love his brother. This verse closes this section on an ominous note, because the mention of "not loving a brother" is going to be illustrated in the next section by Cain's murder of Abel (3:12). Those who damage the community are damaging not just fellow members of a voluntary association but their brothers and sisters in Christ.

Theological Issues

The status of believers as "children of God" is a central component of Johannine theology as well as the Johannine teaching on discipleship (John 1:12–13). But in the same way that believers are called children of God, the author of 1 John also addresses believers as his own children. Second John makes this convention even more explicit. In 2 John 1, the Elder addresses his letter to "the Elect Lady and her children," which interpreters generally understand to be a symbolic reference to a church and its members. Support for this interpretation comes from the close of the letter in 2 John 13, where the Elder speaks of "your Elect Sister and her children," a phrase that clearly refers to the Elder's own church and its members. Christians are children of God, children of their teachers, children collected within churches, and brothers and sisters of one another. The use of family language to describe ecclesiastical relations raises interesting historical questions and provides valuable insight into the social relations of early Christianity, as it seems to reflect an effort to deal with the crisis of conversion to a new faith.

The following paragraphs will explore the significance of this language in all three Letters of John, because familial language seems to be used in order to reinforce communal boundaries in ways quite similar to the use of such language in the Pauline corpus, and yet in ways that are also different from the usage in Paul, due to the particular concerns of 1–3 John.

We can begin by briefly looking more closely at the evidence from 1–3 John. The term *teknia* will be used several other times in 1 John (2:12, 28; 3:7, 18; 4:4; 5:21) and is repeatedly used to address the readers directly. Less common is the related term *paidia*, often translated as "children" (1 John 2:14, 18). In addition to these two related terms in 1 John, all three of the Johannine Letters use the term *tekna* to address the readers or to refer to Christians (1 John 3:1, 2, 10; 5:2; 2 John 1, 4, 13; 3 John 4). Second John, as noted above, refers to Christians as children and sisters (vv. 1, 13) who belong to their mother, the Elect Lady (v. 1).

The terms *tekna*, *teknia*, and *paidia* all appear in the Fourth Gospel. *Tekna* is used three times, twice for those who "are given the power to become children [*tekna*] of God" (1:12; 11:52) and once for the children of Abraham (8:39). *Teknia* is used for the very intimate words of Jesus to his disciples at the beginning of the Farewell Discourse (13:33), when he addresses "his own." This seems to parallel usage in the Letters, where the term is the preferred method of direct address to the author's "own" followers. Jesus also uses *paidia* in the Gospel of John to refer to his disciples (21:5). Each of the three terms for children, thus, has an antecedent in the Gospel.

And yet referring to fellow believers as "children" is not confined to the Johannine orbit. The convention is common in Paul, who calls the various members of his different churches "my children" (*tekna mou*, Gal. 4:19; cf. Philem. 10). For Paul, however, the language is used to emphasize that believers were converted through his efforts. They are his children because he is their father in the faith, as when he says (1 Cor. 4:14–15): "I am not writing this to make you ashamed, but to admonish you as my beloved children [*tekna*]. For though you might have ten thousand guardians in Christ, you do not have many fathers. Indeed, in Christ Jesus I became your father through the gospel." Paul calls his followers "my children" because he is their father. According to Brown (1982, 707), the Johannine tradition seems in some ways different. Believers are not called children because a human apostle is their father. They are children because God is their Father (John 1:12–13; 3:3, 5). But the Elder, as we have seen in a variety of ways, speaks to his communities in the way that Jesus spoke to his followers. The author of the Letters writes in the way that the Jesus of the Gospel speaks, using the various terms for children as a way of "imitating Jesus's affectionate address for his disciples at the Last Supper as he gave them the commandment to love" (Brown 1982, 214).

Wisdom teachers also, of course, used the language of "child" for those whom they addressed. "This pattern was influenced by the fact that the genre of wisdom admonitions had its origins in a father's instructions to his sons" (Brown 1982, 214). Sirach 2:1, for example, says, "My child [*teknon*], when you come to serve the Lord, prepare yourself for testing."

And yet the effect and function of this language in both the Pauline and Johannine corpora may best be explained through recourse to other writings, which use not only the language of children but also all forms of familial relationship. After all, believers are not only called "children" in Pauline and Johannine texts. They are also called "brothers" (1 John 2:9, 10, 11; 3:10, 12–17; 4:20, 21; 5:16; 3 John 3, 5, 10), as when Paul says, "I do not want you to be ignorant, brothers" (Rom. 1:13), a convention that he repeats numerous times. Such use of the language of fathers, brothers, and children reflects what historians call "fictive kinship," a convention in which the language of blood ties is transferred to relationships not defined by blood relations (Stowers 1986, 100–101).

Abraham Malherbe views the use of fictive kinship language as a way to compensate for a trauma in actual kinship relations experienced by converts to a new philosophy or religion experienced in antiquity. He writes, "Conversion was a disturbing experience that did not lead to a placid life in a safe harbor. The radical reorientation . . . required social, intellectual, and moral transformation that often resulted in confusion, bewilderment, and sometimes dejection" (1987, 36–37). Various things could derail a convert to a new philosophical or religious life, but social tension was high on the list of temptations. Plutarch writes about the fledgling Diogenes as he struggles to maintain the discipline of his new philosophical life:

> The Athenians were keeping holiday with public banquets and shows in the theatre and informal gatherings among themselves, and indulging in merry-making the whole night long, while Diogenes, huddled up in a corner trying to sleep, fell into some very disturbing and disheartening reflections how he from no compulsion had entered upon a toilsome and strange mode of life, and as a result of his own act he was now sitting without part or parcel in all these good things. (Plutarch, *Progress in Virtue* 77 E–F, trans. from Malherbe 1987, 40)

But it was not just a desire to live an easier life that vexed the convert to a new philosophical life. Such a person also had to face the scorn and taunts of friends and associates who wished that their friend would return to his old, familiar life. Plutarch continues, "The sober advice of friends and the bitter criticisms of the unfriendly, in the form of scoffing and joking, cause a warping and weakening of purpose, and have even made some persons renounce philosophy altogether" (78 A–C, trans. from Malherbe 1987, 39). The trauma of conversion was not confined to new adherents to the philosophical life. The tension seems to have been even more acute for the new adherents to a minority religion like Judaism. Because ties to religion were the same ties that linked one to family relations and to broader civic bodies, to leave behind the polytheism of Greek and Roman religions to follow the one God of Israel created a vast array of social tensions. The Roman historian Tacitus tells us that these social ties were one of the first things that proselytes to Judaism would cut: "The earliest lesson they receive is to despise the gods, to disown their country, and to regard their parents, children, and brothers as of little account" (*Hist.* 5.5, trans. from Malherbe 1987, 44).

Philo of Alexandria says the same, in a positive way, of proselytes to Judaism, emphasizing the need to provide new familial ties for the associations that such people lose when they leave behind their former religious lives, and all the other ties that are lost with it. Such people are known for "forsaking the ancestral customs in which they were bred. . . . They have crossed over to the pious life . . . [and are] *orphans and widows* because they have lost their protectors." Given this state of affairs, Philo says, "Let them not be denied another citizenship or other ties of *family and friendship*, and let them find places of shelter standing ready for refugees to the camp of piety" (Philo, *Spec. Laws* 1.309; 1.52).

Such a trauma has a special resonance for those in the Johannine orbit. We see them experience such rejection clearly in the Gospel of John. John 15:18–16:2 tells us, for instance, that believers were expelled from synagogues when they entered the Johannine circle of belief, and their anxiety may have been even more personal. When the blind man in John 9 was questioned by the leaders of Israel, his parents abandoned him in his hour of need (9:22–23), hoping to avoid the fate of expulsion that awaited him.

When they entered the Christian fold, these new Christians became brothers and sisters of one another; the author of 1 John can call them his children and the children of the various churches to

A Jewish Proselyte

A newly faithful Jew reflects on the loss of old family ties and the need for new ones:

"Preserve me, O Lord, for I am desolate, for my father and my mother have renounced me, because I destroyed and crushed their gods, and now I am an orphan and desolate. I have no other hope but in Thee, Lord, for thou art the father of orphans, the protector of the persecuted, and helper of the distressed. . . . Look upon my orphan state, Lord, for I have fled to thee." (Jos. Asen. 12.11; 13.1, trans. from Malherbe 1987, 44)

which they belong (2 John 1, 13). Apparently, older members of the community can also be called "fathers" (1 John 2:13–14). This fictive family developed as a response to harsh treatment from actual blood kin. The Johannine community was a new family, formed for people who experienced the trauma of separation from their blood relations and their home in the synagogue. Being children of God and children of the Elder is interchangeable, just as fellowship with God depends on fellowship with the Elder. Now, however, the new family is experiencing its own trauma, and the split in the community is cast in the form of a struggle between brothers and sisters. The statement in 1 John 2:9–11 is instructive. Those who undermine the community are injuring their family, their brothers and sisters. The trauma of this split is a trauma in the family. Just how far this imagery goes in explaining the rift in the community will become clear in the next section of the letter, beginning in 3:11–12, where the paradigmatic figures for family strife are Cain and Abel. Those who injure members of the church are committing nothing less than fratricide.

1 John 3:11–4:21

Love for God, Love for One Another

Introductory Matters

Delineating the rhetorical or narrative units of any biblical text is difficult, and no two interpreters will divide the same book in the same way. This is especially true of 1 John, given its kaleidoscopic use of imagery and the circular flow of the argument. It circles back over the same themes and terminology regularly, adding and changing phrases or words slightly each time, and yet ever seeming to say very similar things (see the "Introductory Matters" section for 5:1–21). Deciding where one unit concludes and another begins is not always easy. Given such problems in separating the material, the present section of this commentary is quite large and deals with many different topics, starting from 3:11 and extending through 4:21. The line that begins the section is one of the clear points of transition in 1 John. We see that 3:11 stands apart as marking a new line of thought in many ways, not least because it is the first verse in 1 John that actually repeats the new commandment from the Gospel, "Love one another." The new stage that begins at 3:11 finally ends at 4:21, which says, "The one who loves God loves also his brother." The rhetorical arc bends from one discussion of love to another. Several smaller units stand between 3:11 and 4:21. The first two sections, 3:11–18 and 3:19–24, focus on the story of Cain and Abel, applying this story to the problems in the community. Verse 23 of chapter 3 gives a double commandment: to believe in the name of Jesus Christ and to love one another. This commandment determines the structure of chapter 4, because these two themes—Christology and love for one another—are dealt with separately in two distinct sections in chapter 4. Thus 4:1–6 addresses the question of true and false belief, and the proper understanding of the identity of Jesus Christ; 4:7–21 returns to the theme of love, and especially the theme of love as a means for abiding in God, with a brief interlude (vv. 13–16) that returns again to the question of true confession and Christology.

---

1 John 3:11–4:21 in the Rhetorical Flow

Introductory prologue (1:1–4)
The light and the darkness (1:5–2:11)
Who are the children of God? (2:12–3:10)
▶ **Love for God, love for one another (3:11–4:21)**
  Love one another (3:11–18)
  Believe in the Son (3:19–24)
  True teaching is "from God" (4:1–6)
  True fellowship is "from God" (4:7–21)

Tracing the Train of Thought

Love One Another (3:11–18)

3:11. For this is the message which you heard from the beginning: to love one another. This verse is selected by Raymond Brown (1982, 467) as one of two major structuring verses in the letter. The other structuring phrase comes in 1:5, which shares with 3:11 a basic similarity in form:

1:5	*Kai estin hautē hē angelia hēn akēkoamen ap' autou*
	And this is the message that you have heard from him
3:11	*Hoti hautē estin hē angelia hēn ēkousate ap' archēs*
	For this is the message that you heard from the beginning

First John 1:5 opens the argument of the entire letter. The close resemblance that 3:11 has with 1:5 reinforces Brown's assumption that 3:11 also marks a major new moment in the argument. The significance of 3:11 within the broad sweep of the letter is reinforced in another way as well. This is the first time in 1 John that we hear the precept "Love one another," the form of the love command given by Jesus (John 13:34; 15:12). Prior to this, the warrant to love fellow Christians has been expressed in terms of loving the brother (1 John 2:10; 3:10). That usage will continue in the present section (3:14; 4:20), but the more common expression in chapters 3 and 4 is the one used here in 3:11: "Love one another" (3:11, 23; 4:7, 11, 12).

The expression "from the beginning" appears in 1:1, the very first phrase in the letter. "The beginning" refers to everything that has been passed down and experienced since the ministry of Jesus. It is fitting to refer to "the beginning" here because 3:11 finally issues the command to love in the formula actually used by Jesus during his earthly ministry. This wording of the promise, in other words, is the one that was actually spoken "from the beginning."

3:12. As soon as the formulation "Love one another" enters the argument, in 3:12 the approach to love is immediately turned back temporarily to the need to love the brother. The brothers in question are Cain and Abel, and especially Cain, who **was of the evil one and slaughtered his brother. And why did he slaughter him? Because his works were evil and those of his brother were righteous.** The exemplary quality of the story of Cain and Abel (Gen. 4:1–16) is entirely negative. Hebrews 11:4 focuses on Abel as a positive example, but Jude 10–11 is more akin to the argument here, using Cain to exemplify a path to be avoided. He is often used for this purpose in ancient Judaism. Philo writes several treatises that deal with Cain and Abel (*The Cherubim, The Sacrifices of Abel and Cain, The Worse Attacks the Better,* and *The Posterity and Exile of Cain*). Other Jewish writers do the same. Josephus (*Ant.* 1.52–62) bears an interesting relation to the present text because his retelling of the story of Cain and Abel uses language similar to 1 John. He describes Abel as being concerned with righteousness (*dikaiosynēs*) and Cain as being most evil (*ponērotatos*), which mirrors 1 John, where Abel's works are said to be righteous (*dikaia*) and those of Cain are evil (*ponēra*). Matthew 23:35 also refers to the "blood of Abel the righteous" (*Abel tou dikaiou*).

Here in 1 John 3, Cain represents the opponents of the author, who are mentioned in the immediately preceding section (3:7–10). Verses 7–10 delineated the difference between God's children (*tekna tou theou*) and the devil's children (*tekna tou diabolou*). Verse 10 closed that section by referring to "the one who does not love his brother." In the broad sweep of 1 John, believers are regularly called brothers (2:9, 10, 11; 3:10, 13, 14, 15, 16, 17; 4:20, 21; 5:16). Those who left the community, the secessionists, must also at one time have been called brothers. But they turned on the community and now hate their brothers, just as Cain turned on his brother. The struggle with the opponents is projected onto the characters of Cain and Abel.

As 3:11 transitions to 3:12, a brief phrase that was not translated above makes this association clear: *ou kathōs Cain.* The construction *ou kathōs* is used rarely in the NT (John 6:58; 14:27; 2 Cor. 8:5). The phrase means "**not like Cain, who was of the evil one.**" The term *kathōs*, which means "like, as," typically carries a positive connotation in 1 John and illustrates how believers should act in a way "just like" a positive exemplar (2:6; 3:3, 7; 4:17). Here the term is used in a negative sense. Cain was a brother to Abel and then slew Abel, precisely like the opponents, who were brothers to the community and then departed from and rejected the community. The paraenetic thrust of the Cain imagery is clear: Do not be like Cain. Do not leave the community.

The imagery and language of John 8:39–44 also lies behind this section. In the Gospel, Jesus argues with his opponents about whether they are children of Abraham or of the devil. Jesus tells them that they do the works of their father, the devil, by wanting to kill him, since the devil was a "murderer [*anthrōpoktonos*] from the beginning" (8:44). The term *anthrōpoktonos* ("murderer") will appear below (3:15). Its only appearances in the NT are here and in the Gospel of John, making the connection with the Gospel clear. But even before the use of that term, the Gospel passage is already relevant here. Cain is not born from God, but from the devil, so he does the works appropriate for one born from the evil one. He does evil.

The story of Judas in the Gospel of John must also lie behind these verses. Judas accomplishes the work of the devil (13:2, 27), and he behaves like Cain. He had been one of the twelve disciples, even though his identity as the betrayer had always been known to Jesus (6:71). Judas had never been a true disciple, but was a disciple in appearance. When he betrayed the Lord, he showed that he had never been anything but a false disciple. The opponents in 1 John did the same and behaved like Judas: "They went out from us, but they were never of us, for if they had been of us, they would have remained with us" (2:19).

3:13. And do not be amazed, brothers, if the world hates you. In two subtle but very real ways, this line continues the imagery of verses 11–12. Although 1 John regularly refers to the readers as "brothers," this is the only time when they are directly addressed as such. With the story of the brother Cain fresh in their minds, they are reminded that they too are brothers and sisters who have been betrayed. The imagery of a brother betrayed from the story of Cain and Abel is being directly projected onto the readers, subtly but clearly. The imagery of the betrayal of Judas is also subtly continued. Judas betrays Jesus during the Farewell Discourses in the Gospel of John, and thus shows the animosity of the world and of the devil (13:1–2, 21–30). In those same discourses, Jesus teaches his disciples that the world would hate them, just as it hated him (15:18–16:2). The betrayal of the secessionists shows the realization of this prophecy.

3:14–15. We know that we have passed from death into life, for we love the brothers. The one who does not love abides in death (3:14). The shift from "you" to "we" in verse 13 has a pedagogical quality, designed to urge the readers to remember that they are still part of the community, still part of the "we"—provided they make the right choice (see discussion of 1:1–4). They can choose to remain within the fold and abide in new life, or to follow Cain and Judas and to abide in the realm of death, following the evil one. This is one of only a few examples where the phrase "abide in" (*menein en*) or "be in" is used to refer to something negative. The formula typically connotes a positive circumstance. In John 12:46, though, we read, "I have come as light into the world, so that everyone who believes in me should not abide in the darkness," and at 1 John 2:9 we are told, "Whoever says, 'I am in the light,' while hating a brother or sister, is still in the darkness." Because God gives life and because God is light, to be in darkness and in death is to be separated from God and thus to be in the realm of the evil one.

Wikimedia Commons/Honolulu Academy of Arts

Figure 8. Cain Killing Abel by Gaetano Gandolfi.

The connection with the devil is more explicit in verse 15: **Everyone who hates his brother is a murderer, and you know that every murderer does not have life eternal abiding in him.** Does this verse imply that real murder is being committed? This is always possible. In John 16:2 Jesus says, "They will put you out of the synagogue; in fact, the time is coming when anyone who kills [*apokteinas*] you will think they are offering a service to God." Some have speculated as to whether the opponents in 1 John have joined league with those who are persecuting Christians here in John 16:1–2, and might actually be killing the members of the community. The suggestion is possible but highly implausible. No other notice exists of real murder being committed. Closer to the point at hand is the saying of the Matthean Jesus in the Sermon on the Mount: "You have heard that it was said to those of ancient times, 'You shall not murder.' . . . But I say to you that if you are angry with a brother or sister, you will be liable to judgment" (Matt. 5:21–22). The betrayal committed by the opponents is so great that murder is the only way to describe it.

3:16. We have known love in this way: he laid down his life for us, and we ought to lay down our lives for the brothers. The contrast with Cain and Judas could not be more pronounced. Cain and Judas took the lives of others. The one who knows the love of Christ not only should avoid the negative examples of Cain and Judas but also should follow the positive example of Christ. Far from taking the life of another, the believer should, on behalf of others, lay down his or her own life. The language of laying down one's life, especially when applied to Christ, draws directly from the Gospel of John. In the Good Shepherd discourse in John 10, Jesus says that the Good Shepherd "lays down [*tithenai*] his life" for the sheep (10:11, 15, 17, 18). Just as in the present text, Jesus will direct his disciples to follow his example and to lay down their lives for one another (15:13). The act of imitation is clarified here by the repetition

Laying Down One's Life

First John 3:16 defines love by insisting that Christians must follow Christ in laying down their lives for one another. Jesus famously tells his disciples to do the same in John 15:13. But there is also a less well-known example of Jesus urging his disciples to imitate his sacrificial death in the Gospel of John, and it is related to 1 John 3:16 by the use of the verb *tithenai*. The relevant scene seems somewhat remote from the act of sacrificial death, and occurs during the footwashing scene in the Johannine Farewell Discourses. After Jesus washes his disciples' feet, he tells them, "I have given you an example, in order that you might do as I have done to you" (John 13:15). In saying this, did Jesus mean literally that the disciples should wash one another's feet? The context of these discourses is the night of Jesus's betrayal, as he reflects on his departure, and so the footwashing unfolds beneath the shadow of Jesus's impending death. Jesus's coming sacrifice further impinges on the scene when one compares the terms Jesus uses for the footwashing to the language he uses in John 10 when the Good Shepherd describes the nature of his ministry. He lays down his life and takes it up again, using the verbs *tithenai* (lay down) and *lambanein* (take up).

> "I lay down my life [tithenai] in order that I might take it up [lambanein] again." (10:17)

> "I lay it down [tithenai], and I have the authority to take it up [lambanein] again." (10:18)

As he washes the disciples' feet in John 13, Jesus acts out the same verbs:

> "He rose from the table, laid down [tithenai] his robe, and took up [lambanein] a towel." (13:4)

> "When he had washed their feet, he took up [lambanein] his robe." (13:12)

Given the verbal parallels, it seems that when Jesus washes his disciples' feet and then tells them to go and do likewise, he is telling them to lay down their lives for one another. First John 3:16 teaches the same message (see Brown 1970, 2.551).

of the verb *tithenai*. Jesus "laid down" (*ethēken*) his life, and believers ought, in the same way, to "lay down" (*theinai*) theirs.

3:17–18. **Whoever possesses the abundant life of the world, and then sees his brother in need, but shuts off from him any of his compassion, how does the love of God dwell in him? Little children, let us love not in word or in speech, but in action and in reality.** The phrase here translated "abundant life of the world" is really just the term *bios*, "life." The translation "abundant life" was chosen partly due to the context, a scenario in which one person has enough to share with another. Also in mind is the use of this term in 1 John 2:16, where it exemplified the presumptuous and self-satisfied sense that the delights of this earthly life can satisfy human longing for the divine. A person so well satisfied with earthly goods should not watch the suffering of others without offering whatever he is able.

The phrase "love of God" is ambiguous and was discussed at length when it first appeared in 1 John 2:5. It could refer to love that comes from God toward us, love that we show toward God, or love that characterizes God. As was said at 2:5, one hesitates to choose one option over the other. First John 4:19 reminds us that human love and divine love are united: "We love because he first loved us." Human love is an extension of God's love. To this can be added as well 4:21: "The one who loves God loves also his brother."

Believe in the Son (3:19–24)

3:19–20. These verses mark a sudden shift into a digression. Verses 11–18 had as their focus the relationship that believers have with one another, especially in light of the departure of the false community members. Verse 19 now turns unexpectedly to the relationship between human beings and God. The section opens clearly enough in 19a: **And in this way, we will know that we are of the truth.** The language and phrasing of this verse are very much at home in the Letters of John in general as well as in this context. In 3:8–9 a distinction was made between those who are "of [ek] the devil" and those who are "of [ek] God." To be "of [ek] the truth" in the present verse is the same as to be "of God."

The assurance that we are "of the truth" seems to be focused against some form of anxiety about the future judgment (Lieu 2008, 154). The nature of this anxiety is explained in verses 19b–20: **And in this we shall know that we are of the truth, and in his presence we will reassure our heart [that], even if our heart condemns us, that God is greater than our heart.** These statements are incredibly difficult to untangle, due to a great number of textual variants and also to a difficulty in understanding the grammar even after a sound text is established. The meaning of every important word is contested, and the translation of the passage as a whole depends on a variety of moving parts being brought into alignment. One thinks of trying to solve a Rubik's Cube. Any panel that moves on one side affects panels on every other side, and only by accounting for the whole can one develop a coherent translation of this verse.

The most basic grammatical problem is the repetition of the word *hoti*, which this commentary translates as "that." It appears in two places where its meaning can be contested, and it has potentially three different meanings. It can mean either "that" or "because," or it could be the indefinite relative pronoun *hoti*, which is formed by blending the relative pronoun *ho* with the indefinite pronoun *ti*, to form the English phrase "in whatever way." All three translations are valid options for the first *hoti* in verse 20a. Only "that" or "because" are options in 20b. The problem can be illustrated by translating everything in the line clearly, while giving all the variations for *hoti* in italics together, as follows:

3:19b		and before him we shall reassure our heart
3:20a	*that/because/with respect to what*	our heart accuses us
3:20b	*that/because*	God is greater than our heart

In the end, no two translators render the phrase in the same way. The translation chosen here understands the word *hoti* as "that" in both 3:20a and 20b. Such a thing is not at all impossible and is called the resumptive use of *hoti*. When a subordinate clause intervenes after the term "that," then the term "that" is stated not only before the subordinate clause but also after it. *Hoti* is "resumed." Even in English we often colloquially employ the resumptive "that," as when we say such things as, "Tell them *that*, if they go to the store and see our friends, *that* they should call us." This is a silly sentence, but the point is made. We often speak like this in English, and the Greeks did the same, whether speaking or writing. This solution seems the easiest and cleanest way to account for the problems associated with *hoti*. The first appearance of the term "that" is placed in brackets in the translation in order to indicate that it is present in the Greek text, but need not be present in an English translation.

Difficulties extend beyond grammar. Many of the important words in this section have contested meanings, beginning with the phrase translated as "in his presence." The Greek word is *emprosthen*, an adverb functioning as a preposition. In and of itself, its meaning is fairly obvious. But in 3:22 the similar term *enōpion* is used. Some have tried to discern a difference in the two words. The variation, however, is purely stylistic and precisely the sort of thing we have seen many times in 1 John (see comments on 2:21).

In 3:19b, the verb translated as "reassure" is *peithein*. The primary sense of the word is "convince, persuade, appeal to" (BDAG 791), but it could also mean to "reassure or calm, set at ease." The word takes its meaning from its context (Lieu 2008, 155), and context suggests that the sense of reassurance seems most likely in the present case, because of what will be said in 3:21 about having boldness before God. Christians need not be ashamed but can stand boldly in the divine presence. This sets the conscience at ease and calms and "reassures" the anxious person. Hence, *peithein* seems to be best rendered as "reassure."

The object of reassurance is the heart. The heart can certainly condemn a person. It is often remarked that, in the Semitic sense of the self, the heart is the seat of moral reflection (Brown 1982, 455). In 1 Sam. 24:5 we read, "David was stricken to the heart because he had cut off a corner of Saul's cloak." Likewise, in Acts 2:37 we read of the people of Jerusalem, "Now when they heard this, they were cut to the heart and said to Peter and to the other apostles, 'Brothers, what should we do?'" In a biblical view, the heart is the seat of moral reflection—and of self-condemnation. The heart, therefore, must be reassured in the face of coming judgment so that it does not condemn a person.

105

The next line is a puzzle. What does it mean to say that God knows all? Why does this help? Two meanings are possible (Brown 1982, 458). First, God's omniscience might not be reassuring at all. It may be precisely the thing that drives one to anxiety. This is certainly the sense of God's omniscience in a text like Prov. 24:12: "If you say, 'Look, we did not know this'—does not he who weighs the heart perceive it? Does not he who keeps watch over your soul know it? And will he not repay all according to their deeds?" The sense of the Proverbs text is that nothing can be hidden from God. His all-knowing eye cannot be avoided, and our sins cannot be hidden. This is not reassuring but daunting. As was just said above, however, verse 21 concludes this section with a note of reassurance that we can have boldness before God. Thus, the fact that God knows all things is meant to reassure believers that they need not fall before God's judgment. In John 21:17, for example, Peter is saddened and alarmed that Jesus asks him a third time whether he loves Jesus. Peter relies on Jesus's omniscience to certify his love. He says, "Lord, you know all things. You know that I love you."

Judith Lieu adds one final thing about the tone of reassurance for Christians in this section, which hearkens back one last time to the discussion of Cain. In his omniscience, God knew about Cain's wicked act (Gen. 4:9–10), and even when Cain is expelled from his home, God does not allow him to be killed by others (4:13–16). If God preserves a murderer, how much more will he preserve those who strive for what is good. As Lieu (2008, 156) writes, "How much more can those who have not shared in Cain's ways be sure that they will continue to enjoy the safety of God's presence."

3:21–22. Beloved, if our hearts do not condemn us, we have boldness before God. This boldness has been discussed before as an eschatological boldness that inspires one to stand firm and confident at the final judgment (see comments at 2:28). But it is also a sign of intimacy with God (see "Theological Issues" following 4:21 below). Boldness is something shared among friends. In the present argument, such intimate boldness is demonstrated by the fact that **whatever we request, we receive from him.** Jesus promises the same thing in the Gospel of John when he says: "I will do whatever you ask in my name, so that the Father may be glorified in the Son. If in my name you ask me for anything, I will do it" (14:13–14), and "If you abide in me, and my words abide in you, ask for whatever you wish, and it will be done for you" (15:7; cf. 15:16; 16:23–24, 26; Matt. 7:7; 18:19; 21:22). This does not mean, of course, that just any request can be made of God, or that just any request will be granted. The requests must be fitting for God. They must be requests that are in line with the warrant to **keep his commandments** and that we **do things pleasing in his sight.**

3:23. And this is his commandment—that we believe in the name of his Son Jesus Christ and that we love one another, just as he gave the commandment to us. The verb *pisteuein* (to believe) is one of the most important words for the Gospel of John, where it occurs roughly one hundred times, and is used in nineteen of the twenty-one chapters of the Gospel. Only chapters 15 and 21 omit the term. This is the first time that the verb has appeared in 1 John, and it will be used only eight more times (4:1, 16; 5:1, 5, 10 [3x], 13). It is never used in 2 or 3 John. The reason for its meager appearance may not be complicated. In the Gospel, the great struggle with opponents was a struggle between belief and unbelief. The term *pisteuein* has a special prominence in such a struggle. In 1 John, by contrast, the struggle is not between belief and unbelief, but between right belief and wrong belief.

As for the content of belief, to believe in Jesus's name is the same as believing in Jesus, and 1 John can alternately refer to "believing in the Son of God" (5:10) and "believing in the name of the Son of God" (5:13). The same object is in view in spite of the different formulations (see comments on 2:12). Here 3:23 also sets out the two themes that will be dealt with separately in chapter 4: the issue of true belief versus false belief (4:1–6) and the theme of Christians' love for one another (4:7–21).

3:24. And the one who keeps his commandments abides in him, and [God abides] in him. Abiding (*menein*) is one of the most important and common words in the Letters of John. The verb *menein* is meant to "connote having a deep and lasting relationship" (von Wahlde 2010, 60; see 60–61 for discussion). The term has occurred many times in 1 John up to this point, with many nuances (von Wahlde 2010). Believers abide in God (2:6; 3:24a), in the Son and in the Father (2:24), and in Jesus (2:28; 3:6). In addition to these personal relationships defined by abiding, the term also defines believers' abiding in the light (2:10) and in love (4:16). A negative relationship can also be defined by abiding. Those who do not love abide in death (3:14). Likewise, certain things are said to abide in a Christian: the word of God (2:14); what was heard from the beginning (2:24); the anointing (2:27); God's seed (3:9); and the love of God (3:17). Negative associations are covered by abiding as well, as when the murderer does not have eternal life abiding in him (3:15). The one who does the will of God will abide forever (2:17).

In the present verse, a totally new sense of abiding is introduced: mutual abiding of the believer and God, a notion that will appear again in 4:12–16. Raymond Brown defines this circumstance well: "[Abide] . . . communicates two important points: first, that the Christian's relationship to God is not just a series of encounters but a stable way of life; second, that the stability does not imply inertia but a vitality visible in the way one walks" (1982, 260).

In the Gospel of John, as Jesus prepares to depart from the world, he tells his disciples in the Farewell Discourses that he will send the Spirit, and the Spirit will abide among them (14:16–17). Here in the final verse of 1 John 3, the Spirit is precisely the entity that makes it clear that God abides in the believer: **And in this we know that he abides in us—he has given to us from his Spirit.**

True Teaching Is "from God" (4:1–6)

4:1. The argument contained in 4:1–6 is a tight unit of thought. It is motivated by the mention of the Spirit in 3:24, which inspires the discussion about whether a given spirit is from God. The section from 4:1 to 4:6 is marked off by a beginning that is mirrored in its ending. The first verse urges the readers to put spirits to the test, and then verse 6 concludes with "in this way we know the spirit of truth and the spirit of deceit," returning to the idea of putting spirits to the test.

In spite of the focus on Christology, the section is still concerned with the relationships that believers have with one another, relationships based in love. For this reason, the line of argument opens by addressing the readers intimately, by calling them **Beloved**. As the instruction continues, they are told that they should **not trust every spirit, but test the spirits, [to see] whether they are from God**. At 2:20–27 the readers were reminded that they have been anointed with the Spirit, by which they "know the truth" (2:20–21). They have no need of anyone to teach them, because they also know that "every falsehood is not of the truth" (2:21). In that discussion in chapter 2, the spiritual discernment of the readers in 2:21, 26 is coupled with a description of the opponents in 2:22–23. The readers are able to discern truth from falsehood because they are taught by the Spirit.

The same logic applies in the present discussion. Immediately after believers are reminded of the gift of the Holy Spirit (3:24), they are urged to test the truth or falsehood of the opponents' theology (4:2–6). The connection between the Spirit and the false theology of the opponents in both chapters 2 and 4 may not be coincidental. In John 14:26, Jesus promises that the Spirit-Paraclete will be sent by the Father, and "he will teach you all things." Later, in 16:12–13, Jesus says, "I have many things to say to you, but you are not able to bear them now. But when he comes, the spirit of truth, he will guide you in all truth." In each of these Gospel passages, the teaching of the Spirit is bounded by the teaching of Jesus. The Spirit does not teach new things, but things that are in accord with what Jesus taught. John 14:26 says that the Spirit will remind the disciples of everything Jesus said, and 16:13–15 says that the Spirit will say nothing on its own but only what Jesus directs. Even so, the promise that the Spirit would have a teaching function after the ministry of Jesus might have inspired people to think that the ongoing revelation of the Spirit would guide them into new territory. This may explain the use of the verb *proagein* ("go ahead") in 2 John 9. The opponents may feel that the revelation of Jesus is being supplemented and pushed forward by further revelation of the Spirit. If this is true, then we have further insight into what it means to say that the opponents are not abiding in what was taught from the beginning (1:1; 2:24).

The criteria for separating truth from falsehood are also provided. The notion that one could establish criteria for determining truth, or for deciding

"By This We Know": The Criterion of Truth

In 1 John 4:1–6, believers are instructed regarding the criteria for distinguishing truth from falsehood. The pursuit of a criterion to separate truth from falsehood was common in ancient philosophy, and the debates of the philosophers influenced the early church. Several philosophical schools contemporary with early Christianity—Epicureans, Stoics, and Skeptics—contended over whether there was such a thing as a "criterion of truth," a final arbiter in determining truth, a factor that did not need to be defended or supported itself, but that could support what is true or convict what is false in other matters (see Lucretius, *Things* 4.469–521). These criteria of truth are not in and of themselves open to debate. They are said to be self-evident. Epicurus is the innovator in this pursuit. The key term in epistemology for Epicurus is *kanōn*. A *kanōn* was a tool for making a straight line or for measuring, much like our modern ruler, and its close synonym in the thought of Epicurus is the term "criterion" (cf. *Letter to Herodotus* in Diogenes Laertius, 10.37–38). The three criteria posited by Epicurus are sensations, preconception (*prolēpsis*), and feelings (*pathos*). If our sensations lead us to make an improper judgment, then the fault does not lie with the sensations, which are accurate, but with the judgment that was founded on them. The Stoics develop this program in a slightly different direction, locating the criterion of truth not in sense impressions themselves, but in the cognitive impressions. The Skeptics chose instead to suspend all judgment (see Plutarch, *Col.* 1122A–F). Their purpose was to destroy any foundation that other philosophers established in order to force their opponents into an ever-expanding infinite regression of argument. They rejected the existence of a criterion of truth.

In the debates between orthodoxy and heresy in the second century, the concern among Hellenistic philosophers for finding a "criterion of truth" became a central concern of early Christian theologians. Irenaeus argues that the gnostics would develop a new line of argument in every debate (*Haer.* 1.18.1; 1.21.5), leading to the same infinite regress that the Stoics and Epicureans tried to avoid when they argued with the Skeptics. In response, Irenaeus and others establish the "rule of faith" as the criterion of truth. With regard to gnostic readings of Scripture, Irenaeus declares, "Anyone who keeps unswervingly in himself the canon of truth [*kanona tēs alētheias*] . . . will restore each of the passages [of Scripture] to its proper order and . . . fit it into the body of truth" (*Haer.* 1.9.4). The "rule of faith" is the baseline that allows meaningful discussion to take place. It is not debatable in and of itself, but it allows meaningful discussion and debate to begin.

And yet the criterion of truth should not be considered to be a merely intellectual matter. It was not for Irenaeus, and it is not for 1 John. When the contemporary ascetical writer Archimandrite Zacharias discusses the pursuit of dogmatic truth, he recognizes the need to avoid error, but he also does not focus solely on theology and biblical hermeneutics. He directs the criterion of truth to the Christian life. As Zacharias (2006, 4) reflects on the work of St. Silouan of Mount Athos, he writes, "With apostolic conviction, St. Silouan . . . says somewhere that the criterion for the presence of the Holy Spirit, the criterion of the truth, is the love for one's enemies."

between truth and falsehood, was common among philosophers contemporary with 1 John. In the effort to avoid endless skepticism and to be able to make positive statements about reality, criteria of truth were sought to serve as the basis for fuller philosophical systems. The criteria of truth were not in and of themselves open for debate. They were the factors that would provide the basis for debate on other matters. In the present discussion in 1 John, the readers must discern the truth or falsehood of the things being taught to them. There are, broadly speaking, two categories of criteria (Black 1998, 426). Verses 2–3 offer a christological criterion that has to do with the identity of Jesus. The truth is present in those who believe particular things, and the truth is absent from those who teach the opposite. Verses 5–6 present a criterion based more on the experience of the community, though the experience is cast in a theological mold.

The reason that believers must test the spirits is given at the end of 4:1, where we read that **many false prophets have gone out into the world**. The opponents are here described in ways that are somewhat similar to, and yet also different from, the description of their activity in chapter 2. The opponents were said at 2:19 to have "gone out," and the same is said here. They were said to have taught what is false (2:21–22), and they are bearers of falsehood here also. But now the nature of their false teaching gains a new dimension. They are not merely false teachers. They are also called false *prophets*. This may be significant. If the teaching of the opponents was inspired by some supposed further teaching from the Spirit-Paraclete, perhaps, under the influence of the Spirit, they have construed themselves as prophets (Rensberger 1997, 109–11). In early Christianity, prophecy was not merely the utterance of ecstatic speech, but also involved teaching under the guidance of the Spirit (1 Cor. 14:1–6, 22–25; Rev. 2:20; 10:11). The opponents may have claimed to be inspired by the Spirit. The readers of 1 John are, for this reason, urged in 4:1 to test the spirits. In Deut. 13:1–5 and 18:20–22, the chief crime that false prophets commit is to say, "Let us follow other gods . . . and let us serve them" (13:2). The teaching of those "who went out" could be construed as the seduction to follow another Christ, since they do not adhere to what has been taught "from the beginning" (2:22–24; 2 John 9). In this sense, they are very much like the false prophets warned against in Deuteronomy.

The notice that the false prophets have gone out into the world is not a casual comment. While the Johannine tradition says that God loves the world (John 3:16; 1 John 4:9), it is also emphatically the case that the world is in rebellion against God (4:19). Everything that is in the world is not "of the Father" (1 John 2:16), and so it is passing away (2:17). Thus those who are "of the Father" are strangers in the world. First John 3:1 says that "the world does not know us because it did not know him [God]." If the opponents, therefore, go out into the world, this says something about their relationship to the Father and to the truth. Brown writes of their going out into the world: "In so doing they found their spiritual home: It was the Evil Spirit that led them to distort Jesus to the point of negation, and the world to which they have gone is the realm of which that Spirit is the Prince" (1982, 503). In the Gospel, the world was the home for all those people who denied Jesus. In 1 John, it is the home for people who so thoroughly distort the identity of Jesus that they actually deny him.

4:2. In this way you know the Spirit of God—every spirit which confesses Jesus Christ as having come in the flesh is from God. The criterion of truth in 4:2–3 is christological. The Spirit of God is clearly present in someone who confesses Jesus Christ as having come in the flesh. The term translated "flesh" here is the Greek word *sarx*, appearing in 1 John only here and in 2:16, which refers to the "desire of the flesh." In that verse, the desire of the flesh was irretrievably associated with the world and was passing away alongside the world. Now the circumstances are different. Those who confess that Jesus Christ has come in the flesh are "of God." This is so because, as was stated in the discussion at 2:16, flesh itself is neutral and represents earthly human existence. The desire of the flesh is negative because it leads one to use earthly human existence in a manner that leads people away from God. But to say that Jesus arrived in the flesh is to say that he has entered human life. This is a basic christological claim of the Fourth Gospel (John 1:14): "The Word became flesh."

What, therefore, is the significance of the flesh in the battle with the opponents in 1 John? What was the teaching of the opponents that required this insistence on Jesus Christ coming in the flesh? Scholarly opinion varies widely. Several things are possible; nothing is certain. It is possible, for instance, that the opponents denied that Jesus really and actually became flesh, along the lines of what we know from certain figures in the second century cataloged under the label docetists (from the Greek *dokein*, "to seem"). If the opponents were docetists, then they would have argued that Jesus did not really take on flesh, did not really become human, but only "seemed" to do so. He put on humanity like a costume, but only a confused person would believe that he really took on human flesh. That is one possibility. Another is the teaching of Cerinthus, who taught that the earthly human Jesus and the heavenly Christ were two different entities. If 1 John argues against such a teaching, then the affirmation "Jesus Christ has come in the flesh" would be a way of uniting the earthly and the heavenly into one figure, since Cerinthus tries to separate them. Finally, it is possible that the opponents represent none of these known heresies and instead believe that Jesus arrived in the flesh, but that his flesh was in no way salvific. Nothing that he did in the flesh mattered for human beings (see Rensberger 1997, 110–11; von Wahlde 2010, 142–43; see also "Setting and Purpose of 1 John" in the introduction).

This is the position championed by several major interpreters regarding the errors of the secessionists (for discussion, see Brown 1982, 505; Schnackenburg

1992, 201; von Wahlde 2010, 142–43). Support for this view comes from what some term the "quasi-technical sense" of the Greek term *erchomai* ("to come/go"; von Wahlde 2010, 142). In 1 John 4:1 and 2 John 7, Jesus is said to have "come in the flesh," while in 1 John 5:6, we hear that Jesus has "come [*elthōn*] in water," and then "in water and in blood." Thus the verb *erchomai* unites the appearance of Jesus in the flesh with his activity in water and in blood, understood as references to his death (John 19:34). The need to defend the significance of Jesus's salvific activity in the flesh could also explain the emphasis given to Jesus's physical death, and especially the fact that his death was a sacrifice endured on behalf of humanity (2:2; 3:5, 8, 16; 4:10, 14; 2 John 7).

4:3. And every spirit that does not confess Jesus is not from God. And this is the spirit of the antichrist, which you have heard is coming. Even now it is already in the world. The opposite of the Spirit of God is the spirit of the antichrist—the devil, the evil one, in whose grasp the whole world is reclining (5:19). As in 2:18, the antichrist is expected. The believers know he is coming (see 2:18) because it is the last hour, and Satan is expected to deceive the world in the time before the return of Christ (Rev. 20:7–8).

The idea that two spirits are at war, representing good and evil, is common in Jewish texts, not always in the manner described in 1 John, but nevertheless in a way that provides interesting background material (Lieu 2008, 174). In the *Testament of Judah*, for example, there are two opposing possibilities in humans, characterized as two spirits: "Recognize, my children, that two spirits are active in humanity, that of truth and that of error. . . . Indeed, those of error and those of truth are inscribed on the human heart" (20.1). A similar sentiment appears in the Qumran *Rule of the Community*: "He [God] created man to rule the world and placed within him two spirits so that he would walk with them until the moment of his visitation: they are the spirits of truth and of deceit" (1QS 3.17–19, trans. in García Martínez 1994). These two spirits dwell within a person, so are not exactly what we see in 1 John, and yet the idea that two spirits are at war, one of truth and one of deceit, is a helpful thing to consider as we try to imagine how the imagery of two spirits entered the Johannine vocabulary. In the Fourth Gospel, there is no such language. There is only one Spirit, the Spirit of Truth, the Paraclete.

> **Opposing Spirits Representing Good versus Evil, Light versus Darkness**
>
> "From of old you appointed the prince of light to assist us, . . . and all the spirits of truth are under his dominion. You created Belial for the pit, angel of enmity; his domain is darkness, his counsel is for evil and wickedness. All the spirits of his lot, angels of darkness, walk in the laws of darkness." (*War Scroll*, 1QM 13.10–12, trans. in García Martínez 1994, 107–8)

4:4–6. The second criterion by which one discerns the Spirit of Truth is articulated in 4:4–6. The logic of this second criterion is simple. Since the opponents have gone out into the world, they are attractive to the world. The world listens to them. By contrast, the members of the Johannine community have not gone out into the world. They are not attractive to the world. The world does not listen to them. Those who are of God, however, do listen to them, and so the readers should heed and adhere to the teaching of 1 John and not the doctrine of the opponents. Verse 4 begins, therefore, by insisting that the readers are "of God." By the end of the section, that they are "of God" should make it very clear to them where the truth resides and to whom they should listen: **You are of God, little children, and you have conquered them, for greater is the one in you than the one in the world (4:4). They are of the world, and so of the world they speak, and the world listens to them (4:5). We are from God. The one who knows God listens to us. The one who does not know God does not listen to us. In this way we know the spirit of truth and the spirit of deception (4:6).**

Verse 1 opens this unit by talking about false prophets, and 4:6 concludes the section by talking about deception (*plane*). The idea that a false prophet will arise to deceive the people has a special significance in the tradition that lies behind 1 John. In the Fourth Gospel, Jesus is pursued and persecuted by those who consider him to be a false prophet who deceives the people. It seems that the imagery of the conflict over the identity of Jesus in the Gospel has provided the vocabulary and the concepts for the debate in 1 John over the identity of Jesus, though that debate is now a very different contest. A brief survey of the material from the Gospel can demonstrate how this might have been so.

Deuteronomy says the following about the prophet to come who will be like Moses:

> The Lord your God will raise up for you a prophet like me from among your own people. You shall heed such a prophet. This is what you requested of the Lord your God at Horeb on the day of the assembly when you said, "If I hear the voice of the Lord my God anymore, or ever again see this great fire, I will die." (18:15–16)

> I will raise up for them a prophet like you from among their own people, I will put my words in the mouth of the prophet, who shall speak to them everything that I command. (18:18)

> But any prophet who speaks in the name of other gods, or who presumes to speak in my name a word that I have not commanded the prophet to speak, that prophet shall die. (18:20)

This coming prophet was one of the expected figures in the eschatological expectations of the first century. When people visit John the Baptist in the wilderness, for example, he first denies being the Messiah, then says that he is not Elijah, and then finally he is asked, "Are you the prophet?" (John 1:19–21).

113

Jesus's foes say that he is not the prophet like Moses. The Fourth Gospel says that Jesus is the prophet like Moses. To be sure, Jesus is much more than the prophet, as the Logos theology of the Prologue makes clear, but he is the expected one who was to come. Several statements of Jesus make direct allusion to Deut. 18:18. For instance, when Jesus says to the Father (John 17:8), "The words [*rhēmata*] that you gave [*edōkas*] to me, I have given to them," he clearly evokes the portion of Deut. 18:18 in which God says, "I will give [*dōsō*] my word [*rhēma*] in his mouth, and he shall say [*lalēsei*] to them whatever I command [*enteilōmai*] him" (LXX). The latter part of Deut. 18:18 seems to have influenced Jesus's statement in John 12:49: "I have not spoken on my own, but the Father who sent me has himself given me a commandment [*entolēn*] about what to say [*lalēsō*] and what to speak" (Meeks 1967, 45–46).

If Jesus is positively viewed as the prophet like Moses who was to come by his followers, however, his opponents see him as the false prophet in Deut. 18:20, the prophet who must be killed. This negative perception of Jesus is reflected in many places, including the following verses in John:

> And there was considerable complaining about him among the crowds. While some were saying "He is a good man," others were saying, "No, he is deceiving [*plana*] the crowd." (7:12)

> So they picked up stones to throw at him, but Jesus hid himself and went out of the temple. (8:59)

Thus Jesus deserves to die like the false prophet in Deut. 18:20 because he deceives (*plana*) the people. The debate over the identity of Jesus involved deciding whether he was the prophet like Moses or a false prophet who deceived the people.

This same Moses imagery may lie behind the debate in 1 John. Only this time, the negative imagery is not attached to those who follow Jesus loyally, but to those who do not. The false-prophet imagery is applied to those who reject Jesus as the one who comes in the flesh. In the Gospel, the language of false prophecy was used against Jesus and his community. Now it is used against the community's opponents. The imagery has been redeployed in a new context, and yet it remains very much the same imagery.

True Fellowship Is "from God" (4:7–21)

First John 4:7 ushers the theme of love once again to the forefront of attention, and the treatment of love continues through 4:21. And yet the new line of thought that begins here is completely connected to what has just preceded in 4:1–6. The discussion of Christology in 4:1–6 and the discussion of love in 4:7–21 are held together as the two halves of the commandment given in 3:23: "And this is his commandment—that we believe in the name of his son

Jesus Christ and that we love one another." That commandment is explicitly referenced at the close of the section, in 4:21, making the association plain (Brown 1982, 542–43). There are three discrete units within this overarching unit: 4:7–12, 13–16, 17–21. Verses 7–12 and 17–21 are exclusively about the revelation and significance of God's love. Verses 13–16 return to the theme of true confession from 4:1–6, but tie this confession into the discussion of love in 4:16.

4:7–8. In the preceding section the false prophets went out into the world because they were at home in the world. They were "of the world." Not so the members of the Johannine community, who are again addressed as **Beloved** and then urged, **let us love one another, for love is from God, and everyone who loves has been born of God and knows God. The one who does not love does not know God, for God is love.** Those who slay their brothers, like Cain did, are murderers (3:15), and so they are "of the evil one" (3:12), who "was a murderer from the beginning" (John 8:44). Such people would abandon their fellow believers and follow the false prophets. By contrast, those who love their brothers are "of God," and born of God, because God is love.

4:9–10. Verses 9–10 demonstrate the definitive act of God's love in sending Jesus Christ, beginning with the incarnation: **In this way the love of God was revealed among us, for God has sent his only begotten Son into the world, in order that we might live through him.** But the matter is not left at the incarnation. The crucifixion, understood as Christ's sacrifice for sins, is brought into view in verse 10: **In this is love—not that we have loved God, but that he loved us and sent his Son as an atonement concerning our sins.**

4:11–12. **Beloved, if God has in this way loved us, we also ought to love one another. No one has ever seen God. If we love one another, God abides in us, and his love has been made perfect in us.** Since verses 9–10 define God's love in the incarnation and crucifixion, events wherein Jesus embodied God's love on earth, so also the followers of Christ continue to embody this love if they are bound to one another by love. If in their lives in the flesh the believers also embody God's love on earth, then their union and love represent an imitation of the incarnation—a pale echo, to be sure, and one that is both qualitatively and quantitatively different—but nevertheless an imitation of the incarnation. The love of God is visible in human flesh, and the love of God "abides" in human flesh. The crucifixion is also in view in the statement that God's love is "perfected" in us. The word here translated "perfected" is the term *teteleiōmenē*. The last words of Christ on the cross were "It is finished" (*tetelestai*, John 19:30); in his Farewell Discourses, Jesus was said to love his disciples "to the end" (*telos*, 13:1). The love required of disciples is a love that imitates the sacrifice of the Lord (see comments on 3:16–18).

4:13–16. The discussion of love is interrupted momentarily in 4:13–16, reminding us that the discussion of love in 4:7–12 is intimately connected to the discussion of true confession and the true gift of the Spirit in 4:1–6. These two topics—true confession and God's love—were introduced together as interconnected halves of a single commandment in 3:23: "And this is his commandment: that we believe in the name of his Son Jesus Christ and that we love one another." **In this way we know that we abide in him and he in us—he has given to us from his Spirit** (4:13). This verse draws our attention back to the gift of the Spirit in 3:24, as well as to the need to discern the spirits in 4:1–6. **And we have seen and testify that the Father has sent the Son as Savior of the world. Whoever confesses that Jesus is the Son of God, God abides in him and he in God** (4:14–15). The emphasis on Christ's coming into the world calls to mind the insistence on professing that Christ has come in the flesh in 4:1–2. The repetition of the term "confess" (*homologein*) also connects us once more to the need for a proper christological confession in 4:2–3, while the next verse (4:16) reminds us of 4:8, where it was said that God is love: **And we have known and testified to the love that God has in us. God is love, and the one who abides in love abides in God, and God abides in him.**

4:17–18. In this way, love has been made perfect with us, so that we might have boldness on the day of judgment, for just as he is, so are we in this world. There is no fear in love, but perfect love casts out fear, for fear carries punishment, and the one who fears has not been made perfect in love. Verses 17–18 return to the emphasis on boldness before God as enunciated in 2:28 and repeated in 3:21. If we love on earth, we can stand boldly before God in heaven on the day of judgment.

4:19. As the discussion draws to a close, the theme mentioned above regarding the divine initiative in love is repeated: **We love because he first loved us.**

4:20–21. The broad sweep of the discussion of love that began with the quotation of the command to love in 3:11 now comes full circle. The section began by turning immediately to the example of Cain, who hated his brother. Cain's behavior was described only to admonish the readers to avoid it. Now 4:20 repeats this admonition, saying, **If someone says, "I love God," and yet he hates his brother, he is a liar. For the one who does not love his brother, whom he sees, is not able to love God, whom he has not seen.** The point seems clear enough. To fulfill the new commandment and "Love one another," believers must show love for fellow Christians and thus remain within the fellowship of the Johannine community (1:1–3). The final clause of the section, in 4:21, makes this point crystal clear: **And we have this commandment from him—that the one who loves God ought also to love his brother.**

Theological Issues

First John 3:21 urges Christians to have boldness (*parrēsia*) before God in their petitions, while 2:28 urges them to live in such a way now that they might have boldness before Christ at his second coming. Then 4:17 and 5:14 return to the theme of boldness before God. Such boldness might seem out of place, and not at all the kind of humility that one should show before God, as though one is demanding to be saved or to be vindicated at the final judgment. A brief survey of the meaning of the term might help to clarify matters (see Fitzgerald 1996; Parsenios 2004).

The Greek noun *parrēsia* is a compound noun consisting of the words *pan* (all, every) and *rhēsis* (statement, utterance). Someone possessed of *parrēsia* feels the freedom to say whatever comes to mind ("every statement"), with no fear of repercussions or punishment. The standard English translations for the word are "boldness" and "frankness." Such boldness was an asset in the political life of ancient Athens. The health of the free democratic life of the city depended on the full participation of all its citizens in government. Everyone was, and had to be, free to speak their mind in public life. Philosophers also depended on *parrēsia*. A philosopher could not be cowed by the powerful and thus be prevented from speaking the truth. A textbook example of the boldness of a philosopher comes from a probably apocryphal story in which Alexander the Great approached the famous Cynic philosopher Diogenes of Sinope (fourth century BCE). Alexander was awed by the philosopher and offered him anything that a great king like Alexander could provide. Diogenes was relaxing in the sun at the time and simply asked Alexander to move a little to the side, because he was blocking the sun (Diogenes Laertius, *Lives* 6.6).

Philosophers also showed boldness to their friends and pupils. Such a teacher could not always treat his disciples mildly; if they were in danger of falling into grave error, one had to reprove them sharply, even boldly. Such boldness was also required among friends, and ancient discussions of bold and frank speech are coupled with discussions of friendship. The Platonist Plutarch (45–125 CE) says that frankness of speech is a "most potent medicine in friendship" (*Flat.* 74D, trans. Yonge, LCL). A friend should always want only what is best for another friend, and so should not allow a friend to fall into grave error or an immoral life. Friends should not allow their friendship to keep them from reproving one another. In fact, the bond of friendship should impel them to save one another from disaster. Further, friends should have boldness before one another in the sense that they do not hold secrets from each other.

These associations between boldness and both friendship and philosophical instruction must lie somewhere behind the use of boldness/frankness/openness in various places in the Gospel of John. Like Diogenes, Jesus is not at all afraid to stand boldly and teach (7:26), even though others were too afraid to speak about him publicly (7:13). In the same manner, he reproves the world boldly (18:20). But in the Farewell Discourses, where Jesus calls his disciples his friends (*philoi*, 15:13, 14, 15), he also speaks to them boldly and openly (16:29) as he expresses his love for them. Neither does he hide unpleasant truths, but warns them openly and honestly about the troubles that await them and the strength that is expected of them (15:18–16:2). Here the boldness that he shows is tied to the intimacy that he shares with his friends. Since Jesus has invited believers into this relationship of intimate friendship, it is no wonder that in 1 John 2:28 disciples are invited to show boldness before Christ when he returns. By doing so, believers are simply responding as friends to their friend. If they live as Christ taught them to live, they will not be ashamed before his presence (2:28). The possibility of such shame is not to be treated casually either.

The term *parrēsia* is well chosen for the relationship to which Jesus invites his disciples, because it is a bold thing to call God a friend. And we possess this boldness, not because we have earned it or achieved it, but because God has given it to us. A text that recognizes how bold it is to address God in such a way is the prayer before the communal recitation of the Lord's Prayer in the Divine Liturgy of St. John Chrysostom, the principal eucharistic service of the Orthodox Church. Just before the Lord's Prayer is recited, the following prayer is said by the clergy: "Make us worthy, Master, with boldness [*parrēsias*] and without condemnation to dare address you, the heavenly God, as 'Father,' and say, . . . Our Father, who art in heaven . . ."

1 John 5:1–21

Testimony and Witnesses

Introductory Matters

As the argument of 1 John draws to its final chapter, a particular characteristic of the letter is obvious now. First John relies on a relatively limited set of terms, themes, and syntactical structures, but it combines and then recombines these limited ingredients in a dazzlingly endless number of combinations. And yet, even as 1 John deploys an ever-greater constellation of images and ways of talking about God and those who believe rightly in God, it almost never strays from saying the same two things repeatedly. The two things ever in mind are expressed in 1:3: (1) "that you also may have fellowship with us," and (2) "our fellowship is with the Father and with his Son, Jesus Christ." These two interrelated elements are a proper belief in and fellowship with God, and the proper fellowship with the other members of the community. First John 3:23 puts the matter in other terms as it claims to provide a single commandment, and then proceeds to offer two: "that we believe in the name of his son, Jesus Christ, and that we love one another." For five chapters, 1 John finds a variety of ways to state these two closely related ideas. By writing like this, 1 John closely resembles the Fourth Gospel, where a great variety of images are used to express a limited set of ideas. The malleability of the images is most obvious in the Good Shepherd discourse. Early in that discourse, Jesus says that he is the Good Shepherd and that the shepherd enters the sheepfold through the gate (10:2). A few verses later, although Jesus is still speaking about shepherds, sheepfolds, and gates, he now says, not that he goes through the gate, but "*I am* the gate" (10:7). The image of

119

"the way" in John 14 is similar. Jesus initially speaks about "the way" on which he goes (14:4–5), but in the very next verse he announces, contrary to expectations, "*I am* the way" (14:6).

Harold Attridge has carefully studied the complicated imagery of the Gospel and believes that this great variety does not distract the reader but rather focuses the reader's attention ever more closely on a limited field of vision. The image of water is a good example. Water appears throughout the early chapters of the Gospel. Jesus is baptized in water in chapter 1, he turns water into wine into chapter 2, and in chapter 3 he urges Nicodemus to be born of water and the Spirit. In chapter 4 Jesus speaks of "living water" to the Samaritan woman, then heals the man in the pool in chapter 5, before walking on water in chapter 6. In chapter 7 Jesus speaks of the living water that rises up from within believers. Water imagery flows in many directions in the early chapters of John, but eventually all these directions lead to the cross. All the manifestations of water in the early chapters of John find their meaning in the water that pours from Jesus's side in John 19:34. Attridge writes:

> It is highly probable that the final deployment [the water in John 19:34] unites and focuses the others. The water that works with the Spirit to give new birth, flows finally from the cross. The wisdom that Christ teaches and reveals who he is flows finally from the cross. . . . What then does the diversity achieve? Like the facets of a gem or the multiple angles of view in a cubist painting, the complex image refracts attention and establishes connections with several other important images and themes within the Gospel. . . . Complexity overdetermines, interconnects by anticipation, and yet at the same time focuses. (2012, 85, 81)

The many manifestations of water that seem to point in so many different directions, in the end focus our attention in one direction only—toward the cross.

The same can be said for the dazzlingly complex imagery in 1 John. Our attention is ever more focused on the interconnected poles of fellowship expressed in 1:3—a proper disposition toward God and a proper disposition toward fellow believers. The images multiply further throughout the letter, as our connection to God is expressed in the images of "being in," "abiding in," "being of," "being born of," and many more. Likewise, the relationship that we share with fellow believers is expressed in the language of family and kinship, in loving one another, in resisting false teaching (which seduces one away from the community), in hating the world and being hated by it, and much more. What Attridge says about the Fourth Gospel applies equally well to 1 John: "Complexity overdetermines, interconnects by anticipation, and yet at the same time focuses." We will see this manner of focusing the reader's attention continue to be employed in the final chapter of 1 John. The chapter unfolds in two roughly distinct sections, 5:1–12 and 5:13–21.

Tracing the Train of Thought

Witnesses (martyriai) *for God's Son (5:1–12)*

5:1. Everyone who believes that Jesus is the Christ has been born of God, and everyone who loves the one who begets loves also the one who has been begotten of him. Judith Lieu (2008, 200) offers a cogent and clear reading of this verse that recognizes the shift in thought it represents. First John 4:7 had defined the one born of God as the one who loves. This verse defines those born of God based on their confession of faith. Believers are still called born of God, but the justification for this status has shifted. This verse also pulls together several strands from the argument that has preceded it. While 4:20 says that the one who does not love is a liar, and 2:22 says that the liar is the one who refuses to believe that Jesus is the Christ, here in 5:1 the positive version of these ideas is expressed. The one who believes that Jesus is the Christ is also the one who loves.

> **1 John 5:1–21 in the Rhetorical Flow**
>
> Introductory prologue (1:1–4)
>
> The light and the darkness (1:5–2:11)
>
> Who are the children of God? (2:12–3:10)
>
> Love for God, love for one another (3:11–4:21)
>
> ▶Testimony and witnesses (5:1–21)
>
> Witnesses (*martyriai*) for God's Son (5:1–12)
>
> Martyrs (*martyres*) for God's Son (5:13–21)

5:2–3. In this we know that we love the children of God—whenever we love God and do his commandments. For this is the love of God—to keep his commandments. And his commandments are not burdensome. The phrase "love of God" has been used already in 1 John (2:5; 3:17), and it has raised a question each time. Does the phrase mean love for God, love from God, or an imitation of the love that God shows? Here the sense is clear. It means to love God, as 5:2 states explicitly.

Why are God's commandments not burdensome (*bareiai*)? The sentiment seems similar to the Matthean phrase "My yoke is easy, and my burden is light" (11:30) and the similarly worded 23:4, "They tie up heavy [*barea*] burdens, hard to bear, and lay them on the shoulders of others." There is considerable speculation about why the commandments of the Lord are not a burden (see Brown 1982, 541). The next verse claims to explain the matter, and yet does not do so in a way that makes things completely plain.

5:4–5. For everything that is born of God conquers the world. And this is the victory that conquers the world: our faith. Who is the one who triumphs over the world if not the one who believes that Jesus is the Son of God? Jesus was the first to conquer the world. In his Farewell Discourses, he says to his disciples, "In the world you face persecution, but take courage, I have conquered [*nenikēka*] the world" (John 16:33). That victory is extended to the disciples.

This is not the first time that 1 John has spoken of the followers of Jesus as "conquering," using the Greek verb *nikan*. The same idea is expressed for conquering the evil one (2:13, 14) and the antichrists (4:4). How this victory keeps the commandment from being burdensome is not entirely clear. Note that 5:4 contains the only use of the noun *pistis* ("faith") in the Johannine literature; the verb *pisteuein* ("to believe") is always used except in this verse.

5:6–8. He is the one who comes through water and blood, Jesus Christ—not in water only, but in water and in blood. And the Spirit is the one testifying, because the Spirit is truth. For there are three who testify, the Spirit and the water and the blood, and the three are in agreement. Four items are drawn together in these three verses, and all four of them—water, blood, the Spirit, and testimony—are present at the crucifixion of Jesus in the Gospel of John. John 19:34–35 says that "one of the soldiers pierced his side with a spear, and at once *blood* and *water* came out. (He who saw this has *testified* so that you also may believe. His *testimony* is true, and he knows that he tells the truth.)" A few verses prior to this, Jesus gave up his spirit as he died (19:30). The rich collection of symbols in 1 John 5:5–7 can point in multiple directions, especially when the entire Gospel is brought to bear on the discussion. Each of these items mentioned has its own life outside the episode of the crucifixion. As the introduction to this chapter showed, the images and language of the Gospel can be combined and recombined in a vast number of arrangements. Interpreters try to draw out the many associations that all these words—water, blood, testimony, and Spirit—might raise (for options, see Brown 1982, 573–78; von Wahlde 2010, 183–88). A particularly common move is to see this verse as referring not only to the crucifixion of Christ but also to Christ's baptism, on the assumption that the opponents accept that Jesus was baptized but that the divine Christ withdrew from him before his crucifixion. They would, in other words, accept that he came in water, but not in blood. Water and blood, by this way of reading, refer to the baptism and death of Jesus, respectively. But even if we do not know whether or how this formulation might have been directed against the secessionist opponents, the cluster of ideas gathered here clearly puts us at the foot of the cross. In 5:4–5 the believers were said to conquer the world. This evokes Jesus's Passion (John 16:33), and now the various elements present at the cross do the same. Perhaps the point is simply to say that the Son of God is none other than the one who died on the cross, and that he offers the victory of his death to those who believe in him (Lieu 2008, 213). The phrase "in agreement" is a compromise translation for the very puzzling Greek phrase *eis to hen*, literally "into the one." In John 17:23 Jesus uses this phrase in his prayer to the Father. He asks that the disciples "be made perfect into one" (*eis hen*) just as Jesus and the Father are one. The context of testimony suggests that this unity should express itself in being "in agreement." But the translation of the phrase is less than certain.

The Johannine Comma

First John 5:7–8 confounds interpreters when it announces, "For there are three who testify: the Spirit and the water and the blood, and the three are in agreement." The phrase was no less puzzling to ancient and medieval interpreters. The unusual phrase "the three are in agreement" was especially suggestive for trinitarian reflection. Over time, additions were made to the text that turned the puzzling phrase in a trinitarian direction. These additions were eventually accepted by the famous thinker and text critic Desiderius Erasmus (1466–1536) and found their way into the King James Version of the Bible. The additions have come to be called the Johannine Comma, where *comma* is the Latin term for "clause." With the additions in italics, the text reads as follows (AT):

Because there are three who testify *in heaven:*
Father, Word, and Holy Spirit;
and these three are one;
and there are three who testify on earth:
the Spirit and the water and the blood;
And these three are in agreement.

The evidence against the authenticity of this addition is irrefutable. No Greek text before 1400 contains the comma, and of the eight that contain it after that date, four do so in the form of marginal notes. The comma appears in the Old Latin text only after the year 600 and in the Vulgate only after 750. Before 1500, it does not exist in Coptic, Ethiopic, and Arabic versions. The comma tells us much more about the history of Christian thought than it does about the history of the text of the NT or the theology of 1 John. It seems to have entered the textual tradition due to trinitarian controversies in Spain and North Africa. (For fuller discussion, see Painter 2002, 301–9; Brown 1982, appendix 4.)

5:9. If we receive the testimony of human beings, the testimony of God is greater. For this is the testimony of God, since he has testified concerning his Son. The idea of God being greater than some other entity has been expressed elsewhere in 1 John. God is greater than our hearts (3:20), and his Spirit is greater than the one that is in the world (4:4). Here in 5:9 his testimony is greater than human testimony. This seems an obvious allusion to John 5:36, where Jesus says that he has testimony greater than that of John the Baptist. In John 5, the works that the Father has given Jesus provide testimony to Jesus's identity (5:36), and such testimony comes even from the Father himself (5:37).

5:10–11. The one who believes in the Son of God has the testimony in himself, while the one who does not believe God has made him a liar. For he has not believed in the testimony that God has testified concerning his Son. What does it mean to say that the believer has the testimony "in himself"?

Are we speaking of some sort of inner spiritual guidance? This question will be answered in verse 12, but the final line of verse 11 describes the content of the testimony: **And this is the testimony, that God gave eternal life to us and this life is in his Son.** Once we learn that this is the content of the testimony, a careful correlation is clear between verses 10 and 12.

5:12. The one who has the Son has life. The one who does not have the Son of God does not have life. Having the testimony is equivalent to having life, because the content of the testimony is that God gave eternal life through his Son (5:11). Thus to "have" the testimony in verse 10 is to have eternal life.

Martyrs (martyres) for God's Son (5:13–21)

5:13. I wrote these things to you, who believe in the name of the Son of God, in order that you might know that you have eternal life. This expression draws 1 John gradually toward its close in a way very similar to the ending of the Gospel of John. As the Gospel winds toward its final chapter, John 20:30–31 says: "Now Jesus did many other signs in the presence of his disciples, which are not written in this book. But these [*tauta*] are written so that you may come to believe that Jesus is the Messiah, the Son of God, and that through believing you may have life in his name." This statement of purpose in the Fourth Gospel resembles the statement of purpose here in 1 John: "I wrote these things [*tauta*] to you, who believe in the name of the Son of God, in order that you may know that you have eternal life" (5:13). Both texts refer to "these things" which are "written," and both texts connect "belief" in the "Son of God" to "having" either "life" or "eternal life." Third John 13 has a similar resonance, though in a slightly more muted form (see comments there).

5:14–15. And this is the boldness that we have before him—that whatever we might request, if it be according to his will, he hears us. And if we know that he hears us, in regard to whatever we might ask, we know that we obtain the requests that we have requested of him. Boldness (*parrēsia*) before God has come up before (2:28; 3:21–22; 4:17). In 3:21–22, boldness was connected to making requests of God, as it is here.

5:16–18. If someone sees his brother committing a sin that is not unto death, he will ask and he [God] will give him life—for those who commit sins not unto death. There is sin unto death, and I am not saying that someone should ask in regard to this. Every injustice is sin, and there is sin not unto death. We know that everyone who has been born of God does not sin, but the one who is born of God preserves himself, and the evil one does not touch him. These verses present yet another version of the problem regarding human sin in 1 John. Chapter 1 insists that Christians must confess their sins and that they must acknowledge that they sin (1:8–10), while 1 John 3:9 insists that Christians are unable to sin. Here again we see that sin can exist in the community, even as it should not (see "Theological Issues" after 1:5–2:11). But another issue must be briefly addressed here, and that is the question of sins that are unto death, and sins that are not. Many commentators have long understood this distinction in relation to OT texts that speak of sins and violations of the law of Moses that do or do not lead to death (Num. 18:22; Deut. 22:26). The next and final verses might explain the sin unto death in a very different way, though, and in a way that is connected to the opponents and their departure from the community.

5:19–20. We know that we are of God, while the whole world lies in sin. We know that the Son of God is coming and has given to us insight, in order that we might know the one who is true. And we are in the true one, in his Son, Jesus Christ. This one is the true God and eternal life. It is possible that the sin unto death might be explained in relation to the eternal life among those who have the life that comes from Jesus. To sin unto death is to reject the life that Christ offers—by leaving the community. The secessionists have returned to the world, which lies in sin. If this is the case, it would explain why one is forbidden to pray for those who sin unto death (5:16), because they are to be denied all the consideration of brothers and sisters as and members of the community, as in 2 John 10–11.

5:21. Little children, guard yourselves from idols. This last verse is confusing. Early Christians struggled in various ways with idolatry, and especially with the problem of dealing with food offered to idols (Acts 7:41; 15:29; 1 Cor. 8:4, 7; 10:19; 12:2; 2 Cor. 6:16). First John 4:1–2 refers to the opponents as false prophets who do not guide one closer to the true God. To follow their teaching would, consequently, be equivalent to following false idols. In this sense, the final line of the letter is roughly metaphorical. The greatest support for this reading lies in the statement in 5:20: "This one is the one true God and eternal life." To believe in Jesus as he is outlined in 1 John is to believe in the one true God. Any other Jesus is a false Jesus and an idol.

John Painter (2002, 329–30) clearly and cogently argues, though, that the phrase is not merely metaphorical. He believes that 1 John specifically connects the opponents with the worship of idols, because of the specific nature of the threat that seems to lie behind the description of the opponents in 4:1–2 and here in 5:1: "Everyone who believes that Jesus is the Christ has been born of God." First John would not need to affirm that Jesus is the *Christ*, unless any sense of the Jewish messianic hope had been lost as Christians moved into a more and more gentile world. The theology of the Gospel of John is deeply rooted in the theology of the OT, but its Logos theology is also very amenable to the popular Platonist and Stoic speculations about the universe that existed at the time when this document was written. When the Elder says in 2 John 9 that certain people are "going ahead" and not adhering to what had been taught "from the beginning," could this mean that they are moving forward in such a way that they have lost any sense of Jewish messianic faith? Such a reading is certainly possible, and Painter defends the thesis in a very convincing fashion. But as with any attempt to define too carefully what the beliefs of the opponents are in 1 John, the evidence does not allow us to arrive at any amount of certainty.

Theological Issues

The introduction to this commentary examined the relationship that exists between 1–3 John and the Gospel of John from several different perspectives. Now that the commentary has covered all of 1 John, it is possible to pause and reflect again on several other features shared by the various texts that have been addressed individually up until now throughout the commentary but would helpfully be collected into a single place. The introductory chapter listed connections that exist between the texts on several different levels of abstraction in order to show that the associations were both broad and deep. The following four categories of evidence were surveyed there and are mentioned here in abbreviated form for the sake of completeness (for greater detail see in the introduction the sections titled "The Relationship of the Letters to the Gospel" and "The Rhetoric of the Letters: *Sententiae* and Social Division"). The four categories are the following:

1. Shared vocabulary: not only is a series of key terms used in the Johannine literature more than in other books, but these terms are used with greater frequency than in the other works in the NT. For example, words like truth/reality (*alētheia*), testimony (*martyria*), love (*agapē*), abide (*menein*), and others have a distinctly Johannine character.
2. This shared vocabulary not only appears more often and with greater density in the Johannine literature but is combined into similar constructions. For example, not only is the word "truth" an oft-repeated Johannine term but it is also configured into characteristically Johannine phrases, like "spirit of truth," or "do the truth."
3. Larger structuring devices are also shared in common. Terms for testimony or testify appear in the opening and closing sections of three of the four Johannine texts discussed in this commentary: the Gospel of John, 1 John, and 3 John. This is not a casual or easily dismissed device.
4. The texts rely on a similarly "sententious" rhetorical style but, even more, seem to do so for the same purpose: to force a decision on their readers. Orators typically use *sententiae* in order to frame boundaries between groups. The Gospel and Letters of John seem at first to do this—when they set up stark realities that are polar opposites, like light and darkness, sight and blindness, and so on. If this was all the *sententiae* did, then the Gospel and Letters would both resemble their contemporaries and be not at all unique. But this is not all that they do.

They certainly use *sententiae* to establish sharp distinctions, but they do not do this in order to prevent people from moving from the one to the other. They do it in order to force people to choose.

These issues are all interesting and helpful to be reminded of. The evidence of the greatest significance to my mind, though, appears in the deeper mechanisms of thought that are shared among the various texts. These deeper mechanisms have been noted several times in this commentary, and some of them will be covered in greater detail in the commentary on 2 and 3 John, as noted below. Such devices reflect deeper patterns and mechanisms that are shared by the various Johannine texts and so are worthy of consideration. No single one of them is convincing enough to demonstrate a relationship between the texts, but when read collectively they offer a compelling body of proof. The most salient of these are the following:

1. Rhetorical variation (*variatio*) characterizes both texts, where variation means that two or more different words signify the same reality. See the discussions in the commentary at 1 John 2:3, 26–27; 3:19b–20, and especially at 2:20–21, where the matter is dealt with at the greatest length. To be sure, any good author, whether from today or in antiquity, would seek to vary vocabulary in order to avoid lulling the reader to sleep. But the Gospel and Letters have a knack for using two or more words to signify the same reality. A telling example from the Gospel comes near the end of the narrative. When Jesus questions Peter, for instance, at 21:15–17, Jesus uses not only two different words for love (*agapan, philein*) but also two terms for caring for a flock (*boskein, poimainein*), two words for the flock (sheep, *probata*; lambs, *arnia*), as well as two interchangeable verbs for the expression "to know" (*ginōskein, eidenai*). The same mechanism occurs several other times in the Letters of John, as in 3 John, where there is the same variation between two words for love: *agapan* and *philein* (see discussion at 3 John 15). The device occurs regularly in 1 John as well, using multiple terms for the concept of knowing, *ginōskein* and *eidenai*. In chapter 2 especially, *ginōskō* appears several times (vv. 3, 4, 5, 13, 14, 18, 29) alongside of *eidenai* (vv. 11, 20, 21, 29). Interpreters have tried to assign different senses to the different verbs, but their efforts do not stand up to serious scrutiny.

2. Second, both the Gospel and 1 John have a dialectical approach to theology (see "Theological Issues" discussion after 1:5–2:11). In the Gospel, opposing theological propositions are held in tension with one another, and that tension is never resolved. In Christology, for instance, Jesus is one with the Father, but the Father is greater than him (14:28). Signs, likewise, are narrated in order to encourage faith (20:30–31), but sometimes those who believe signs are rejected (2:23–24) and sometimes

those who seek signs are rebuked (4:48). Every major theological theme in the Gospel operates in the same way, as a way to initiate readers into the Gospel's profound exposition on the incarnation, where the Word becomes flesh, the creator enters the creation, and eternity enters time. Jesus's entire ministry is characterized by such a dialectic, and in 1 John the lives of his believers manifest the same dialectic. If Jesus is caught between opposing realities when the eternal one enters time, so are believers caught between opposing realities when creatures are invited to ascend to God. This dialectical mode explains why 1 John says in chapter 1 that believers must confess their sins (1:8–10) while chapters 3:4–9 and 5:14–17 insist that believers cannot sin. As in the case of Jesus in the Gospel, both sets of opposing statements are true, reflecting the fact that believers are caught between human and divine life in their ascent to God, in the same way that Jesus was caught between heaven and earth when he descended to the world.

3. Both the Gospel of John and 1–2 John operate on multiple temporal planes (see discussion in "Theological Issues" following 2 John). The Gospel of John, for instance, refers to the death and resurrection of Jesus as his glorification (John 12:28), and he is not glorified until he ascends the cross and rises from the dead. But then, surprisingly, Jesus already reveals his glory in the wedding at Cana when he changes water into wine. That scene ends with the notice, "Jesus did this, the first of his signs, in Cana of Galilee, *and revealed his glory*; and his disciples believed in him" (2:11).

The Gospel regularly reminds us that Jesus cannot be properly understood until after the resurrection (2:22; 7:39; 12:16). In order to provide this insight, the Gospel narrates the pre-resurrection life of Jesus from this post-resurrection perspective. In statements like that in 2:11 from the wedding at Cana, the post-resurrection perspective of greater insight and understanding intrudes into the pre-resurrection life of Jesus. The purpose of this is to emphasize that he can only be understood rightly if he is understood in the light of the resurrection. After establishing a strict boundary between the pre- and post-resurrection perspective on Jesus, the Gospel crosses this boundary for specific didactic purposes. Something similar seems to be at work in the temporal tensions in the Letters of John. The boundary separating past and present is crossed in order to show the readers that they can only understand their own present from the perspective of the past. The repeated emphasis on things that were "from the beginning" (1:1) emphasizes continuity with the past and with the ministry of Jesus that took place in the past. But the boundary separating past and present is sometimes transgressed. When describing the incarnation, for example, 1 John 4:2 refers to Jesus as "having come in the flesh," while 2 John 7 refers to Jesus in the present as one "who comes." This latter phrase adopts the temporal perspective of the Gospel, which uses the same phrase to refer to Jesus many times in his ministry (*erchomenos*; 1:15, 27; 3:31; 6:14; 11:27; 12:13).

The Letters also sometimes refer to the "new commandmant" to love one another (John 13:34; see also 15:12, 17) as the old commandment—because it originated in the past in the ministry of Jesus—and sometimes also call it the new commandment, which again adopts the temporal frame of the ministry of Jesus (1 John 2:7–11; 2 John 5). Second John 9 explains the logic of this move: "Anyone who goes ahead and does not remain in the teaching of Christ does not possess God." The secessionists seem to have developed a theological profile that is unmoored from the message of Jesus. First John 2:24 makes the same point by way of admonition: "You, what you heard from the beginning, let that in you abide. If what you heard from the beginning abides in you, then you also abide in the Son and in the Father." If the opponents have erred by developing an understanding of Jesus that deviates from one that was passed down "from the beginning," meaning from the ministry of Jesus himself, the Letters underscore the indispensability of seeing Jesus "from the beginning" by casting their readers into a past perspective. Thus the temporal tensions in the Letters seem to serve the same didactic and rhetorical purpose as the temporal tensions in the Gospel. In the Gospel the shift in time zones emphasizes that one misunderstands Jesus by knowing him only before the resurrection, while the temporal transitions in the Letters emphasize that one misunderstands Jesus just as badly by moving so far forward in one's theology as to become unmoored from the actual earthly life and ministry of Jesus.

The first of these three rhetorical and theological postures is not unique to the Johannine literature, but it does help to round off a collection of factors that seem to link the texts in uncanny ways. More compelling are the second and third categories, especially because, even as they show use of the same two mechanisms, they show those mechanisms being applied in vastly different circumstances. The use of two such idiosyncratic devices is a compelling thing to confront, and can reasonably be seen to reflect the work of the same mind (or group of minds) at work in the various texts, responding to different situations to be sure, but nevertheless with the same set of tools. In the end, perhaps no single piece of data bears much persuasive force, but cumulatively they make a compelling case. I do not expect this evidence to close the door on questions of authorship, of course. What these data do accomplish, however, is to provide at least a basic and reasonable basis for assuming that the Gospel and Letters of John are the product of the same mind, and are linked at a very deep level of abstraction.

2 John

A Letter to the Elect Lady

Introductory Matters

Second John is both more and less mysterious than 1 John. It is less mysterious in the sense that it follows more closely the conventions associated with ancient letter writing than does 1 John. It has a clearly marked sender and recipient, and its brevity accords well with the standard length of a typical ancient letter. Second John can even be classified as a particular type of ancient letter, the paraenetic type. The Greek word *parainesis* means "exhortation" or "advice," and 2 John seems very much like a typical paraenetic letter.

When we look beyond the form of the document, though, and try to understand the historical circumstances in which it was written, we are met with even more confusion than we encountered in reading 1 John. We see in 2 John the same secessionists we encounter in 1 John, but we are no nearer to understanding who they are or precisely what they believe. We now also face the additional fact that the contents of 2 John merely duplicate the contents of 1 John. This fact begets a natural question: Why was 2 John written at all? Some scholars suggest that 2 John was written before 1 John, which would mean that 2 John represents a quick, hurried response to the schism, to be followed later by 1 John, which responds in greater detail to the problem after a longer period of reflection. Or perhaps 2 John was sent to a different community than was 1 John. Maybe it even accompanied 1 John or was even written after 1 John. There is no way of choosing one option over the others with any certainty. In addition to asking the same questions, therefore, that we ask when reading 1 John, we encounter even further uncertainties when we read 2 John.

Before exploring these and other questions further in the commentary proper, a word or two more needs to be said about the nature of paraenetic letters. In his textbook on *Epistolary Styles* (5), Libanius defines the paraenetic letter as having two basic intentions: to urge people to adopt certain kinds of behaviors, and to dissuade them from adopting others. Second John does precisely these two things. On the positive side, the letter urges its readers to love one another (v. 5) and to walk in the commandments (v. 6) and also to abide in the teaching that they have received. On the negative side, the readers are told to reject and avoid anyone who tries to turn them toward another teaching (vv. 7–11).

Another key feature of paraenetic discourse is present in 2 John. Writers and speakers who compose paraenetic texts and speeches not only acknowledge but also often freely admit that the advice they encourage people to follow is not new or novel but something that the recipient of the instruction already knows (Isocrates, *Nic.* 40–41; cf. Malherbe 2000, 82; 1986, 125). In his third oration, Dio Chrysostom revels in the traditional nature of his paraenesis, because his concern is to preserve eternal truths, in the manner of 2 John. Dio says:

> (26) And if anyone shall say that I always say the same things, this will be the same charge that was laid against Socrates. For the story runs that once Hippias of Elis, who had been listening for some time to the words of Socrates about justice and virtue and to his wonted comparisons with pilots, physicians, cobblers and potters, finally made the exclamation natural to a sophist, (27) "The same things once more, Socrates!" to which the other replied with a laugh, "Yes, and on the same subjects. Now you by reason of your wisdom probably never say the same about the same things, but to me this appears a thing most excellent. We know that liars say many things and all different, while those who stick to the truth cannot find anything else to say than just the truth." (*Or.* 3.26–27, trans. Cohoon 1959, LCL)

This aspect of paraenetic discourse is common in NT texts, and especially in 1 Thessalonians, where Paul repeatedly encourages the Thessalonians simply to keep doing what they already know to do (1:5; 2:1, 2, 5, 11; 3:3–4; cf. Malherbe 2000, 82). People may know what to do, but they still need to be reminded or encouraged to do it.

As a context for both 2 and 3 John, we have to imagine the Elder who writes these epistles as having authority over a network of churches in a particular area (see Malherbe 1983, 100–101; 2000, 344–45). We know, for instance, that in Rome the Christians were gathered into several different house churches, perhaps as many as three (Rom. 16:5, 14, 15) or five (Rom. 16:10–11; Jewett 2006, 59–69). Different households are also united within the one church in Corinth (Acts 18:1–3, 7, 8; Rom. 16:23). It is possible that the same circumstance prevails in Thessalonica as well, and that when Paul says that he wants 1 Thessalonians to be read to "all the brethren" (5:27), he means to have it

---

Libanius on the Paraenetic Letter

"The paraenetic style is that in which we exhort someone by urging him to pursue something or to avoid something. Paraenesis is divided into two parts, encouragement and dissuasion. Some also call it the advisory style, but do so incorrectly, for paraenesis differs from advice. For paraenesis is hortatory speech that does not admit of a counterstatement, for example, if someone should say that we must honor the divine. For nobody contradicts this exhortation were he not mad to begin with. But advice is advisory speech that does admit of a counterstatement, for example if someone should say that we must wage war, for much can be gained by war. But someone else might counter that we should not wage war, for many things result from war, for example, defeat, captivity, wounds, and frequently the razing of a city." (Epis. Styles 5, trans. Malherbe 1988)

"The paraenetic letter. Always be an emulator, dear friend, of virtuous men. For it is better to be well spoken of when imitating good men than to be reproached by all men while following evil men." (Epis. Styles 52, trans. Malherbe 1988)

---

read among the various Christian groups gathered in and around Thessalonica (Malherbe 2000, 345). The evidence is not easy to clarify, and conclusions are provisional, but these examples do suggest a situation in which several different households host churches in a particular area, and that the various churches in a given area are joined by informal bonds. A similar circumstance seems to operate in the present case, with the Elder writing letters to dispersed churches within his orbit of activity. He writes 2 John as a figure of authority in light of the schism created by those who have left the community (1 John 2:19; 2 John 7), in order to ensure that the church addressed in this letter remains within the fold.

2 John in the Rhetorical Flow

Epistolary prescript (1–3)

The true faith and the true way of life (4–6)

The false faith and the false way of life (7–9)

False teachers and hospitality (10–11)

Epistolary farewell (12–13)

Tracing the Train of Thought

Epistolary Prescript (1–3)

1–3. The Elder, to the Elect Lady and her children, whom I love in truth—and not I alone, but all who have come to know the truth, because of the truth that abides in us and will be with us forever. With us will be grace, mercy, peace—from God the Father and from Jesus Christ, the Son of the Father in truth and love. The letter begins with a typical epistolary opening, identifying its sender and the recipient. But not everything in this opening period is typical. One immediately questions, for example, the use of the title "the Elder" for the sender. In fact, the use of this title elicits not one question, but many. First, it is not at all unusual for an author to use a title alongside his name in a letter. Paul regularly adds a title to his name when he writes to his churches, whether apostle (1 Cor. 1:1; 2 Cor. 1:1; Gal. 1:1) or slave and apostle (Rom. 1:1). The only time he does not use a title for himself is when he lists the names of Silvanus and Timothy alongside his own in 1–2 Thessalonians. So the use of a title is not unusual in a letter opening. The use of a title without a name attached to it, though, is very unusual, and this manner of identifying the senders of the letter returns our attention once more to the anonymity of the author of these letters (see "Theological Issues" after 1 John 1:1–4).

Second, if the only identifying title given is "Elder," what are we to assume this means? The English word *elder* literally translates the Greek comparative *presbyteros*. The title *presbyteros* was common in early Christianity for identifying various authority figures (Acts 14:23; 15:2–6, 22–23; 20:17; 1 Tim. 5:17–19; James 5:14; 1 Pet. 5:1). Commentators generally assume that the use of the title here implies a certain status on the part of the sender of the letter, but the precise nature of the status is unclear. Raymond Brown has an interesting hypothesis that both respects the ancient tradition connecting these letters to John the son of Zebedee and deals responsibly with how this letter is attributed to someone named the Elder. Several times Irenaeus speaks of figures whom he calls "elders" (*Haer.* 3.3.4; 4.27.1; 5.33.3) and specifically mentions *presbyteroi* who saw and knew John. It is possible that one of these elders writes the present letter to a church in the Johannine orbit of influence for this letter (Brown 1982, 651). Even if this is not certain, the title implies authority.

The title for the recipient, "Elect Lady," is no less opaque than the title Elder, but it is easier to explain in its immediate context. Attempts to connect this title to an actual person are unnecessary. The title "Elect Lady" represents the church to whom the Elder writes, following a long-standing precedent of referring to God's people in the person of a woman, especially in the OT, where Jerusalem is often depicted as a woman (Isa. 54; Bar. 4–5; 2 Esd. [*4 Ezra*] 9–10; cf. Lieu 1986, 66). Especially vivid is Paul's description of the heavenly and earthly Jerusalems as Sarah and Hagar, respectively (Gal. 4:21–31). If the Elect Lady is the church, the "children" are its members. The same image resurfaces as the letter draws to a close (v. 13), where the members of the Elder's church are labeled in turn "the children of your Elect Sister." The Elect Lady of verse 1 and the Elect Sister of verse 13 are therefore churches, and their children must be the members of the churches.

The adjective "elect" (*eklektē*) is regularly applied to believers in the NT (Rom. 8:33; Col. 3:12; 2 Tim. 2:10; Rev. 17:14). In John 15:16 Jesus says to his disciples, "You did not choose [*exelexasthe*] me, but I chose [*exelexamēn*] you." Given this background, 2 John addresses the church to which it is sent as "elect" in order to remind its recipients of their status in the community as well as of the fact that they were called to this community by the Lord himself (Brown 1982, 651).

It seems significant as well that the Elder here refers to both the collective body of the church as a whole (the Elect Lady) and the individual members of the church (her children). This is a reminder that the one is composed of many, and that the individual members of the church should live in concord and harmony. Paul does a similar thing in 1 Corinthians. Usually Paul writes either to the collective body of the church/churches as a whole (2 Cor. 1:1; Gal. 1:1; 1 Thess. 1:1) or to the many members of the church individually (Rom. 1:7; Phil. 1:1). In 1 Cor. 1:2 he does something different by referring first to the collective body as a whole ("To the church of God that is in Corinth"), and then to the individual members ("to those who are sanctified in Christ Jesus"). Since the church of Corinth was being rent by factionalism and division, Paul subtly reminds the Corinthian Christians that the many members of the church are called to live in unity in the one body (Mitchell 1993, 193). Second John faces a similar crisis of schism and division, and the similar phrasing could have the same purpose.

The expression "whom I love in truth" extends this train of thought. In 3 John 1 a similar expression is directed toward Gaius. The phrase might be nothing more than a warm greeting at the beginning of the letter, but a few things suggest a more profound significance. The phrase "whom I love," with the plural relative pronoun, immediately evokes the Gospel of John's phrase "the disciple whom Jesus loved," with a singular pronoun (John 13:23–25; 19:26–27; 20:1–10; 21:1–25). The Elder loves the members of this church in imitation of the love of Jesus. Further, Jesus urges all his disciples to "love one another" (John 13:34; 15:12), a commandment that appears again in 1 John (3:11, 23; 4:7, 12) and will be repeated below at 2 John 5.

The Elder does not merely love the members of the church; he also loves them "in truth." The phrase could be taken in the adverbial sense "truly love," but this would not convey the full Johannine sense of the term (Brown 1982, 655–56). The noun "truth" is very common in the Johannine literature, appearing twenty-five times in the Fourth Gospel and nine times in 1 John. "Truth" appears five times in this brief letter, including four times in these opening three verses. Truth is usually contrasted with what is false (1 John 1:6, 8; 2:4, 21; 4:6). That sense is implicit here, as a preparation for the argument that will follow regarding the falsehood of those who left the community. Verse 2 explains that the truth which the Elder here defends is not only a truth for the present age but also will last forever.

Verse 3 shows the influence of the Pauline Epistles on later Christian epistolography. In his letters, Paul had already modified the standard Greek greeting formula in several ways. For example, he greeted his readers with the standard

Semitic greeting, "Peace be to you," and then he set aside, or rather replaced, the standard Greek verb *chairein*, "greetings/rejoice," with the related noun "grace" (*charis*), which carries considerable theological significance. A typical Pauline greeting was thus, "Grace and peace to you from God . . . and from Jesus Christ" (1 Cor. 1:3; Gal. 1:3; Lieu 2008, 247). Later Christian books follow this Pauline innovation, as in Rev. 1:4, "Grace to you and peace from him who is . . ." Other letters add further innovations (1 Pet. 1:2; 2 Pet. 1:2), including the word "mercy" (1 Tim. 1:2; 2 Tim. 1:2). Thus 2 John wishes "grace, mercy, and peace" to the Elect Lady. A Johannine element is nevertheless added to this Pauline phrase. When Paul speaks of grace and peace "from" God the Father and Jesus Christ, he uses the preposition *apo*. Here 2 John relies on the more common Johannine preposition *para*, which Jesus uses in the Gospel of John to refer to his origin in the Father (6:46; 7:29; 17:7–8). Finally, the opening greeting is rounded off with a further repetition of truth and love.

The True Faith and the True Way of Life (4–6)

4–5. I was exceedingly glad because I have found some of your children walking in truth, just as we received a commandment from the Father. And now I ask of you, Lady, not as one writing a new commandment to you, but the one that we have had from the beginning—that we love one another. Verse 4 opens with an expression that will be repeated in slightly different form in 3 John 3, where the Elder will also be "exceedingly glad" at the manifestation of truth. In 3 John, the truth that is on display is the offering of hospitality to visiting missionaries. Here in 2 John, the Elder is exceedingly glad because the members of the church he addresses are "walking in the truth." Living the Christian life is often described as "walking" (*peripatein*) in 1–3 John (1 John 1:6; 2:6, 11; 3 John 3, 4) and in the Bible generally (Pss. 1:1; 15:2; Rom. 6:4; 8:4; 14:15). It should be understood in relation to the similar expression "Do the truth" in 1 John 1:6–7, where the phrase refers to showing one's faith in concrete actions, and also to the need to avoid the falsehood of those who have left the community (cf. Painter 2002, 346; also see comments on 1:6–7).

Walking in truth, we are next told, means to obey "the commandment." Like the term "truth," which is repeated with tremendous frequency in the thirteen verses of this letter, the term "commandment(s)" is also used with considerable density in 2 John, appearing four times (4, 5, 6 [2x]). The commandment is expressed in verse 5: "that we love one another." This at first seems straightforward, since Jesus gave his disciples the "new commandment" to love one another (John 13:34; 15:12). The same commandment is given here, to love one another, but the label "new" is rejected. As in 1 John 2:6–7, the commandment is not new at all but, rather, is the same commandment that was held "from the beginning." Insisting that the commandment is not new seems jarring, since Jesus himself said it was new. The solution to this dilemma resides in the formulaic statement "from the beginning" (see comments on

1 John 2:6–7). In 1 John 1:1 the expression "from the beginning" stresses that the teaching of these letters had its origin in the ministry of Jesus. The origin of the teaching in the ministry of Jesus explains how the commandment is not "new." It has been passed down from the Lord himself "from the beginning." It is not new in the sense that it is not an innovation of the Elder. The play on words, in which the novelty of the "new commandment" is disavowed, indicates that the "new commandment" is not new at all, but comes from the ministry of the Lord himself. The value of this line of argument will be seen in verse 9, in the problem presented by those who "go ahead" and who do not "abide in the teaching of Christ." They do not respect what was given "from the beginning."

6. And this is love—that we walk according to his commandments. This is the commandment, just as you heard from the beginning—that you walk in it. The basic intention of verse 6 is clear enough. Readers are urged to adhere to the commandment to love one another. This clear direction could not have been expressed, however, in a more confusing construction. The content of the commandment is also unusual, or it is at least presented in an unusual fashion, precisely because the term "commandment(s)" is repeated so many times. Coming right after verse 5, the repetition of the commandment in verse 6 creates what appears to be a tautology. Verse 5 says that the commandment is to love one another. Verse 6a says that love means to walk in the commandments. To obey the command, in other words, is to love (v. 5), and to love means to obey the command (v. 6).

In verse 6b–c, one also wonders how to render the phrase **This is the commandment, just as you heard from the beginning—that you walk in it.** Two problems come especially to the fore. First, in which direction does the "this" at the start of verse 6b point? Does it refer to the previous clause or to the following one? The word "this" often has its meaning explained and completed by a phrase that follows it (see comments on 1 John 2:3), and yet it might also explain a clause that precedes it. In the present verse, neither option is ideal. Brown translates the term as "that," in order to make verse 6b refer to the previous clause. In such a rendering, though, the phrase "that is the commandment" (v. 6b) explains the phrase "this is love" (v. 6a), which creates yet another tautology. The present translation follows Martin Culy (2004, 146) in making verse 6b refer to the clause that follows.

The second problem in this line concerns the antecedent for the last word in the verse: the pronoun "it" (*autē*). The pronoun could grammatically refer either to "commandment" or to "love" in verse 6, or to the word "truth" last mentioned in verse 4. No solution is ideal because the syntax is neither smooth nor clear. The key Johannine terms "love," "walk," and "commandment" tumble quickly after one another, so that it is difficult to render the phrases clearly. The impression one gets is that the mere repetition of phrases is precisely the point. Ernst Wendland (1991, 32–33) refers to the "intentional ambiguity

---

A Standard Paraenetic Letter

"Aquila to Sarapion, greetings. I was overjoyed to receive your letter. Our friend Callinicus was testifying to the utmost about the way of life you follow even under such conditions—especially in your not abandoning your austerities. Yes, we may deservedly congratulate ourselves, not because we do these things, but because we are not diverted from them by ourselves. Courage! Carry through what remains like a man! Let not wealth distract you, nor beauty, nor anything else of the same kind: for there is no good in them, if virtue does not join her presence, no, they are vanishing and worthless. Under divine protection, I expect you in Antinoopolis. Send Soteris the puppy, since she now spends her time by herself in the country. Good health to you and yours! Good health!" (P.Oxy. 3069 [third/fourth century CE], trans. Stowers 1986, 99)

---

of these verses," and Duane Watson (1989a; 1989b) seems rightly to see here the Johannine tendency toward rhetorical amplification, and specifically *expolitio*. *Expolitio* is defined as "dwelling on the same topic, and yet seeming to say something ever new" (anonymous, *Rhet. Her.* 4.42.54). The idea is to draw attention to a topic by repetition and thus to reinforce its significance. Judith Lieu (2008, 252) states the matter plainly: "On any reading of these verses, with a greater or lesser degree of clarity the author is most concerned to evoke familiar concepts and phrases—'from the beginning,' 'the command,' 'love one another,' 'this is'—packing them together to create a close-knit framework defined in terms of obedience and of continuity with the past."

The False Faith and the False Way of Life (7–9)

7. For many deceivers went out into the world, those who do not confess Jesus Christ coming in the flesh. Such a person is the deceiver and the antichrist. Throughout the Johannine literature, those who are "of the world" are set apart from those who are in the community, and those in the community do not belong to "the world." The Fourth Gospel makes the point even more strongly, saying that the world hates the followers of Christ (15:18–16:2). First John 2:15 follows this rhetorical arc and says, "Do not love the world, nor the things in the world; if someone loves the world, the love of the Father is not in him" (cf. 2:16; 3:1, 13, 17). All this should be borne in mind when 2 John 7 refers to those who have left the community as having gone out "into the world." While in the community, they were opposed to the world. Now that they have left the community of fellowship, they are one with the world (cf. 1 John 4:1).

Much of the discussion of the secessionists in these verses echoes and evokes the discussion of their activity in 1 John, though there are notable differences.

In 1 John 4:1, for example, the secessionists were called "many" (*polloi*), just as they are now, but they were further defined as false prophets: "Many false prophets have gone out into the world." Here, after they are called "many," they are defined in a different way, as "deceivers" (*planoi*). The noun *planoi* will appear again in the singular (*planos*), at the end of this verse. Though the word occurs nowhere else in the Johannine literature, the verb form *planan* (to deceive) is used three times in 1 John (1:8; 2:26; 3:7), and the noun *planē* (deceit) once (4:6). These deceivers are also said to have "gone out" (*exēlthon*). This description seems significant and colors their behavior in a dark shade. When Judas leaves the supper in the Gospel of John to betray the Lord, he also "went out" (*exēlthen*; John 13:30).

The teaching of the opponents is presented in a slightly different form in this verse, which at first might seem like just another example of standard Johannine variation (see comments at 1 John 2:20), but it does create a bit of a puzzle if one takes the change seriously. In 1 John 4:2, the description of the false teaching referred to Jesus Christ as "having come [*elēlythota*] in the flesh." Second John 7 is different. It (literally) refers to "Jesus Christ coming [*erchomenon*] in the flesh," with a present participle. Does this matter? It has certainly mattered to scholars. Not all the proposals for explaining the different tenses of the participles are equally convincing, but attending to the various arguments will prepare us to see a rich and profound understanding of the theology of the Johannine Letters.

Scholarly approaches to this problem have different starting points and rely on different evidence, but one can still classify opinions into broad categories (Painter 2002, 349–50). Some interpreters believe that there is no difference between this present participle in 2 John 7 and the perfect participle in 1 John 4:2. Both texts refer to the same debate with the same figures, and they both defend the theology of the incarnation. Jesus Christ is the Word who became flesh (John 1:14). This position is mostly correct. It finds support in the fact that 1 John elsewhere alters verb tenses when describing the incarnation. First John 4:9–10, for example, uses first the perfect "has sent" (*apestalken*) and then the aorist "sent" (*apesteilen*) to describe the entry of Christ into the world. So we cannot assume too strict an adherence to tenses in the Johannine Letters (Rensberger 1997, 153).

However, a real difference separates these two passages. It should not be ignored that the participle form does change. The perfect participle from 1 John 4:2 has become the present participle of 2 John 7, and scholars have found various ways to account for this change. Some, for instance, believe that the change in tense means that the present participle in 2 John cannot refer to the incarnation. For these interpreters, the present tense of the participle in verse 7 is a reference to the real presence of Christ in the Eucharist, a not utterly implausible view if one coordinates what is said here with the possible Eucharist reference in 1 John 5:6 as well as with the eucharistic passage in chapter 6 of the Gospel of John. The plain sense of the text does not support such a reading, though. There is no hint that a debate over the Eucharist is in view in 2 John.

Other efforts also see the present participle as significant, but in different ways. George Strecker (1996, 234–36) writes that the present participle points not to the present but to the future. He argues that the change in tense of the participle means that 2 John 7 is to be separated utterly from 1 John 4:2. The present participle here in 2 John 7 refers to Jesus as the "coming one," and thus points to the parousia, in the manner of texts like Rev. 20:1–3 and 1 Cor. 15:23–24. Like the eucharistic interpretation, though, this interpretation seems to import concerns that have little to do with the debates engaging the Elder in 2 John 7.

Judith Lieu (1986, 86–87) offers a different way forward (cf. Brown 1982, 670). She argues that 2 John 7 alters the language in 1 John 4:2, and that the alteration has nothing to do with a polemic against opponents. It is simply a redeployment of the language of the Fourth Gospel, which refers to Jesus as "the one who comes" (1:15, 27; 3:31; 6:14; 11:27; 12:13). This is a compelling claim, but the denial of any polemic intent seems to go a bit too far, because the Elder boldly declares that those who hold this position are antichrists and deceivers. The polemic intent seems clear (Rensberger 1997, 153). However, Lieu's proposal that 2 John 7 borrows its phraseology from the Gospel opens up a broad area of inquiry that coordinates the change in participles here with the broader argument of the Johannine Letters. When 2 John 7 refers to Jesus as the one who "comes in the flesh," it simply adopts the temporal perspective of the Gospel evident in the various places where the Gospel refers to Jesus as "the one who comes," such as 3:31: "The one who comes [*ho erchomenos*] from above is above all; the one who is from the earth belongs to the earth, and speaks as one from the earth. The one who comes [*ho erchomenos*] from heaven is above all." Such an example helps us to hear differently the reference in 2 John 7 to "Jesus Christ coming [*erchomenon*] in the flesh," because 2 John 7 employs both the tense and time frame of the Gospel. It speaks of Christ's coming as a present reality, as though the incarnation is happening in the author's present, even though it was in his past. As we have seen, a similar circumstance prevails with the "new commandment." The Letters speak of this commandment as "new" because it was the new commandment in the ministry of Jesus, thereby adopting the time frame of the Gospel. But when the commandment is also called "old," the letters are conscious of how they are not written from within the ministry of Jesus, which happened in the past. The temporal posture of the letters thus speaks of the ministry of Jesus as something that happened in the past, as well as something that is right now happening in the present. This is why 1 John 4:2 speaks of Christ as "having come," while 2 John 7 speaks of him as the "one who is coming." The temporal perspective on the incarnation has changed, but the focus on the incarnation remains the same. For more on the temporal shifts involved in this verse, see the discussion below in "Theological Issues."

Second John 7 shifts our focus from the plural "many deceivers" to the singular "antichrist." This is the opposite of the shift in person that takes place in 1 John 2:18, where the singular "antichrist" becomes the plural "antichrists." The point seems to be the same in both cases, though (Brown 1982, 670). All those false teachers who peddle a false Christology are anti-Christ, that is, enemies of Christ, and working according to the pattern of the great deceiver who is to come at the end of time (see comments at 1 John 2:18).

8. Watch yourselves, in order that you do not lose the things for which we have labored, but instead receive the full reward. The teaching of the opponents is not something to be taken casually. Now that the opponents' Christology has been mentioned once more, the readers are brought to a point of decision with "Watch yourselves." They are being urged to recognize the falsehood of the opponents and to remain within the fold of the Elder. The shift in person likely carries great significance. The verbs here rendered as "watch," "lose," "labored," and "receive" alternate on a pattern: you, you, we, you. A similar shift in the person of pronouns and verbs occurred in 1 John 1:1–10. The point here is the same as it was there. The author refers to his readers as "you" in order to urge them to be part of the "we" of the true community. By first referring to them as though they are not part of "we," but of "you," he reminds them that they have a choice, but then by referring to them suddenly as part of the "we," he makes it clear that the choice lies with them and they have the ability to choose where they stand (see "The Rhetoric of the Letters: *Sententiae* and Social Division" in the introduction).

The idea that the faithful will receive (*lambanein*) a reward (*misthos*) is thoroughly Johannine. John 4:35–36 reads, "The fields are ripe for the harvest; the reaper is already receiving [*lambanein*] his reward [*misthos*]." The only difference is that 2 John projects this reward into the future as an eschatological hope, while the Gospel sees it as the enjoyment of the gifts of eternal life now ("the reaper is already receiving"). In this sense, 2 John is closer to the phraseology and thought of other early Christian writers (Matt. 5:12; Mark 9:41; 1 Cor. 3:8–9).

9. Anyone who goes ahead and does not remain in the teaching of Christ does not possess God. The one who remains in the teaching—this one possesses both the Father and the Son. The term here translated "goes ahead" is the Greek word *proagein*, which literally means "to advance," "go forward," or "move ahead." As the latter part of the verse makes clear, the term refers to those who do not abide in the teaching that has been passed down but move ahead and beyond that teaching. To use an expression repeatedly used in the Letters of John, they do not abide in what was "from the beginning" (1 John 1:1; 2:7, 13, 24; 3:8, 11; 2 John 5, 6). Hence they "go ahead," as the verb is translated here (cf. Culy 2004, 150).

False Teachers and Hospitality (10–11)

10–11. If someone comes to you and does not bring this teaching, do not receive him into your house and do not say to him, "Greetings!" For the one who says to him, "Greetings," has fellowship with his wicked deeds. The teaching here is clear, and the reference to "have fellowship" (*koinonei*) recalls the fellowship that believers share with the Father and with one another in 1 John 1:3. Holding on to the true faith and showing love for the members of the community—this is the path to fellowship with the true community and with the true God. Sharing in the work of the false teachers is the path to fellowship with false believers and a false divinity.

Something further is implied by the term "have fellowship." As Christianity spread throughout the Roman Empire, its communities were scattered far and wide. The communities were in contact, but because they were often separated by some distance, the members of one community did not always know those of another location. Hence the traveling missionaries and teachers who visited these communities often did so as strangers to the people they visited. This could lead to abuses. Traveling missionaries might be frauds who duped people into supporting them. To prove their good faith, therefore, itinerant evangelists would often carry letters of recommendation from people who knew the Christians in a given city, in order that the traveler might be given hospitality. Third John refers to precisely this act of hospitality and praises Gaius for supporting missionaries, praising him as a coworker in the ministry of such missionaries because of the material support he has given them. To support a true missionary is to be a coworker with the truth (3 John 8). As we

---

Teaching from the *Didache* on Traveling Missionaries

Rules on Proper Teaching

"¹So, if anyone should come and teach you all these things that have just been mentioned above, welcome him. ²But if the teacher himself goes astray and teaches a different teaching that undermines all this, do not listen to him. However, if his teaching contributes to righteousness and knowledge of the Lord, welcome him as you would the Lord." (*Did.* 11.1–2 [first century CE], trans. Holmes 2007, 361)

Rules on Proper Behavior

"⁸However, not everyone who speaks in the spirit is a prophet, but only if he exhibits the Lord's ways. By his conduct, therefore, will the false prophet and the [true] prophet be recognized. ⁹Furthermore, any prophet who orders a meal in the spirit shall not partake of it; if he does, he is a false prophet. ¹⁰If any prophet teaches the truth, yet does not practice what he teaches, he is a false prophet." (*Did.* 11.8–10, trans. Holmes 2007, 363)

see here in 2 John, the opposite can also be true. To provide material support for a false teacher is to have fellowship with falsehood. The teachers who have "gone ahead" and left behind the teaching that was "from the beginning" seem to be visiting the churches in the Elder's care. He wants the faithful to be careful, therefore, about whom they welcome and support.

Epistolary Farewell (12–13)

12. Although I have many things to write to you, I did not want [to communicate] through paper and ink. Instead, I hope to be with you and to speak face-to-face, so that our joy might be complete. The letter ends in ways that are typical for ancient letters, but in those same ways the letter also shows its uniquely Johannine character. For instance, the statement about wishing to speak face-to-face, rather than through a letter, is a common epistolary formula, but it is also shared by 3 John 14. Likewise, the phrase "that our joy might be complete" sounds at first like a typical expression of joy at the close of a letter, but it also calls to mind Johannine expressions of joy elsewhere. In the Fourth Gospel, the disciples "rejoiced" (20:20) when they saw the risen Lord. First John 1:4 urges unity in the Johannine churches, "so that our joy might be complete." At 1 John 1:4, the fulfillment of joy was connected to the integrity of the community. The same concern operates here, and the need to preserve the true fellowship is present in this phrase

13. The children of your Elect Sister greet you. As noted at the start of the commentary on 2 John, the term "sister" here probably refers to the Elder's church, and the children are the members of the church (see "Theological Issues" after 1 John 2:12–3:10).

Theological Issues

The commentary on 2 John has brought into sharp relief the temporal tensions that appear in both 1–2 John. The temporal perspective of the author is not uniform but alternates between past and present. Or rather, the author sometimes writes as though the past *is* the present. The shifting temporal postures are obvious in the treatment of the "new commandment" and of Jesus's appearance in the flesh. In some places, the author writes as though the ministry of Jesus is in the past. Thus at 1 John 4:2 he refers to the incarnation by saying, "In this way you know the Spirit of God—every spirit which confesses Jesus Christ as having come in the flesh is from God," where the phrase "having come" translates the perfect participle *elēlythota*. In 2 John 7, however, the temporal perspective on the incarnation has shifted. Now, Jesus did not come in the flesh in the past tense, but rather "Jesus Christ is coming in the flesh," where *erchomenon* is a present participle. Many different proposals have been made to explain this, but Judith Lieu (1986, 86–87) has insightfully shown that this use of the present participle is a way of adopting the temporal perspective of the Gospel's presentation of Jesus, where Jesus is referred to as "the one who comes" using the same present participle (*erchomenos*; 1:15, 27; 3:31; 6:14; 11:27; 12:13). The temporal perspective in 2 John 7, then, is no longer that of the author's present time, but of the ministry of Jesus.

Something similar seems to happen in the jarring protestations that the "new commandment" is not actually a new commandment at all, but an old commandment. First John 2:7–11 says, "Beloved, I do not write to you a new commandment, but an old commandment that you had from the beginning; the old commandment is the word that you heard. Again, I write to you a new commandment." Second John 5 makes a similar move by saying, "And now I ask of you, Lady, not as one writing a new commandment to you, but the one that we have had from the beginning—that we love one another." The new commandment obviously refers to the new commandment that Jesus gave in the Gospel of John, when he said, "I give you a new commandment, that you love one another" (13:34; see also 15:12, 17). Sometimes the letters speak of this commandment as though it is old, meaning that it was passed down to them in the tradition and is therefore an "old" commandment that they received from the past, and sometimes they accept the temporal frame of the Gospel and call it a new commandment. Thus, in these two instances, the temporal perspective of the letters shifts back and forth from its own time to the present time of the Gospel. Sometimes the ministry of Jesus seems to be happening in the present, and sometimes it is in the past. What does this mean? What is happening here?

To answer these questions we first have to recognize that a similar temporal flexibility operates in the Gospel of John. John seems at first to unfold according to a very strict temporal horizon that separates two distinct "time zones." The boundary dividing the time zones is the hour of Jesus's glorification. Several different texts signal the separation of different temporal periods. When Jesus cleanses the temple early in John (2:13–22) he announces that he will rise from the dead in three days, only to baffle his interlocutors. A comment of the Evangelist explains that understanding would come after the resurrection: "After he was raised from the dead, his disciples remembered that he had said this; and they believed the scripture and the word that Jesus had spoken" (2:22). A similar explanatory note accompanies the triumphal entry into Jerusalem on Palm Sunday, "His disciples did not understand these things at first; but when Jesus was glorified, then they remembered that these things had been written of him and had been done to him" (12:16). Finally, John 7:39 also establishes a strict separation between the reality that prevails after the resurrection and the reality before the resurrection, as follows: "Now he said this about the Spirit, which believers in him were to receive; for as yet there was no Spirit, because Jesus was not yet glorified." These verses insist that before the resurrection there is a failure to understand Jesus properly, the Spirit has not been given and Jesus is not yet glorified. These realities only appear after the resurrection. But after establishing this firm temporal horizon, the Gospel also violates it in two key episodes. The glorification of Jesus is only supposed to take place in the moment of his death and resurrection (7:39; 12:16), and yet when Jesus turns water into wine in the wedding at Cana, the following comment is appended to the episode: "Jesus did this, the first of his signs, in Cana of Galilee, and revealed his glory" (2:11). The post-resurrection glory of Jesus is manifest in his pre-resurrection ministry.

A similar violation of temporal horizons occurs in the Farewell Discourses. Past, present, and future are mingled together inscrutably in the Farewell Discourses. A few examples can demonstrate the confusion. Jesus announces his departure by informing the disciples, "Little children, I am with you only a little longer" (John 13:33); and yet, in his prayer to the Father he has already left them behind, saying of the disciples: "While I was with them . . ." (17:12). Jesus also refers to his death as a coming conflict with Satan ("Behold, the ruler of this world is coming," 14:30) but soon thereafter heralds his success in the conflict as a past event: "Take heart, I have overcome the world," in the perfect tense (16:33). Later, Jesus opens chapter 17 by praying, "Father, the hour has come; glorify your Son" (17:1; cf. 17:5), and yet already insists earlier in chapter 13, "Now the Son of Man has been glorified" (13:31), in the aorist tense. Finally, Jesus can announce his imminent departure from the world by saying, "In a little while, the world will no longer see me" (14:19) but then conversely announces, "And I am no longer in the world" (17:11). It is as though two discourses have been blended together, one that Jesus delivers around the table on the night of his betrayal, and one that he delivers from the realm of the Father after the ascension. Jesus is alternately here and there, before and after, above and below.

What is the meaning of this temporal confusion, in which post-resurrection realities intrude into the pre-resurrection life of Jesus? Does this mean, as some have suggested in the history of scholarship, that the resurrection is meaningless in John? If Jesus can already reveal his glory in the wedding at Cana, does this make the revelation of glory on the cross superfluous? I believe the opposite is true (see discussion in Parsenios 2005b, 16–17). It is not that the resurrection is meaningless for understanding Jesus, but that it is the only meaningful lens through which to interpret his life. He is only known correctly when he is known as the crucified, resurrected, and glorified Lord. The post-resurrection perspective of the Gospel, signaled in verses 2:22; 7:39; and 12:16 is meant to impress upon us the insight that we are wrong if we try to appreciate Jesus by examining only his pre-resurrection life. We understand his earthly ministry wrongly if we understand it from a pre-resurrection perspective. We can only understand his life prior to the resurrection by viewing it from a standpoint after the resurrection. To project this perspective into the narrative, John violates the strict temporal horizon that he establishes, narrating post-resurrection realities already in the wedding at Cana in John 2 and in the Farewell Discourses.

Something similar seems to be at work in the temporal tensions in the Letters of John. The boundary separating past and present is crossed in order to show the readers that they can only understand their own present from the perspective of the past. The repeated emphasis on things that were "from the beginning" shows the desire to be in continuity with the past. And the basic assumption is that the ministry of Jesus is something that happened in the past. But the various devices that are used to treat the ministry of Jesus as though it is the present, and to adopt the temporal perspective of the Gospel, must also serve a didactic purpose related to the struggle with the secessionists. Second John 9 explains the logic of this move: "Anyone who goes ahead and does not remain in the teaching of Christ does not possess God." The secessionists seem to have developed a theological profile that is unmoored from the message of Jesus. First John 2:24 makes the same point by way of admonition: "You, what you heard from the beginning, let that in you abide. If what you heard from the beginning abides in you, then you also abide in the Son and in the Father." If the opponents have erred by developing an understanding of Jesus that deviates from one that was passed down "from the beginning," meaning from the ministry of Jesus himself, the letters underscore the indispensability of seeing Jesus "from the beginning" by casting their readers into a past perspective.

Thus, the temporal tensions in the letters seem to serve the same didactic and rhetorical purpose as the temporal tensions in the Gospel. In the Gospel, the shift in time zones emphasizes that one misunderstands Jesus by knowing him only before the resurrection, while the temporal transitions in the letters emphasize that one misunderstands Jesus just as badly by moving so far forward in one's theology as to become unmoored from the actual earthly life and ministry of Jesus.

3 John

A Letter to the Beloved Gaius

Introductory Matters

Third John, with its fifteen verses, is the shortest letter in the NT. The letter is not only brief but also focuses on an apparently mundane matter—showing hospitality to travelers. The Elder begins the letter by praising and thanking Gaius for the hospitality he has shown to missionaries in the past (vv. 5–8). He condemns Diotrephes for withholding the same hospitality (vv. 9–10), and he urges Gaius to support the missionary named Demetrius (vv. 11–12). Then the letter ends (vv. 13–15). In various ways scholars have tried to tease some deeper significance out of these few details. An especially fruitful area of inquiry explores the social conventions regarding the proper treatment of ambassadors and messengers in the Greco-Roman world in general, and within Christianity in particular (Malherbe 1983; Mitchell 1998). It was common in antiquity to support traveling agents of a foreign ruler or dignitary, and the technical language associated with this practice is fully present in 3 John. The offering of hospitality to traveling evangelists was common among early Christians, and the practice seems to have inspired frequent controversy (*Did.* 11–15). It is no wonder that we see the practice causing disagreements here. But if 3 John fits neatly within ancient discussions over hospitality, it fits far less neatly within the theological debates of 1–2 John. Third John is generally considered to be the least "Johannine" of the Johannine Letters. It was also the last of the letters to be circulated in the development of the canonical Scripture (Lieu 1986).

Vocabulary presents a particular problem in associating 3 John with the other letters. On the one hand, while key Johannine terms appear in 3 John, such as "love" (vv. 1, 6), "truth" (vv. 1, 3, 4, 8, 12), true (v. 12), and "testify/ testimony" (vv. 3, 6, 12 [3x]), the density and frequency of Johannine vocabulary is not nearly as pronounced as in 1 and 2 John. On the other hand, 3 John is a short letter. The shallower concentration of Johannine terms in it can be explained as a function of the document's brevity. Yet a lack of Johannine vocabulary is not the only matter that causes people to question the Johannine quality of this letter. There is at the same time a good deal of language that is more common in other Christian circles. Words and phrases like "send on" (v. 6), "for the sake of the name" (v. 7), and "coworkers" (v. 8) are common in Acts and in the Pauline corpus but much less at home in the Johannine literature. Third John is also the only document in the Johannine corpus that uses the term "church" (*ekklēsia*, vv. 6, 9, 10).

An even greater difficulty arises when one tries to discern how the struggle with Diotrephes in 3 John relates to the struggle with the secessionists in 1–2 John. Third John does not raise doctrinal issues, much less the particular issues that are so prominent in 1–2 John. Even when 3 John uses the Johannine language mentioned above, it fills a term like "truth" with content that does not reflect the theological concerns in 1–2 John. The truth at issue in 3 John seems more to reflect a personal struggle between the Elder and Diotrephes. For some, because no explicit links join the problems in 3 John to those circulating around 1–2 John, no identification between the three letters can be attempted. Raymond Brown (1982, 701–27) and John Painter (2002, 361–86) are more positive about making connections among the various letters. They recognize that the documents are joined by no *explicit* links, but insist that there are strong *implicit* ones. This commentary will follow them in finding a reasonable set of connections between 3 John and 1–2 John.

Furthermore, the Johannine quality of the letter is more pronounced than at first it seems. Third John has to do with showing hospitality to missionaries sent from one church to another. Receiving those who are "sent out" has a particular prominence in Johannine thought, because Jesus is regularly identified as the one "who was sent" (Mitchell 1998, 319). The Fourth Gospel describes Jesus as the agent whom the Father has sent into the world (3:17, 34; 4:34; 5:23, 30, 36, 38; 6:29, 57; 7:16, 29, 33; 8:29, 42; 10:36; 12:44, 45, 49; 14:24; 15:21; 17:3, 8, 18, 21, 23, 25; 20:21; etc.). And although Jesus is sent to his own, his own do not receive him (John 1:11), while those who do receive him are "given the power to become children of God" (1:12). To receive (or reject) Jesus when he is sent into the world is to receive (or reject) the Father who sent him. Giving honor and respect to the one sent is a sign of respect for the sender. This special status of "being sent" is extended to the disciples when Jesus says, "Very truly, I tell you, whoever receives one whom I send receives me; and whoever receives me receives him who sent me" (John 13:20). Showing hospitality to the disciples acknowledges their connection to Jesus—which is really to honor the Father. Seen in this light,

3 John is readily understood as a debate over the proper appropriation of the message of the Fourth Gospel. This commentary will read 3 John as being closely connected to the other documents in the Johannine corpus in general as well.

If the place of 3 John within the larger Johannine corpus is contested by some, its place in the broader body of ancient epistolography is much more certain. Third John more closely resembles other ancient letters than either 1 or 2 John does, and more than almost any other letter in the NT. The length of 3 John is a principal feature that especially connects it to other ancient letters. The vast majority of letters that survive from antiquity, either in random collections of papyrus or in edited personal collections, are relatively short. Like 3 John, they would fit on one page of papyrus.

Third John also fits neatly into the very well-known category of ancient letters of recommendation/introduction (*systatikai epistolai*). These letters have been studied closely, and they have a typical pattern (Stowers 1986, 153–65). While the more rhetorically sophisticated letters that survive in the private collections of well-educated writers shows some variety, the papyrus letters gathered from Egypt fairly closely adhere to this particular scheme:

I. Opening
   A. Salutation (e.g., "Musonius to Nilus, greetings")
   B. Wish for well-being (e.g., "If you are well, we also are well")
II. Background
   A. Identification of the one recommended
   B. Background proper (e.g., reason for the writer recommending the person)
III. Request period
   A. Request clause (e.g., "you would do well"; "you will be doing me a favor")
   B. Circumstantial clause (e.g., "if he has need of anything")
   C. Purpose and causal clauses (e.g., "so that you might introduce him to Tyrannus"; "for he is a trusted friend")
IV. Appreciation (only in some papyri, but often in Latin letters; e.g., "by doing this, you will have my gratitude")
V. Closing
   A. Wish for well-being (e.g., "take care of yourself so that you might be in good health")
   B. Salutation (e.g., "farewell"; "good luck")

This pattern roughly corresponds to the textbooks of Libanius and Demetrius, which define various types of letters appropriate to various social situations, including the letter of recommendation. Demetrius quickly summarizes this type of letter, then provides an example, as follows:

The commendatory type, which we write on behalf of one person to another, mixing in praise, at the same time also speaking of those who had previously been unacquainted as though they were (now) acquainted. In the following manner:

So-and-so, who is conveying this letter to you, has been tested by us and is loved on account of his trustworthiness. You will do well if you deem him worthy of hospitality both for my sake and his, and indeed for your own. For you will not be sorry if you entrust to him, in any manner you wish, either words or deeds of a confidential nature. Indeed, you, too, will praise him to others when you see how useful he can be in everything. (*Eloc.* 2, trans. Malherbe 1988)

Libanius writes:

The commending genre is that in which we commend someone to someone. It is also called the introductory genre.

The letter of commendation. Receive this highly honored and much sought-after man, and do not hesitate to treat him hospitably, thus doing what behooves you and what pleases me. (*Epis. Styles* 8, 55, trans. Malherbe 1988)

These patterns and rules should be kept in mind as we read 3 John, in order to recognize how the general model is deployed in this particular context. Especially significant is the fact that both textbook definitions assume that the letter of introduction is being conveyed by the person whom it recommends. The letter is proof of support for a person abroad, a passport of sorts, identifying that the person should be treated in a particular way and given a certain kind of privilege. Given this background, we should assume that 3 John is being carried by Demetrius as he travels to Gaius. Judith Lieu (2008, 280–81) questions this possibility, but cites evidence both for and against it. The most reasonable assumption remains that Demetrius is bearing the letter.

> **3 John in the Rhetorical Flow**
>
> **Epistolary opening (1–4)**
>
> **Hospitality for missionaries (5–8)**
>
> **The inhospitality of Diotrephes (9–10)**
>
> **The recommendation of Demetrius (11–12)**
>
> **Epistolary closing (13–15)**

Tracing the Train of Thought

Epistolary Opening (1–4)

1. In keeping with standard epistolary procedure, 3 John opens by naming its sender and recipient: **The Elder, to the beloved Gaius, whom I love in truth.** The identity of "the Elder" has already been addressed in the opening of 2 John. Unlike that letter, 3 John mentions its recipient, Gaius, by name. The name was very common in the Roman world, and its most famous owner was Gaius Julius Caesar. The NT knows several figures named Gaius (Acts 19:29; 20:4; Rom. 16:23; 1 Cor. 1:14), but none of these other persons is credibly considered to be the Gaius mentioned here (Brown 1982, 702–3). If 3 John follows the typical letter format in some ways, it deviates by including a greeting. Equally atypical is the use of the verb "I love" in the first person, which breaks the standard third-person form of epistolary openings (*x* to *y*, greetings).

And yet if this latter phrase marks a deviation from typical epistolary style, it fits nicely within Johannine style, where love is one of the definitive terms and concepts binding believers to one another. The adjective *agapētos* that is applied to Gaius is also significant in this regard. The use of *agapētos* as an adjective is not unheard of in ancient letters, as in the opening, "Irenaeus to Apollinarius, his dearest brother, many greetings" (Lieu 2008, 267). Contemporary translations of 3 John, in light of this epistolary procedure, render the term as an ancient equivalent of the modern letter opening, in the form "To my dear friend, Gaius" (NIV). But the term has a Johannine quality that suggests it should be translated in the form "beloved" (NRSV). The term *agapētos* is used throughout the NT writings as an adjective to modify the name of fellow Christians (Rom. 16:5, 8, 9, 12). In the LXX this adjective was also applied to the people of God (Jer. 6:26; Ps. 127:2), and in the NT to Jesus (Mark 1:11; 9:7). But in the Johannine usage it evokes several things, including at least a distant echo from the epithet of the author of the Fourth Gospel, who is referred to only in John as "the disciple whom Jesus loved" (John 13:23–25; 19:26–27; 20:1–10; 21:1–25). In the same way that Jesus loved this disciple, the Elder loves his disciple Gaius (3 John 1). Love is the definitive principle of relationships in the Johannine orbit. Jesus urges all of his disciples to "love one another" (John 13:34; 15:12), a commandment that appears again in the Johannine Letters (1 John 3:11, 23; 4:7, 12; 2 John 5). The love of God and the love of disciples come explicitly together when 1 John 4:11 says, "Beloved, if God so loved us, we in turn ought to love one another." Whatever the personal connotations that the adjective *agapētos* carries, therefore, its primary referent is this Johannine sense, in which Gaius is one of God's beloved. This places him squarely within the Johannine circle of believers.

The opening clause of the letter ends by affirming that the Elder not only loves Gaius but that he loves him "in truth." The phrase should be understand here in the same way that it was in 2 John 1, where it does not simply carry the adverbial sense "truly," but rather evokes the importance of the word "truth" (*alētheia*) in the Johannine literature. First and foremost, Jesus is understood as the Truth (John 14:6). First John provides an even more immediate context, when we read, "Let us love, not in word or speech, but in action and in reality [*alētheia*]" (3:18). To love in truth is, thus, to demonstrate one's love in concrete acts. First John 4:19–20 makes the same point even more elaborately: "We love because he first loved us. If someone says, 'I love God,' and yet hates his brother, he is a liar. For the one who does not love his brother whom he sees, is not able to love God whom he has not seen." When the Elder calls Gaius his beloved and insists that he loves him in truth, he evokes all these associations with love and truth. The purpose of the letter, consequently, is to ensure that Gaius displays that love through the real-life course of action that the Elder encourages him to follow.

2. Beloved, I pray that you fare well and enjoy good health in every regard, just as your soul is faring well. The verse opens with the term "beloved" from the previous line, now in the vocative case as a direct address to Gaius. This same direct address will be used two more times in the letter (vv. 5, 11). Like verse 1, verse 2 is characterized by, on the one hand, a close correspondence to typical epistolary procedure and, on the other hand, minor but significant deviations from the expected letter form. The use of the verb "I pray" (*euchomai*) and a wish for good health (*hygiainein*) are typical in a Greek letter, as evidenced by a papyrus (P.Oxy. 292, 11–12; cf. Painter 2002, 368) that reads, "I pray [*euchomai*] that you enjoy good health [*hygiainein*]." The translation of *euchomai* as "I pray" should thus not be given too great a religious expression. It is a standard term in the opening line of Greek letters. So is the wish for good health. Less standard is the verb *euodousthai*. It is here translated "to fare well," because it carries connotations of traveling on a journey (*eu* = well + *hodos* = road, path). The Christian life is often construed as a way of "walking" (*peripateite*) in the Johannine Letters (1 John 1:6, 7; 2:6, 11; 2 John 4, 6), and this idea is perhaps present in the wish for Gaius to "fare well."

At the end of the verse, the reference to the soul presents a puzzle. It seems to turn the phrase into a wish for both physical and spiritual health. The health of the body, in this way of reading, would be covered in the wish "to enjoy good health" (*hygiainein*), while the reference to the soul is a wish for spiritual well-being (Brown 1982, 704). One should not, however, imagine a dualism between body and soul, where the two represent opposing or unrelated entities. Instead, one should see a wish for the health of the entire person—body and soul (Schnackenburg 1992, 292). And this does not seem to be a casual statement. It is based on the connection that is commonly made in NT texts between physical and spiritual well-being (see 1 Cor. 11:29–30; James 5:13–16).

The final phrase, "just as your soul is faring well," begins with the Greek word *kathōs*, where *kathōs* resembles its use in 1 John 2:6: "The person . . . ought himself to walk just as [*kathōs*] Christ walked." Gaius's behavior shows that he is faring well in his soul, and the hope of the letter's greeting is that he fares just as well in his physical health.

3–4. Verse 3 builds on the spiritual health of Gaius when it announces, **For I was exceedingly glad when the brothers arrived and testified to your truth, even as you walk in truth.** The spiritual health mentioned briefly in verse 2 is explained here, and verses 2 and 3 are connected by the Greek particle *gar*, "for." Thus the Elder can speak of spiritual health in verse 2 because of what the brothers reported in verse 3. Fellow believers have returned from Gaius to the Elder, and they testify that Gaius is "walking in the truth." His spiritual health is assured, but it is assured because of his physical actions. He has provided material support for those who were sent to him, as we learn in verses 6–8.

The phrase "I was exceedingly glad" is the exact phrase in Greek (*echarēn lian*) that we find in 2 John 4, which also mentions "walking in truth." In that verse, walking in truth is connected to keeping the commandments, and then the single commandment "to love one another" is repeated. To walk in truth means to love one another. Here in 3 John, to walk in truth means to show hospitality to the brothers. The connection between 2 John and 3 John on this point makes it plain that the command to love one another in 2 John finds its expression in the support given to traveling missionaries in 3 John. Could even more be implied than this? Could the reference to "truth" have to do with a question of doctrine as well? In the Johannine Letters the word "truth" can be attached to questions of both belief (1 John 2:21–23; 4:2, 6; 5:20) and behavior (1 John 1:6; 2:4; 3:18–19), so one should not entirely rule out the doctrinal element. It is certainly the case that the Elder would not refer to Gaius's walking in the truth if Gaius held to a faulty Christology. And yet the content of Gaius's theology does not seem to be specifically in view. The truth in which Gaius walks is contrasted to the opposite status in Diotrephes, and there seems to be no stated theological deficiency in Diotrephes. Diotrephes's fault is a failure of action, not of belief. It would seem, then, that the truth in which Gaius walks is his proper behavior, and especially his behavior toward missionaries. The Elder then amplifies his joy by repeating himself, saying in verse 4, **I have no greater joy than to hear that my children are walking in the truth.**

Hospitality for Missionaries (5–8)

5–8. Verses 5–8 offer insight into the social realities that lie behind both 3 John and the earlier communication to Gaius mentioned in verses 1–4. Verse 5 says, **Beloved, you act faithfully in whatever you might have done for the brothers, and this toward strangers.** The verse opens by repeating the connection between faith and action in verses 1–4. It closes with an interesting point by saying, "and this toward strangers." The emissaries sent from the Elder were strangers to Gaius. They were not known by Gaius. This little detail reminds us how active early Christian missionaries were as they traveled throughout the Roman Empire to spread the message of the gospel to the ends of the earth (Acts 1:8). We see evidence of the networks that Christians used to spread information in anecdotes like the one reported in 1 Thess. 1:7–8. When Paul praises the Thessalonian Christians, he tells them that he is not alone in honoring them: "you became an example to all the believers in Macedonia and Achaia. For the word of the Lord has sounded from you not only in Macedonia and Achaia but in every place." Christian networks of

Christianity Spreads throughout the Roman Empire like a "Contagion"

Pliny the Younger was the Roman governor of Pontus and Bithynia in 111–13 CE. He describes how quickly Christianity spread in the following letter to the Roman emperor Trajan.

"The matter seemed to me to justify my consulting you, especially on account of the number of those imperiled; for many persons of all ages and classes and of both sexes are being put in peril by accusation and this will go on. The contagion of this superstition has spread not only in the cities, but in the villages and rural districts as well; yet it seems incapable of being checked and set right." (Letter 10.96.9, trans. Bettenson 1967, 4)

information and support provide help to missionaries as Christianity spreads rapidly throughout the empire.

As they traveled, these missionaries relied on the hospitality of local churches. So common was the practice that "a virtually technical vocabulary developed to describe the hospitable reception . . . and sending on . . . of those individuals who were spreading the faith" (Malherbe 1983, 96). A key term was *propempō*, "to send forward." Here 3 John 6 gestures toward this practice: **They have testified to your love in the presence of the church, and you will do well to send them on [*propempsas*] in a manner worthy of God.** The verb *propempō* has no other meaning in the NT except "sending a departing traveler on his way" (Malherbe 1983, 96n11). Precisely what it meant to send travelers on their journey could vary. In Acts 20:38, for instance, Paul leaves Miletus to go to Jerusalem. The Ephesian Christians are sad at his departure and travel with him as far as they can, even to the point that "they accompanied [*proepempon*] him to the ship." In Acts 15, Paul and Barnabas are not accompanied as they start their journey, but are authorized to go to Jerusalem by the church in Antioch to correct false teaching. They are sent out by the Antiochian church with the explanation, "So Paul and Barnabas were appointed, along with some other believers, to go up to Jerusalem to see the apostles and elders about this question. The church sent them on their way [*propemphthentes*]" (15:2–3).

More often than not, however, the meaning of the verb is to provide material and moral support while sending a missionary further on his travels in the service of the gospel. The most conspicuous use of the word in this sense comes from Paul's letter to Rome. Like the missionaries sent to Gaius in 3 John, Paul had never been to Rome and was unknown to the majority of the Christians there. But he hoped to come to them so that they might send him on his way for further missionary work in Spain. He writes, "But now, with no further place for me in these regions, I desire, as I have for many years, to come to you when I go to Spain. For I do hope to see you on my journey and

---

Peregrinus and the Abuse of Hospitality Given by Christians to Missionaries

Lucian of Samosata, a satirist who wrote in the second century CE, describes the career of the charlatan Peregrinus, who dupes various people into believing he has special wisdom and powers. Lucian describes his deception of Christians as follows:

"It was then that he learned the wondrous lore of the Christians, by associating with their priests and scribes in Palestine. And—how else could it be?—in a trice he made them all look like children, for he was prophet, cult-leader, head of the synagogue, and everything, all by himself. He interpreted and explained some of their books and even composed many, and they revered him as a god, made use of him as a lawgiver, and set him down as a protector, next after that other, to be sure, whom they still worship, the man who was crucified in Palestine because he introduced this new cult into the world." (Lucian, *Peregr.* 11, trans. A. M. Harmon, LCL)

Peregrinus then goes traveling about, with support from Christians as he goes:

"He left home, then, for the second time, to roam about, possessing an ample source of funds in the Christians, through whose ministrations he lived in unalloyed prosperity. For a time he battened himself thus; but then, after he had transgressed in some way even against them—he was seen, I think, eating some of the food that is forbidden them, they no longer accepted him." (Lucian, *Peregr.* 16, trans. A. M. Harmon, LCL)

---

to be sent on [*propemphthēnai*] by you, once I have enjoyed your company for a little while" (Rom. 15:23–24). The verb has this same sense elsewhere in the Pauline corpus (1 Cor. 16:6; 2 Cor. 1:16; Titus 3:13) and even outside the NT in such documents as Polycarp's *Letter to the Philippians* (1.1).

And yet if a network of Christian missionary supporters existed throughout the empire, so did a ready supply of people who were willing to abuse the support that they so readily offered. The *Didache* (11–12) lists several potential problems that could be encountered by a local church playing host to a traveling missionary.

The best way to ensure that a missionary would be received hospitably and without suspicion was to send him on his way with letters of introduction. It was said above that Demetrius is probably carrying 3 John with him as he visits Gaius. The same must have been the case when envoys visited Gaius, and he welcomed them so warmly. They were carrying letters of recommendation from the Elder. Gaius welcomed them based on their introductory letters. How can we know this? Letters of recommendation were very commonly used among all people in the Greek cities of the Roman Empire, including Christians and Jews. They have several standard and regularly used technical

---

Letters of Introduction in the Book of Acts

Saul Seeks Letters of Introduction from the High Priest

"Meanwhile, Saul was still breathing out murderous threats against the Lord's disciples. He went to the high priest and asked him for letters to the synagogues in Damascus, so that if he found any there who belonged to the Way, whether men or women, he might take them as prisoners to Jerusalem." (Acts 9:1–2)

Apollos Receives Letters to Travel from Ephesus to Achaia

"When Apollos wanted to go to Achaia, the brothers and sisters encouraged him and wrote to the disciples there to welcome him." (Acts 18:27a)

---

terms, and these standard terms are peppered throughout the brief comments of 3 John 5–8 (Malherbe 1983, 102–3). Such letters, for example, would often label the person addressed as a potential "coworker," using some form of the verb *synergeō* (PSI 376, 969), and 3 John 8 urges Gaius to accept missionaries in order to be **coworkers** (*synergoi*) with them. Often there is also a request to receive the person bearing the letter, with some form of *lambanein*, "to receive" (PSI 520), and 3 John 8 reads, **Therefore, we ought to receive [*hypolambanein*] such people**. Specific requests for hospitality are often expressed by some compound of the verb *dechesthai*, "to receive," and this verb is used twice in verses 9–10. Yet another feature of these letters that appears in verses 5–8 is the claim that the people who are shown hospitality will be able to testify about the good care given to them by their hosts, using some form of the verb *martyrein*, "to testify" (P.Oslo 55; P.Flor. 173); and 3 John 3 and 6 mention the testimony (*martyrein*) that "the brothers" have shared regarding the hospitality they received from Gaius.

When two local churches were living in concord with each other, the practice of sending emissaries from the one to the other would work smoothly, and no stumbling blocks would prevent the giving and receiving of hospitality. The emissaries would be sent on their way (*propempein*), and the response of those whom they visited would be to accept or receive them, expressed by *epidechesthai* or cognate verbs (*dechomai* in Mark 6:11; Col. 4:10; *apodechomai* in Acts 18:27; 21:17; *anadechomai* in Acts 28:7; *hypodechomai* in Acts 17:7). An example of the procedure is neatly illustrated in the following scenario described in Acts 15:1–4:

> Certain individuals came down from Judea and were teaching the brothers: "Unless you are circumcised, according to the custom taught of Moses, you cannot be saved." And after Paul and Barnabas had no small dissension and debate with them, Paul and Barnabas and some of the others were appointed to go up

to Jerusalem to discuss this question with the apostles and elders. So they were sent [*propemphthentes*] on their way by the church, and as they passed through both Phoenicia and Samaria, they reported the conversion of the Gentiles and brought great joy to all the believers. When they came to Jerusalem, they were welcomed by the church [*paredechthēsan*] and the apostles and elders.

This seems to be precisely what took place when emissaries went from the Elder to Gaius. Although previously unknown to Gaius, they were received by him graciously and sent profitably on their way.

Two other matters deserve attention. First, after these traveling missionaries visited Gaius, and then apparently other believers as well, they returned to the Elder and "testified" about the love shown to them by Gaius (v. 6). Interestingly, they did so "in the presence of the church." The phrase seems out of place in the Letters of John. What is the sense of "church" (*ekklēsia*) here? Among 1–3 John, the term appears only in this letter (here and in vv. 9–10), and it occurs nowhere in the Fourth Gospel. One should not make too much of the word's absence from the Gospel, since it is also absent from Mark and Luke (Brown 1982, 710). The term is used much more commonly in the epistolary literature of the NT, and its presence here represents the intrusion of language more common in the broader vocabulary of early Christianity (cf. 1 Cor. 14:19, 35). The term will appear again in referring to the community led by Diotrephes (3 John 9–10), so here it seems naturally to refer to the community led by the Elder. This is supported in that the traveling missionaries returned to the Elder in order to report about their treatment at the hands of Gaius.

Second, Gaius is said to be a **coworker in the truth** (v. 8b) because he supported the traveling missionaries (v. 5). This is important. One of the principal problems in interpreting 3 John is its failure to mention any of the dogmatic concerns that fill every page of 1–2 John. Third John seems to have no theological interest at all. But this phrase means that it has more than we might at first imagine. There is no immediate doctrinal concern in the letter, or in the activity of Gaius, but his support for those who do have missionary and theological concerns (the traveling missionaries) means that he is a coworker in their effort to spread the truth of the gospel. The support for traveling missionaries is inherently connected to the theological work of the missionaries. To support missionary work is to be a coworker in it. But not everyone was a coworker of the missionaries. Diotrephes did not receive them.

The Inhospitality of Diotrephes (9–10)

9–10. Prior to verse 9, this letter is characterized by friendly and warm sentiments. Verses 1–8, on the one hand, praise Gaius for supporting traveling missionaries, and on the other hand, they explain why offering such support is so worthy of praise. Praise and friendship fill the first part of the letter. Verses 9–10 are very different. They are combative and admonitory. As soon as the Elder mentions the name Diotrephes, he calls Diotrephes someone **who loves to put himself first** (v. 9, *philoprōteuōn*), and someone **who slanders us with wicked words** (v. 10). The Elder and Diotrephes are locked in combat. That much is clear. The cause of their conflict is less clear. The history of scholarship has seen a variety of ways to explain the circumstances that lie behind the tense tone of these verses, and the variety of explanations can be summarized in three overarching categories (Mitchell 1998, 299). The Elder and Diotrephes could have battled over (1) a theological dispute, (2) a dispute over some personal matter, or (3) a dispute over ecclesiastical authority.

Before we can speculate about the broader nature of their conflict, however, we need to focus on the precise language of 3 John. Understanding the offense that Diotrephes commits is possible only once we understand the verb *epidechesthai*, which appears in verse 9 and again in verse 10. Although the same verb is repeated twice in these two verses, it is never rendered the same way in any recent translation. In verse 10, *epidechesthai* is always translated as "receive" or "welcome," as in **Diotrephes . . . does not receive/welcome us.** Verse 9 is more complicated. The following translations show the great variety of ways of rendering *epidechesthai* in verse 9:

Diotrephes . . . does not accept what we say. (NASB)

Diotrephes . . . will have nothing to do with us. (NEB, NIV)

Diotrephes . . . refuses to accept us. (JB)

Diotrephes . . . ignores us. (NAB)

Diotrephes . . . does not acknowledge us. (NABRE)

Diotrephes . . . does not acknowledge my authority. (RSV)

Diotrephes . . . does not acknowledge our authority. (NRSV)

This variety reflects a modern dilemma and does not exist in older translations (Mitchell 1998, 300). Jerome, in the Latin Vulgate, translates the verb in the same way each time with the Latin term *recipio*. The King James Version does the same, rendering *epidechesthai* into English as "receive" in both verses 9 and 10.

When translators of verses 9–10 assume that *epidechesthai* implies something different in verse 9 from what it means in verse 10, they assume that this verb provides yet another example of Johannine paronomasia, the literary device wherein the various meanings of a word are exploited within close range of one

3 John 9–10
in the King James Version

"I wrote unto the church: but Diotrephes, who loveth to have the preeminence among them, receiveth us not. . . . Neither doth he himself receive the brethren, and forbiddeth them that would, and casteth them out of the church."

another (wordplay). The clearest example of this device within the Johannine tradition comes in John 3:8, where Jesus uses the term *pneuma* to refer within the same verse to both the wind and the Spirit of God. Paranomasia could be at play in 3 John 9–10, however, only if the verb *epidechesthai* referred to the many different realities suggested by the various translations given to it. The dictionary tradition has generally held that *epidechesthai* carries different nuances and various meanings, and this includes even dictionaries like the rightly authoritative *Greek-English Lexicon of the New Testament and Other Early Christian Literature*, edited by W. Bauer and others (BDAG). But Mitchell has carefully and meticulously shown that the dictionary tradition is wrong. *Epidechesthai*, in this context, can mean only "to receive" (Mitchell 1998, 305–16).

Attempts to fill the term with greater meaning than this are designed to read some larger narrative into the verb. When the NASB translates "does not accept what we say," this seems to evoke a theological debate over doctrine. The several translations that represent some variation on the phrase "does not accept our authority" (NAB, RSV, NRSV) seem to develop a different theory, one in which ecclesiastical politics is at stake. In this proposed scenario, one leader of a church (Diotrephes) does not recognize the authority of the other (the Elder). But all these translations import meaning into the verb *epidechesthai* that it cannot bear. It means "to receive." *Epidechesthai* means the same thing in verse 9 that it does in verse 10. This means that we are given no explicit evidence whatsoever about why Diotrephes would not receive the letter and the emissaries. We do not know if he questioned the Elder's theology, or if he questioned the Elder's authority, or even if he simply had a poor personal relationship with the Elder. We do not know *why* he rejected the Elder. We only know that he *did*. Verse 9 should thus read, **I have written something to the church, but Diotrephes, who likes to put himself first, does not receive us.**

To insist on this plain meaning of the verb *epidechesthai* does not mean that we are stuck with a plain and colorless historical circumstance. In the first place, we can piece together the social realities behind the problems based on the discussion above. The Elder had sent emissaries to Gaius and to Diotrephes. Other churches may have been included, but they are not mentioned. Gaius received the emissaries. Diotrephes did not receive them. To receive agents sent from abroad, along with the letters of recommendation that accompany them, is the same as receiving the sender of the letters himself. To reject the letters is to reject the sender. Something like this sentiment surely stands behind Paul's insistence in his Letter to Philemon when he tells Philemon to accept Onesimus: "Welcome him as you would welcome me" (v. 17). Malherbe defines the social reality well when he writes,

> In letters of recommendation such as the letter referred to in vs. 9 had been, the request on behalf of the persons recommended was that they be received

> ## Accepting a Bearer of a Letter of Introduction
>
> To accept someone bearing a letter of introduction was to accept not only the person sent but also the sender, as these two letters demonstrate.
>
> > *"Heracles to his dearest Musaeus, greetings. I request you to regard as introduced to you Dioscurus, who will deliver the letter to you; he is a very close friend of mine. By doing this, you will be conferring a favor on me. Farewell."* (Egypt, first century CE, trans. Stowers 1986, 156–59)
> >
> > *"To Publius Caesius. I most earnestly recommend to your favour my very intimate friend Publius Messienus, a Roman knight, who is distinguished by every valuable endowment. I entreat you, by the double ties of that love which I enjoy with you and your father, to protect him both in his fame and his fortunes. Be assured you will in this way win the affection of a man highly deserving of your friendship, as well as confer a most acceptable obligation upon myself. Farewell."* (Cicero, *Ep.* 13.76 [first century CE], trans. Stowers 1986, 156–59)

for the sake of the writer. . . . The reception of the letter and its bearer proved the goodwill of the recipient toward the writer. It is such an understanding of *epidechesthai* that is present in vss. 9 and 10. Diotrephes had shown his ill will toward the Elder by refusing his letter and his emissaries. (1983, 106–7)

If the verb *epidechesthai* can tell us nothing further about the conflict between Diotrephes and the Elder, many scholars assume that we can simply know nothing further about their debate. In the history of interpretation, several positions have been held on the issue (see Malherbe 1983, 92–93; Brown 1982, 732–39). Some interpreters have imagined that here in 3 John we have a spotlight into the development of church hierarchy. The earlier churches of the Pauline mission seem to have relied on traveling missionaries to spread the gospel. Later letters, like the Pastoral Epistles, seem to move toward a more local, hierarchical church structure. Thus in 3 John we might have a competition between two figures as they struggle to accommodate the change from traveling leaders to more permanent local hierarchies.

Others have argued that the theological debates in 1–2 John lie behind the actions taken by Diotrephes in 3 John. This argument has certain strengths. In the first place, the rejection of traveling missionaries immediately draws our attention to 2 John 10, where we read, "If anyone comes to you and does not bring this teaching, do not receive him into your house." This seems to be precisely what Diotrephes has done. The missionaries he rejected, though, are not the missionaries who opposed the Elder, but the missionaries of the Elder himself. Then 3 John 10 says that he **expels them from the church.** It would assume too much in terms of structure and hierarchy to see here a form of excommunication as later understood, but Diotrephes clearly does not welcome the agents of the Elder. In addition to this parallel in procedure is a striking parallel in vocabulary. In 2 John, those who welcome a false teacher are said to share in that teacher's evil works (v. 11, *tois ergois autou tois ponērois*). Is it mere coincidence, then, that in 3 John 10 the Elder refers to the works of Diotrephes (*autou ta erga*) and then to his evil words (*logois ponērois*)?

For Painter (2002, 364–65), this parallel shows that Diotrephes is one of the teachers whom 2 John opposes. The struggle over authority in 3 John does not reflect a different struggle from the one in 1–2 John, but a different perspective on the same struggle. This is a compelling parallel, and Painter's suggestion is a reasonable reading of the material. Yet this proposal is not without its problems. First and foremost, this is a vague and allusive way to connect the two texts. In no way were 1 and 2 John reluctant to describe the theological errors of unnamed individuals, and to do so in some detail (Brown 1982, 737). Why then, when one of those individuals is actually named, would all theological detail be absent? Second, if Diotrephes is one of the secessionists whom the Elder refuses to accept in his midst, why is he sending emissaries to Diotrephes? The similar terms in 2 and 3 John create a compelling connection between the two texts, but the extent of that connection is difficult to determine. The same language is used to describe both opponents, but this does not imply that they are thus all the same opponents. What seems more likely is that the same language is used to describe all the opponents of the Elder, whether their offense be generated by theological irregularity, as in 1–2 John, or by a deviation in church order, as in 3 John.

Brown (1982, 738) also offers a very reasonable suggestion. He argues that both the Elder and Diotrephes host house churches formed according to the Johannine tradition. Such house churches are accustomed to showing hospitality to traveling missionaries. Those who have broken from the Johannine tradition in 1–2 John have thus created a dangerous circumstance. Local church leaders do not know whom to trust. As already noted, the *Didache* (11–12) instructs people to be wary of traveling missionaries. Perhaps Diotrephes takes this warning more seriously than most. In his confusion over the debate reflected in 1–2 John, and in his desire to avoid error, he accepts no emissaries. He is not himself a part of the secessionist group, but in his effort to avoid falling into error, he also has shunned the agents of the Elder. In this way of reading, Diotrephes is not himself a member of the secessionist party, but the problem of the secessionists sparks the problem with Diotrephes. Since Diotrephes does not know whom to trust, he trusts no one. The advantage of this theory is that it respects the evidence of the letter and does not create an implausible scenario by reading too much into small details, and yet it neatly connects the struggle in 3 John to the struggle in 1–2 John. In the end, no proposal can be proved beyond all doubt.

The Recommendation of Demetrius (11–12)

11–12. Since so much attention is paid by scholars to the problems circulating around Diotrephes, it would be easy to forget that the person whose activity really motivated the writing of the letter is Demetrius. Verses 11–12 move to the obvious purpose of the letter proper, the recommendation of Demetrius. Given the procedure typical of letters of recommendation cited above, Demetrius is very likely carrying 3 John to Gaius. He is a traveling missionary, like the ones described in verses 5–8.

Verse 11 reads, **Beloved, do not imitate the evil, but the good. The one who does good is of God; the one who does evil has not seen God.** This verse provides one more example of how 3 John may or may not have been written specifically against the same opponents as 1–2 John but nevertheless employs the same language and themes common to 1–2 John (Strecker 1996, 265). Not only does the letter repeatedly refer to "testimony" and "truth"; the letter also grounds the admonition in verse 11, to do what is good and to avoid what is evil, in a typical Johannine phrase: "being from/of God" (*ek theou*). For example, 1 John 5:19 says, "We know that we are of God," reminding believers what was said in 1 John 1:1–4: to have fellowship with the Elder and his community is to have fellowship with God. Those who share the Elder's faith share the same status: "Everyone who believes that Jesus is the Christ is born of God [*ek theou*]" (1 John 5:1). First John urges its readers to test the spirits in order to see if they are "of God" (4:1–4). Therefore, as the Elder urges Gaius to perform what is good in this verse, and thus show that he is "of God," he is actually urging Gaius to test the spirit of Demetrius properly. He should receive Demetrius and thus show that he shares fellowship with the Elder and with God. To receive Demetrius is to receive the Elder.

Verse 11 also says that those who do evil "have not seen God." This statement is a puzzle. In Johannine theology, it is not only evildoers who do not see God; all human beings have never seen God. When 1 John 4:12 says, "No one has ever seen God," it expresses a basic tenet of Johannine theology (John 1:18; 5:37; 6:46). Why does 3 John 11 apply this reality to evildoers only? Brown (1982, 721) solves the problem well. First, he observes that one could not reverse this negative statement into a positive statement that says, "Whoever does what is good has seen God." That would be wrong. The Elder seems, rather, to have in mind here what the Johannine tradition elsewhere says about how those who have seen Jesus have seen the Father (John 14:9). Those who do evil, however, have chosen darkness over light (John 3:19; 9:39, 41). They cannot see Jesus. Indeed, 1 John 3:6 says specifically, "Everyone who commits sin has never seen him [Jesus] or come to know him." Diotrephes has chosen to do evil, and his behavior results in his inability to see Jesus. Gaius, if he continues to choose what is good, will show that he is of God. The aphoristic character of the phrase creates a dualism between what is good and what is evil. But the way in which the phrase is crafted shows that these are not realities into which people are immovably placed. Gaius chose well in the past, and he needs to choose well again. The choice of showing hospitality to missionaries or rejecting them is a choice with serious implications.

Verse 12 offers testimony to Demetrius, and in a way that evokes the language of the Fourth Gospel. Verse 12 closely resembles John 21:24. A comparison of the two verses shows the similarity:

> This is the disciple who testifies to these things and who wrote them down. We know that his testimony is true. (John 21:24)

> **Testimony is given for Demetrius by everyone and even by the truth itself. We also testify, and you know that our testimony is true.** (3 John 12)

The person of the verbs and pronouns has changed, but the notion of testimony is very Johannine, and here it is expressed in a Johannine fashion. Precisely how the truth itself testifies to Demetrius is not clear. But here again, we see how the circumstances in 3 John are described by using the weightiest expressions in the Johannine arsenal.

Epistolary Closing (13–15)

13–15. The same Johannine character underlies verse 13, which also brings the letter to a close in a way that evokes the closing of the Fourth Gospel: **I had many other things to write to you, but I hope to see you presently, and we will speak in person.** This line is similar to John 20:30. The claim to have many more things to write is similar to the claim that the Fourth Evangelist had many other things to say about Jesus, even though the world lacked the space to contain everything that could be written. In 3 John, however, this Johannine expression is cast in an epistolary form. Or rather, a standard epistolary format is cast in a Johannine way. To apologize for the brevity of a letter was normal. Third John makes this apology in a way that sounds Johannine, and then in verse 14 promises to follow the letter with a visit. Paul also promises to follow a letter with a visit in 2 Cor. 12:14; 12:20–13:4 (Lieu 2008, 282).

The letter closes with verse 15: **Peace to you. The friends greet you. Greet the friends by name.** The wish of peace is found as a farewell in other letters (Eph. 6:23; 1 Pet. 5:14). A greeting to "friends" (*philoi*) is so common at the end of a letter as to be unremarkable (Rensberger 1997, 164). But both of these elements are evocative of Johannine language. First, the risen Jesus greets his disciples with the wish "Peace to you" (John 20:19, 20, 26). Second, the language of friendship is very Johannine. One immediately thinks of the words of Jesus: "You are my friends [*philoi*] if you do what I have instructed you" (John 15:14–15). The members of Gaius's church and the members of the Elder's church are thus all characterized as friends.

The Johannine quality of the final clause is even more interesting if one reads it in light of the Gospel (Brown 1982, 726). In Jesus's final scene, he questions Peter and asks him three times (John 21:15–17), "Do you love me?" In the process, he shifts from the verb *agapan* to the verb *philein*. The same shift characterizes the title of "the disciple whom Jesus loved." The term "love" for that disciple's title is usually *agapan* (13:23; 19:26; 21:7), but it shifts to *philein* as well (20:2). This is a typical Johannine preference for stylistic variety (Parsenios 2010, 72–78). The same shift, however, takes place over the course of 3 John. Gaius is greeted as *agapētos* ("beloved") at the start of the letter, and then addressed with the same word throughout the letter (vv. 1, 2, 5, 11). Now, as the letter closes, the members of his church are called *philoi*.

Theological Issues

The Johannine Letters open in 1 John 1:1 with one of the richest theological reflections on the incarnation that the NT has to offer. But the trio of letters ends here in 3 John on a very different note, with a letter that carries no theological argument whatsoever. And if 3 John seems remote from the soaring theology of 1 John, it seems even more remote from the concerns of contemporary readers. When a colleague heard that I was writing a commentary on these letters, for example, one of his first questions was, so why is 3 John in the Bible? He asked this question because the letter has a specific focus on a specific problem, and its very particularity seems to confine its meaning to its ancient context, with little to offer by way of teaching or encouragement for modern readers. Its message seems irrevocably and completely confined to the life and times of the Gaius to whom it was written.

But is it necessarily so? Can one view the matter from a slightly different perspective? Is it possible for this letter to have any significance for Christian faith and life beyond its original setting? I believe that it is possible. To explain how this is so, I would like to look for a moment at a similar circumstance in the Letters of Paul with the Letter to Philemon. Third John and Philemon share several features in common. They are two of the shorter letters in the New Testament, and they are both letters of recommendation. They also share in being considered less than equal to the more meaningful works attributed to John and Paul, respectively (Brown 1982, 727). By seeing how interpreters have responded to the case of Philemon, I believe we can see the particularity of 3 John in a new light.

Before turning our attention specifically to Philemon, though, I would like to recognize that the problem of "particularity" applies to the entire *Corpus Paulinum*. All of Paul's letters are addressed to specific people or congregations. They are all "particular." As the first Christians circulated these letters in the wake of Paul's ministry, and to readers distant from Paul's original congregations, certain manuscripts seem to have been modified in order to remove their original destinations, thereby opening them to a broader readership (see Dahl 1962). For example, the phrase "in Rome" has been deleted from Rom. 1:7, 15 in some manuscripts (G, Origen) effectively giving the letter a universal audience (see Metzger 1994, 446, 447; Dahl 1962, 267–68). Excising two words was all it took to transform a letter addressed specifically to the Romans into a letter written for the whole world.

The Letter to Philemon presented bigger challenges. Well into the fourth century people still wondered why they had to read this book, and their concerns resemble the questions people still raise. In the opening lines of his homilies on Philemon, John Chrysostom acknowledges the feelings of his congregation when he says,

> But because some say that it was superfluous that this Epistle should be included, since [Paul] is making a request about a small matter in behalf of one man, let them learn who make these objections that they are themselves deserving of very many censures. (*Homiles on Philemon*, 1, NPNF)

The complaints of Chrysostom's congregation continue today, and commentators on Philemon regularly take time to explain the letter's ongoing value for readers other than Philemon. The way in which N. T. Wright comments on this matter has special relevance for our present interest in 3 John (1986, 168). If the Letter to Philemon seems to have very little explicit theological depth, Wright draws its implicit theological wealth to the surface by reading Philemon in the light of other Pauline texts, especially 2 Cor. 5:16–21. In 5:16 Paul announces, for example, that "from now on . . . we regard no one from a human point of view," signaling a change in perspective exactly like the one that Paul urges in Philemon (vv. 11, 16). The most significant connection between 2 Cor. 5 and Philemon is the notice that Christ has reconciled human beings to God "through Christ" (2 Cor. 5:18) and has passed the ministry of reconciliation on to Christian believers. This ministry of reconciliation is precisely the thing that Paul actualizes in his dealing with Philemon, because if Christ is the one through whom human beings are personally reconciled to God, then Paul is the one in whose person Philemon is reconciled to Onesimus. The Letter to Philemon, read from this perspective, represents a practical application of Pauline theology.

In this same way, 3 John couches its very practical concerns in the theologically rich vocabulary of the Fourth Gospel and of 1–2 John, using and reusing words like "truth" and "testify/testimony." This not only secures the Johannine quality of the letter and shows its natural fit within the Johannine corpus but also shows how this letter articulates one of the more surprising, yet characteristic, expressions of Johannine theology. One cannot only know the truth but must also "do the truth" (1 John 1:6; John 3:21). If 2 John urges its readers not to invite the secessionists into their midst with hospitality in order to avoid sharing in their false teaching, 3 John urges Gaius to invite the true teachers into his church in order to share in the truth, and so be a "coworker" (*synergos*) in the truth (*alētheia*), which echoes the sentiment of 1 John 3:18, which urges, "Let us love, not in word or speech, but in action (*ergō*) and in reality/truth (*alētheia*)." No less than Philemon, 3 John represents the practical application of a profound theological vision.

Bibliography

Allison, Dale C., Jr. 2013. *A Critical and Exegetical Commentary on the Epistle of James*. International Critical Commentary 14. London: Bloomsbury, T&T Clark.

Anderson, Paul. 2007. "On Guessing Points and Naming Stars: Epistemological Origins of John's Christological Tensions." In *The Gospel of John and Christian Theology*, edited by Richard Bauckham and Carl Mosser, 311–45. Grand Rapids: Eerdmans.

Attridge, Harold W. 2006. "The Cubist Principle in Johannine Imagery: John and the Reading of Images in Contemporary Platonism." In *Imagery in the Gospel of John: Terms, Forms, Themes, and Theology of Johannine Figurative Language*, edited by J. Frey, J. G. van der Watt, and R. Zimmermann, 47–60. Wissenschaftliche Untersuchungen zum Neuen Testament 212. Tübingen: Mohr Siebeck.

———. 2012. *Essays on John and Hebrews*. Grand Rapids: Baker Academic.

Barrett, C. K. 1982. "The Dialectical Theology of the Gospel of John." In *Essays on John*. Philadelphia: Westminster.

———, ed. 1989. *The New Testament Background*. San Francisco: HarperSanFrancisco.

Bauckham, Richard. 2007. *The Testimony of the Beloved Disciple: Narrative, History and Theology in the Gospel of John*. Grand Rapids: Baker Academic.

———. 2008. *Jesus and the Eyewitnesses*. Grand Rapids: Eerdmans.

Bettenson, Henry, ed. 1967. *Documents of the Christian Church*. London; New York: Oxford University Press.

Betz, Hans Dieter. 1995. *The Sermon on the Mount*. Hermeneia. Minneapolis: Fortress.

Black, C. Clifton. 1986. "The Johannine Epistles and the Question of Early Catholicism." *Novum Testamentum* 28:131–58.

———. 1998. "The First, Second and Third Letters of John." Vol. 12. *The New Interpreter's Bible*, 363–469. Nashville: Abingdon.

Boer, Martinus de. 1991. "The Death of Jesus and His Coming in the Flesh." *Novum Testamentum* 33:326–46.

Brock, Sebastian. 1992. *The Luminous Eye: The Spiritual World Vision of Saint Ephrem the Syrian*. Rev. ed. Kalamazoo, MI: Cistercian Publications.

Brooke, Alan E. 1912. *A Critical and Exegetical Commentary on the Johannine Epistles*. International Critical Commentary. New York: Scribner's & Sons.

Brown, Raymond. 1966. *The Gospel according to John*. Vol. 1. Anchor Bible 29. New York: Doubleday.

———. 1970. *The Gospel according to John*. Vol. 2. Anchor Bible 29A. New York: Doubleday.

———. 1979a. *The Community of the Beloved Disciple*. Mahwah, NJ: Paulist Press.

———. 1979b. "The Relationship to the Fourth Gospel Shared by the Author of 1 John and by His Opponents." In *Text and Interpretation: Studies in the New Testament Presented to Matthew Black*, edited by E. Best and R. M. Wilson, 57–68. Cambridge: Cambridge University Press.

———. 1982. *The Epistles of John*. Anchor Bible 30. New York: Doubleday.

Bultmann, Rudolf. 1973. *The Johannine Epistles*. Translated by R. Philip O'Hara. Hermeneia. Philadelphia: Fortress.

Carey, Christopher, ed. and trans. 1992. *Apollodoros against Neaira: (Demosthenes) 59*. Warminster, UK: Aris & Phillips.

Charlesworth, James H., ed. 1983. *The Old Testament Pseudepigrapha*. Vol. 1, *Apocalyptic Literature and Testaments*. New York: Doubleday.

Charlesworth, James H., ed., with Henry W. L. Rietz, Michael T. Davis, Brent A. Strawn, and Muzeon Yisrael. 1996. *The Dead Sea Scrolls: Rule of the Community*. Philadelphia: American Interfaith Institute/World Alliance.

Cohoon, J. W., trans. 1959. *Dio Chrysostom, Discourses*. LCL. Cambridge, MA: Harvard University Press.

Constas, Nicholas, ed. and trans. 2014. *Maximus the Confessor, On Difficulties in the Church Fathers: The Ambigua*. Vol. 1. Dumbarton Oaks Medieval Library 28. Cambridge, MA: Harvard University Press.

Culpepper, R. Alan. 1975. *The Johannine School*. Missoula, MT: Scholars Press.

Culpepper, R. Alan, and C. Clifton Black, eds. 1996. *Exploring the Gospel of John: In Honor of D. Moody Smith*. Louisville: Westminster John Knox.

Culy, Martin M. 2004. *I, II, III John: A Handbook on the Greek Text*. Baylor Handbooks on the Greek New Testament. Waco: Baylor University Press.

Dahl, Nils. 1962. "The Particularity of the Pauline Epistles as a Problem in the Ancient Church." In *Neotestamentica et Patristica: Eine Freundesgabe, Oscar Cullmann zu seinem 60 Geburtstag*, by A. N. Wilder et al., 261–71. Supplements to Novum Testamentum 6. Leiden: Brill.

Dodd, C. H. 1937. "The First Epistle of John and the Fourth Gospel." *Bulletin of the John Rylands Library* 21:129–56.

———. 1946. *The Johannine Epistles*. New York: Harper & Bros.

Edwards, M. J. 1989. "Martyrdom and the First Epistle of John." *Novum Testamentum* 31:164–71.

Ehrman, Bart. 1988. "1 John 4:3 and the Orthodox Corruption of Scripture." *Zeitschrift für die neutestamentliche Wissenschaft* 79:221–43.

Engberg-Pedersen, Troels, ed. 2001. *Paul beyond the Judaism/Hellenism Divide.* Louisville: Westminster John Knox.

Fish, Stanley. 1980. *Is There a Text in This Class? The Authority of Interpretive Communities.* Cambridge, MA: Harvard University Press.

Fitzgerald, John T., ed. 1996. *Friendship, Flattery and Frankness of Speech.* Supplements to Novum Testamentum 67. Leiden: Brill.

García Martínez, Florentino. 1994. *The Dead Sea Scrolls Translated.* Leiden: Brill.

Gore, Charles. 1920. *The Epistles of St. John.* London: John Murray.

Griffith, Terry. 2002. *Keep Yourselves from Idols: A New Look at 1 John.* Journal for the Study of the New Testament: Supplement Series 233. Sheffield: Sheffield Academic Press.

Hamburger, Jeffrey F. 2002. *St. John the Divine: The Deified Evangelist in Medieval Art and Theology.* Berkeley: University of California Press.

Hengel, Martin. 1989. *The Johannine Question.* Translated by John Bowden. Philadelphia: Trinity Press International.

Hill, Charles E. 2004. *The Johannine Corpus in the Early Church.* Oxford: Oxford University Press.

———. 2006. "The Fourth Gospel in the Second Century: The Myth of Orthodox Johannophobia." In *Challenging Perspectives on the Gospel of John*, edited by John Lierman, 135–69. Wissenschaftliche Untersuchungen zum Neuen Testament 2/219. Tübingen: Mohr Siebeck.

Hill, David. 1967. "The Interpretation of *hilaskesthai* and Related Words in the Septuagint and in the New Testament." In *Greek Words and Hebrew Meanings: Studies in the Semantics of Soteriological Terms*, 23–48. Society for New Testament Studies Monograph Series 5. Cambridge: Cambridge University Press.

Holloway, Paul. 1998. "Paul's Pointed Prose: The *Sententia* in Roman Rhetoric and Paul." *Novum Testamentum* 40:32–53.

Holmes, Michael W., ed. and trans. 2007. *The Apostolic Fathers: Greek Texts and English Translations.* 3rd ed. Grand Rapids: Baker Academic.

Hutchins, Francis. 1967. *The Illusion of Permanence: British Imperialism in India.* Princeton, NJ: Princeton University Press.

Jewett, Robert. 2006. *Romans: A Commentary.* Hermeneia. Philadelphia: Fortress.

Johnson, Luke Timothy. 2003. *The Creed: What Christians Believe and Why It Matters.* New York: Doubleday.

———. 2004. *Brother of Jesus, Friend of God: Studies in the Letter of James.* Grand Rapids: Eerdmans.

Keck, Leander. 1996. "Derivation as Destiny: 'Of-ness' in Johannine Christology, Anthropology and Soteriology." In *Exploring the Gospel of John: In Honor of D. Moody Smith*, edited by C. C. Black and R. A. Culpepper, 274–88. Louisville: Westminster John Knox.

Keener, Craig. 2003. *The Gospel of John: A Commentary*. 2 vols. Peabody, MA: Hendrickson.

Kierspel, Lars. 2006. *The Jews and the World in the Fourth Gospel*. Wissenschaftliche Untersuchungen zum Neuen Testament 2/220. Tübingen: Mohr Siebeck.

Klauck, Hans-Josef. 2006. *Ancient Letters and the New Testament*. Waco: Baylor University Press.

Layton, Bentley, ed. and trans. 1995a. *The Gnostic Scriptures: A New Translation with Annotations and Introductions*. Anchor Yale Bible Reference Library. New Haven: Yale University Press.

———. 1995b. "Prolegomena to the Study of Ancient Gnosticism." In *The Social World of the First Christians: Essays in Honor of Wayne A. Meeks*, edited by L. Michael White and O. Larry Yarbrough, 334–50. Minneapolis: Fortress.

Lieu, Judith. 1986. *The Second and Third Epistles of John*. Edinburgh: T&T Clark.

———. 1988. "Blindness in the Johannine Tradition." *New Testament Studies* 34:83–95.

———. 1991. *The Theology of the Johannine Epistles*. New Testament Theology. Cambridge: Cambridge University Press.

———. 1993. "What Was from the Beginning: Scripture and Tradition in the Johannine Epistles." *New Testament Studies* 39:458–77.

———. 2008. *I, II, III John*. New Testament Library. Louisville: Westminster John Knox.

Lincoln, Andrew. 2000. *Truth on Trial*. Peabody, MA: Hendrickson.

Malherbe, Abraham. 1983. *Social Aspects of Early Christianity*. Philadelphia: Fortress.

———. 1986. *Moral Exhortation: A Greco-Roman Sourcebook*. Philadelphia: Westminster.

———. 1987. *Paul and the Thessalonians*. Philadelphia: Fortress.

———. 1988. *Ancient Epistolary Theorists*. Atlanta: Scholars Press.

———. 2000. *The Letters to the Thessalonians*. Anchor Bible 32B. New York: Doubleday.

Malina, Bruce J. 1986. "The Received View and What It Cannot Do: III John and Hospitality." In *Social Scientific Criticism of the New Testament and Its Social World*, edited by J. H. Elliott, 171–89. Semeia 35. Decatur, GA: Scholars Press.

Martyn, J. Louis. 2003. *History and Theology in the Fourth Gospel*. New Testament Library. Louisville: Westminster John Knox.

Meeks, Wayne. 1967. *The Prophet-King: Moses Traditions and the Johannine Christology*. Supplements to Novum Testamentum 14. Leiden: Brill.

Metzger, Bruce. 1994. *A Textual Commentary on the Greek New Testament*. 2nd ed. Stuttgart: Deutsche Bibelgesellschaft.

Minear, Paul. 1970. "The Idea of Incarnation in First John." *Interpretation* 24:291–302.

Mitchell, Margaret. 1993. *Paul and the Rhetoric of Reconciliation: An Exegetical Investigation of the Language and Composition of 1 Corinthians*. Hermeneutische Untersuchungen zur Theologie 28. Tübingen: Mohr Siebeck, 1991; Louisville: Westminster John Knox.

———. 1998. "Diotrephes Does Not Receive Us": The Lexicographical and Social Context of 3 John 9–10." *Journal of Biblical Literature* 117:299–320.

————. 2003. "The Corinthian Correspondence and the Birth of Pauline Hermeneutics." In *Paul and the Corinthians: Studies on a Community in Conflict; Essays in Honour of Margaret Thrall*, edited by T. J. Burke and J. K. Elliott, 17–53. Supplements to Novum Testamentum 109. Leiden: Brill.

————. 2010. *Paul, the Corinthians and the Birth of Christian Hermeneutics*. Cambridge: Cambridge University Press.

Muir, John V. 2009. *Life and Letters in the Ancient Greek World*. Routledge Monographs in Classical Studies. New York: Routledge.

Nongbri, Brent. 2005. "The Use and Abuse of $\mathfrak{P}^{52}$: Papyrological Pitfalls in the Dating of the Fourth Gospel." *Harvard Theological Review* 98:23–48.

Painter, John. 2002. *1, 2, and 3 John*. Sacra pagina. Collegeville, MN: Liturgical Press.

Parsenios, George L. 2004. "Adaptability and the Good Shepherd." *Princeton Seminary Bulletin* 25:248–53.

————. 2005a. *Departure and Consolation: The Johannine Farewell Discourses in Light of Greco-Roman Literature*. Supplements to Novum Testamentum 117. Leiden: Brill.

————. 2005b. "'No Longer in the World' (John 17:11): The Transformation of the Tragic in the Fourth Gospel." *Harvard Theological Review* 98:1–21.

————. 2010. *Rhetoric and Drama in the Johannine Lawsuit Motif*. Wissenschaftliche Untersuchungen zum Neuen Testament 1/258. Tübingen: Mohr Siebeck.

————. 2012a. Review of *The Gospel and Letters of John*, by Urban C. von Wahlde, *Review of Biblical Literature* 14:315.

————. 2012b. "A Sententious Silence: First Thoughts on the Fourth Gospel and the *Ardens* Style." In *Portraits of Jesus: Essays in Honor of Harold W. Attridge*, edited by Susan Myers, 1–17. Wissenschaftliche Untersuchungen zum Neuen Testament 2/321. Tübingen: Mohr Siebeck.

Perkins, Pheme. 1979. *The Johannine Epistles*. New Testament Message 21. Wilmington, DE: Glazier.

Phillips, Peter. 2006. *The Prologue of the Fourth Gospel: A Sequential Reading*. Library of New Testament Studies. London: T&T Clark.

Piper, Otto. 1947. "1 John and the Didache of the Primitive Church." *Journal of Biblical Literature* 66:437–51.

Pollard, Thomas E. 2005. *Johannine Christology and the Early Church*. Society for New Testament Studies Monograph Series 13. Cambridge: Cambridge University Press.

Rensberger, David K. 1988. *Johannine Faith and Liberating Community*. Philadelphia: Westminster.

————. 1997. *1 John, 2 John, 3 John*. Abingdon New Testament Commentaries. Nashville: Abingdon.

Roberts, Rhys W., and Ingram Bywater, trans. 1954. *The Rhetoric and Poetics of Aristotle*. New York: Modern Library.

Robinson, John A. T. 1962. "The Destination and Purpose of the Johannine Epistles." In *Twelve New Testament Studies*, 126–38. London: SCM.

171

Rosenmeyer, Patricia. 2006. *Ancient Epistolary Fictions*. Cambridge: Cambridge University Press.

Said, Edward. 2005. "The Pleasures of Imperialism." In *Edwardian and Georgian Fiction*, edited by Harold Bloom, 245–78. Bloom's Period Studies. New York: Chelsea House.

Scafuro, Adela. 1997. *The Forensic Stage: Settling Disputes in Graeco-Roman New Comedy*. Cambridge: Cambridge University Press.

Schnackenburg, Rudolf. 1992. *The Johannine Epistles: Introduction and Commentary*. Translated by Reginald Fuller. New York: Crossroad.

Schoedel, William R. 1985. *Ignatius of Antioch*. Hermeneia. Minneapolis: Fortress.

Sinclair, Patrick. 1995. *Tacitus the Sententious Historian: A Sociology of Rhetoric in Annales 1–6*. University Park: Pennsylvania State University Press.

Smalley, Stephen S. 1984. *1, 2, 3 John*. Word Biblical Commentaries 51. Waco: Word.

Smith, D. Moody. 2009. "The Epistles of John: What's New since Brooke's ICC in 1912?" *Expository Times* 120:373–84.

Solzhenitsyn, Aleksandr I. 1992. *The Gulag Archipelago, 1918–1956: An Experiment in Literary Investigation*. Vol. 2. New York: Harper & Row.

Sommerstein, Alan. 1989. *Aeschylus, Eumenides*. Cambridge Greek and Latin Classics. Cambridge: Cambridge University Press.

Staley, Jeffrey. 1988. *The Print's First Kiss: A Rhetorical Investigation of the Implied Reader in the Fourth Gospel*. Society of Biblical Literature Dissertation Series. Missoula, MT: Scholars Press.

Stowers, Stanley. 1986. *Letter Writing in Greco-Roman Antiquity*. Philadelphia: Westminster.

———. 2001. "Does Pauline Christianity Resemble a Hellenistic Philosophy?" In *Paul beyond the Judaism/Hellenism Divide*, edited by Troels Engberg-Pedersen, 81–102. Louisville: Westminster John Knox.

Strecker, George. 1996. *The Johannine Epistles*. Hermeneia. Minneapolis: Fortress.

Thomas, John Christopher. 1995. "The Order of the Composition of the Johannine Epistles." *Novum Testamentum* 37:68–75.

———. 1998. "The Literary Structure of 1 John." *Novum Testamentum* 40:369–81.

Trapp, Michael B. 2003. *Greek and Latin Letters: An Anthology, with Translation*. Cambridge Greek and Latin Classics. Cambridge: Cambridge University Press.

Unger, Dominic J., ed. and trans. 1992. *St. Irenaeus of Lyons: Against the Heresies, Book 1*. Ancient Christian Writers. Mahwah, NJ: Paulist Press.

Von Wahlde, Urban C. 2010. *The Gospel and Letters of John*. 3 vols. Eerdmans Critical Commentary. Grand Rapids: Eerdmans.

Watson, Duane. 1989a. "1 John 2.12–14 as *Distributio, Conduplicatio*, and *Expolitio*: A Rhetorical Understanding." *Journal for the Study of the New Testament* 35:97–110.

———. 1989b. "A Rhetorical Analysis of 2 John according to Greco-Roman Convention." *New Testament Studies* 35:104–30.

———. 1989c. "A Rhetorical Analysis of 3 John: A Study in Epistolary Rhetoric." *Catholic Biblical Quarterly* 51:479–501.

———. 1993. "Amplification Techniques in 1 John: The Interaction of Rhetorical Style and Invention." *Journal for the Study of the New Testament* 51:99–123.

Wendland, Ernst R. 1991. "What Is Truth? Semantic Density and the Language of the Johannine Epistles with Special Reference to 2 John." *Notes on Translation* 5:21–60.

Whitmarsh, Timothy. 2001. *Greek Literature and the Roman Empire: The Politics of Imitation*. Oxford: Oxford University Press.

Wright, N. T. 1986. *The Epistles of Paul to the Colossians and to Philemon*. Grand Rapids: Eerdmans.

Yonge, C. D., trans. 1993. *The Works of Philo Judaeus*. Peabody, MA: Hendrickson.

Zacharias, Archimandrite. 2006. *The Enlargement of the Heart: "Be Ye Also Enlarged" (2 Corinthians 6:13) in the Theology of Saint Silouan the Athonite and Elder Sophrony of Essex*. Edited by Christopher Veniamin. South Canaan, PA: Mount Thabor Publishing.

Index of Subjects

Index of Modern Authors

Index of Scripture and Ancient Sources